Alan Mullery MBE made his Fulham debut aged 17 and played over 200 games. He signed for Spurs in 1964 and won the FA Cup, League Cup and UEFA Cup, plus 35 England caps, including the infamous 1970 World Cup quarter-final against West Germany in which he scored the opening goal. A final spell at Fulham featured an amazing cup run to Wembley, alongside his great friend Bobby Moore. Mullers then became a manager, notably with Brighton, with whom he achieved two promotions in a five-year spell which took them to the top league, then Charlton, Crystal Palace, QPR and Brighton once again. He is now a successful pundit on Sky Sports. www.alanmullery.com

Tony Norman, who worked with Alan Mullery on the writing of this book, is a freelance writer and broadcaster specialising in sport and music. He has worked with many famous names from Bobby Moore and Bryan Robson to The Beatles and the Rolling Stones. But according to Tony, Mullers is the greatest raconteur of them all. www.tonynorman.com

ALAN MULLERY

The Autobiography

Alan Mullery

With Tony Norman

headline

First published in 2006
by HEADLINE PUBLISHING GROUP

First published in paperback in 2007
by HEADLINE PUBLISHING GROUP

1

Cataloguing in Publication Data is available from the British Library

ISBN 978 0 7553 1482 9

Typeset in Bembo by Palimpsest Book Production Limited,
Grangemouth, Stirlingshire

Printed and bound in Great Britain by Mackays of Chatham plc, Chatham, Kent

Headline's policy is to use papers that are natural, renewable and recyclable
products and made from wood grown in sustainable forests.
The logging and manufacturing processes are expected to conform to the
environmental regulations of the country of origin.

HEADLINE PUBLISHING GROUP
A division of Hachette Livre UK Ltd
338 Euston Road
London NW1 3BH

www.headline.co.uk
www.hodderheadline.com

Alan Mullery loves football with all his heart. His enthusiasm was an inspiration on the field and he scored some wonderful goals that I would have been proud of. He was a great team mate, a great manager and a great friend. One of the real characters of the game.

Martin Chivers

CONTENTS

PROLOGUE

When I look back at my playing career, three very special times stand out.

Winning the UEFA Cup with Spurs, playing in the 1970 World Cup finals in Mexico, with England and Sir Alf, and reaching one last Wembley FA Cup final with my friend, Bobby Moore.

I'll start this book with those experiences.

But they are just part of the story. I've been blessed with the life I've lived. There has never been a dull moment, from my childhood in war-torn London to the present day. As a kid I dreamed of winning the FA Cup and playing for England at Wembley. It all came true.

I've travelled the world as a player and manager. I've talked about the game on TV and radio. My memory teems with incredible matches and great players. I've been through soaring highs and rock-bottom lows.

When this book is published, I will be nearly sixty-five. The thought of picking up my pension makes no sense to me. I don't feel old enough. But this has been the perfect time to write my life story. Other than my family, nothing means more to me than football. I loved it as a kid and I love it still. It has given me an amazing life.

Looking back now, it's hard to believe it all really happened to a war baby whose life nearly ended before it had really begun . . .

ROLLERCOASTER: UEFA CUP FINAL 1972

Smiling faces. Thousands of smiling, cheering faces, all looking up at me. It felt like a dream, but this was reality: 17 May 1972. Over 54,000 fans had packed into White Hart Lane to see if Spurs could win the UEFA Cup. And I had scored the vital goal against Wolves to add another glory glory night to Tottenham's history.

Thousands of Spurs supporters were streaming on to the field and lifting me shoulder high for a victory parade around the ground. I felt like I was floating on air. It was my night. After a long spell out in the cold, I'd proved all the doubters wrong. I was back where I belonged as Spurs' captain.

This all happened over thirty years ago, but I can still remember the roars of celebration echoing around White Hart Lane. It was deafening. That lap of honour with the UEFA Cup remains one of the happiest memories from my playing days.

But drama and tension were simmering beneath those thrilling scenes. I had been on an emotional rollercoaster for most of the season. An awful injury had kept me out of the Spurs first team for five months. Out on loan at Fulham, it seemed Tottenham had forgotten all about me. I seriously wondered if I would ever play for the club again.

Some of the wounds from those dark days would never heal. My relationship with Spurs' manager, Bill Nicholson, would never be the same again.

The night Spurs won the UEFA Cup I was a hero. But how many of those cheering fans would have guessed I had just played my last game for the club? That's professional football for you. In your moments of greatest triumph, you are riding for a fall . . .

Just a few weeks before the UEFA Cup final, I had felt totally abandoned by Spurs and Bill Nicholson. The trouble all started in the opening weeks of the 1971–72 season.

I drove home after training one day in early September and, as I got out of the car, I felt a terrible pain in my groin that cut through me like a knife. I had played with and against some of the hardest players in the world. I was no stranger to fierce tackles in the heat of a big match. But now I was nowhere near a football pitch . . . and I was in agony. I sat back in my car and waited for the pain and shock to pass. The sharp, shooting pains in both sides of my groin were a total mystery.

I replayed recent games in my mind, trying to think of anything that might have caused this trouble. There were no obvious answers, so I tried to push it all to the back of my mind. I loved playing for Tottenham. Leading the team out at White Hart Lane was always a thrill. The new season was coming alive and all I wanted to do was play football.

So I struggled on through September and October, but things got progressively worse. My groin was sore after every game. If I got out of the car quickly, without thinking, the stabbing pains came back. Even simple things, like walking upstairs, were a problem.

I'd been a professional footballer for nearly fourteen years and thought it might all be something to do with getting older. I was a midfield player and I did a lot of running. Maybe you had to expect a few aches and pains at my age. I didn't really know.

I asked our physio, Cecil Poynton, for help. He was dismissive. 'Oh, we've had all this before,' he said. 'Dave Mackay had it. You'll get over it, you'll run it off.'

The truth was, Cecil didn't really have a clue what was wrong with me. So I kept playing and coming off after matches, in excruciating pain. It spread from the groin area up into the stomach as well. Cecil gave me a corset to wear, which caused more leg-pulling than sympathy with the other lads in the team!

Despite all the problems, I played my part in the early stages of our UEFA Cup campaign. We beat Keflavik of Iceland 6–1 away in the first round, on 14 September 1971. I scored two of the goals and Alan Gilzean got a hat-trick. Two weeks later, we beat them 9–0 at White Hart Lane. This time Martin Chivers got a hat-trick and Gilly got two more goals. I don't remember much about Keflavik, other than that they were bloody awful and we were good. The aggregate score, 15–1, tells its own story.

In the second round we played Nantes, who were a very useful French side. The first leg was away on 20 October and we drew 0–0. I got sent off just before half-time. I used to put myself about a bit in away games and I tackled their centre-forward on the halfway line. He was a big man called Henri Guy. As we hit the floor, he deliberately kicked me in the face and cracked one of my front teeth. As we both scrambled to our feet, I gave him a right hander. It was instinctive. The ref ran over and sent us both off.

Henri Guy ran straight off to the dressing rooms. I took a bit longer. The kick in the face had left me a bit dazed. As I was walking off the pitch to the tunnel, I heard the ref blow for half-time. Bill Nick got up from the dugout just in front of me. He didn't say anything. He didn't need to, his look said it all. I'd got myself sent off and he was not impressed. To be honest, I knew I'd let the team down.

Bill walked up the tunnel just ahead of me. In the silence between us, I could hear my studs on the concrete slope. As Bill Nick turned the corner at the top of the tunnel, Henri Guy jumped out and hit him smack in the face. He was obviously expecting me! To give Bill his due, he defended himself and flew at Henri Guy. I dived in to help and managed to thump Guy a couple of times, too. Then all the other players arrived and it was a bit like the Wild West until it all calmed down.

I think the aggravation at half-time made our lads even more determined not to lose and they held out for a goalless draw. Spurs won the home leg 1–0 on 2 November with a goal from Martin Peters, but by then I was out of the side with my mystery injury.

These days, a player would never be expected to carry an injury for so long. But, in the early seventies, football was a much harder and more physical game. Players lived with pain for most of the season. You were always recovering from cuts and bruises. That was the norm.

When I'm trying to explain to younger fans what the game was like in England when I was playing, I always tell them to watch a DVD of the replay of the 1970 FA Cup final between Chelsea and Leeds, which was played at Old Trafford. Chelsea's captain, Ron Harris, nearly cuts Leeds winger, Eddie Gray, in half with a tackle in the first five minutes. A couple of minutes later, Harris hits Gray again and sends him into the cinder track around the pitch.

In the modern game, Harris would have been sent off for the first tackle, let alone the second. But at Old Trafford the referee just gave a free kick both times. Harris wasn't even booked. After that, Gray was never in the match and Chelsea went on to win the Cup 2–1, with goals from Peter Osgood and David Webb.

That was the way it was. There was a lot of rough justice in the game. You had to learn to look after yourself and you were expected to play through pain. I knew that and I was as tough as most players. It took a lot to stop me playing. But the pain in my groin was above and beyond anything I'd faced before. I knew, in my own mind, this was one injury I would not be able to ignore for ever.

The crunch came on 30 October 1971, when we played Stoke away in a First Division game. The ball was hit over the top of our defence and Terry Conroy, the Republic of Ireland international, broke through. Terry was nippy, but normally I'd reckon to catch him. This time I was treading water. Terry left me for dead and he was one-on-one with Pat Jennings, who made a great save.

Big Pat came out and gave me a terrible rollicking, which he had every right to do, but it wasn't my fault. A couple of minutes later, the ref blew for half-time. When I got back to the dressing room, both sides of my groin were aching like mad. Bill Nick was ready to have a go at me for letting Conroy break away.

'What's the problem?' he asked.

'You know what the problem is,' I said. 'The same as it has been the last few weeks. I'm in so much pain, I can't move out there.'

Even then, Bill Nick didn't take me off.

'See how it goes in the second half,' he said.

I didn't argue. I went out and tried my best, but it was hopeless. I felt like Jim Peters, when he collapsed at the end of the marathon in the 1954 Commonwealth Games in Vancouver. Peters made it to the stadium, then staggered round the track. He had no control over his legs whatsoever. That's how I felt. I was usually so fit and strong, but now all my power had gone. I played on until the seventy-sixth minute, when Bill sent John Pratt on in my place.

Nick wasn't happy about me coming off. Neither was I, to be fair. I hated sitting on the bench. If I'd realised I had just played my last first-team game for Spurs for five months, I would have been heartbroken.

Stoke were a good home side. We never came away from the Victoria Ground with much. We ended up losing 2–0, which made me feel even worse. On the way home, I sat with Bill Nick in the front of the team bus as usual. I got travel sick if I sat in the back.

'I can't go on like this, Bill. I need to see somebody who can sort this injury out.'

Bill said, 'Have a word with Brian Curtin [the club doctor]. See what he has to say.'

Brian Curtin told me to rest for a few days, then I should be fine, but it didn't work out that way. I spent the whole of November trying to get fit again. Cecil Poynton would give me heat treatment on the physio's table for three or four days and the pain in my groin would ease. Then, as soon as I started running again, the pain would come straight back.

All the treatment was done at White Hart Lane. I can remember jogging round the edge of the pitch, dreading the pain coming back. What made it worse was running up and down the empty terraces, which left me in agony. Cecil Poynton kept saying I needed to push myself harder. But when you play sport for a living, you get to know your own body. And all my instincts were telling me everything Spurs were telling me to do was a painful and pointless and damaging waste of time. As it turned out, running up and down steps was the worst thing I could possibly have done.

After about five weeks, I agreed to play for the reserves to see how things went. I had three games in mid December. The last was away to QPR, just four days before Christmas. I came off in terrible pain again and spoke to Bill Nick the next day.

'Cecil told me about the game,' said Nick.

'I'm really struggling,' I told him.

'You'd better see a specialist then.'

'I think that's what I need, Bill.'

Bill nodded and walked away. I was left standing there, feeling like I'd done something wrong and let Bill down in some way. It was strange. I was worried and confused about the injury, but Bill made no effort to encourage or reassure me.

It may seem easy to say Cecil Poynton should have helped me more, but you need to see things in the context of the times. In the sixties and seventies, most physios were old players who'd been given a job by their club at the end of their careers. They were given the bucket and sponge and told to get on with it. They had great knowledge and experience of the game as players, but no medical training.

Cecil Poynton was like that. It was his job to keep players playing, even if they had an injury. I remember going into the treatment room at Spurs on my first day at the club, back in March 1964. I wanted some plasters to stop me getting blisters from my new boots. There were three players on the treatment tables including England centre-forward, Bobby Smith, whose ankle was really bruised and swollen.

Bill Nick walked in and said, 'Who's fit for Saturday then, Cecil?'

We were playing Manchester United, my first game. Cecil didn't want to tell Nick none of the players was fit, although that was the truth. Nowadays the physios are paid to give an honest medical opinion, which is so much better. But Cecil would never side with the players against the manager.

In the end, Bobby Smith, who was a real tough guy, said, 'It doesn't look like anyone else wants to volunteer, Bill, I'll play Saturday.' And that's what happened. Bobby had a cortisone injection before the United game and went out and played. Cecil should never have let Bobby take that risk, but he didn't want to cross Bill Nick.

That was the relationship between managers and physios in the seventies and not just at Spurs, but all over the country: keep the players playing, come what may. That was the golden rule. No wonder I had such a struggle to convince Bill I needed expert medical advice. Current first-team stars at Spurs have a team of four medical experts caring for them in terms of health, physio-therapy and massage. It's all so different now.

As you can imagine, it was not the happiest Christmas I've ever had. I was used to playing lots of games over that period. It was nice to have Christmas lunch at home with the family, but then what? Fall asleep in the armchair? I didn't want to be inactive, I wanted to play.

Finally, a few days after Christmas, Cecil Poynton took me to see a surgeon called Nigel Harris. He was a typical Harley Street specialist, very smart in a pinstriped suit, collar and tie. He was well spoken and had a real air of authority, the kind of man who inspired confidence the minute you met him. He asked me questions about what I'd been going through, then did a series of X-rays, from the top of my head down to my toes. It was similar to what they do now with MRSI scans. He was very thorough and I felt at ease with him.

Nigel Harris pinned the X-rays up on the screen and told me I was suffering from an arthritic condition of an area of the pelvis called the symphysis pubis. He showed me jagged edges on the two bones either side of my groin. The cartilage where the bones met had softened and the whole groin area was inflamed and sore.

He explained it was caused by years of wear and tear playing football. The only cure was a period of complete rest for at least a month. After that, I could start light jogging and I should be back playing in three months. I would be fine in the long term, but only if I followed his advice to the letter. I was depressed by the news, but relieved to know what was actually wrong.

Cecil and I went back to the club to see Bill Nick. Cecil gave him the X-rays and the specialist's report. Bill stared at me as if to say, 'You're not the man Dave Mackay was. He got over this, but you're not that tough. You're dropping out just when I need you.'

I've never forgotten the look in his eye that day.

Bill Nick felt I was bottling out and that hurt. It annoyed me, too. I'm not a quitter, never have been. I'd played through pain for weeks and done my best for the team. Bill should have given me some credit for that but, if you couldn't play, he didn't want to know you.

In those days, big clubs like Tottenham had upwards of forty players on their books. As soon as Bill Nick knew I was out for a long spell, his mind moved on to who was going to take my place. He had no time for sentiment. (Bill Nicholson lived for success, not for himself, but for the club. He was totally loyal to Spurs and proud of the club's traditions. His first game as manager, in 1958, was a sparkling 10–4 win over Everton. That set the template for his reign at Tottenham. It wasn't enough for his teams to win: they had to win in style and entertain the public.

That philosophy came from Arthur Rowe's 'push and run' Spurs team who were First Division champions in 1950–51. Bill Nick was a linchpin of that side. A terrific wing-half, who never shirked a tackle. Bill's job was to win the ball and give it to Eddie Baily, who was a brilliant, creative inside forward. Eddie became Nick's assistant manager at Spurs. They saw things the same way and formed a good partnership.

Bill bought players to do a specific job for the team. He had a very logical approach. That's how he built the Spurs Double-winning side of 1960–61. Danny Blanchflower and Dave Mackay were the perfect wing-half combination who combined power, flair and mutual understanding. The Double team was compared to the likes of Real Madrid and the great Hungarian and Brazilian sides of the 1950s. Every player had a role and all the pieces fitted perfectly.)

Bill was still striving for that same level of perfection when I was at the club. If we all did what he told us to do in a match, we'd win. It was as simple as that in his mind. But players are only human. When things went wrong, he could say some harsh things.

Trouble was, he wasn't so quick to give praise when things went right. I think anyone who played for Nick would say the same.

Bill was a difficult man to get to know on a personal basis. He lived for Tottenham Hotspur. He had a little house in White Hart Lane, five minutes' walk from the ground. He'd start work no later than eight in the morning and he'd be there until eight at night. He also drove all over the country to see midweek games, not getting home until the early hours, but he'd still be in the ground first thing the next morning. The club filled his life six days a week and he'd sometimes go in on a Sunday as well. I think his family just fitted in and went along with it.

Bill was happily married to his wife Darkie for over sixty years. She was a lovely lady, so down to earth. You would see her cycling along Tottenham High Road and she'd give you a wave, or stop for a chat. She was totally different from Nick, very warm and friendly. She'd give you a kiss on the cheek and have a laugh and joke. I really liked her, all the players did.

I'm sure Bill loved his family, but football was his life.

They say that when his first daughter got married, he cried at the wedding because he suddenly realised he hadn't seen her growing up. He'd always been away working. That's how fanatical Bill was about the club. His life revolved around making Tottenham Hotspur successful.

So, when I came back from Harley Street and Nick heard I wouldn't be able to play for up to three months into the New Year, he was not sympathetic.

I said I was sorry I'd be out for so long.

'We'll have to find someone to take your place then, won't we?' he said.

And that was it. Meeting over.

I must admit, I came away feeling very low. Some managers today are wary of their players. Bill Nicholson was never wary of his players. He always kept you in your place.

I was sent home to rest and told to have a complete break from playing and training for the whole of January, which wasn't as easy as it sounds. I hate wasting time. I couldn't drive the car. I wasn't even allowed to walk upstairs. (So much for running up and down the terraces!) We had to have a bed moved downstairs so I could sleep in the lounge. Within a week, I was like a bear with a sore head, a nightmare to live with.

When the club asked me to do some scouting, I was delighted. I was driven to Swindon Town to see them play Carlisle United, whom Spurs had drawn in the third round of the FA Cup. I went home and wrote a detailed report for Bill Nick on exactly how Carlisle played, their set-piece plays and so on. It was very thorough and I felt I'd done a good job.

A week later, I was at White Hart Lane to see Carlisle hold Spurs to a 1–1 draw. They had changed everything from what I'd seen at Swindon. Hugh McIlmoyle, their big centre-forward, played centre-half. The centre-half played centre-forward. The right back played outside right. Everything I'd put in my report was wrong. It was the same with set plays. If I'd said they would hit a long ball in my report, they hit it short on the day.

I remember looking up after about ten minutes and seeing Bill Nick in the directors' box. The look on his face said it all. He never asked me to scout again. In his eyes, I couldn't even do that right.

That meant I was trapped at home with nothing to do. I don't know how my wife June put up with me. June and I were happily married, but we weren't used to being cooped up together all day. We got on each other's nerves and argued a lot. June had our little daughter Samantha to look after and I felt in the way. It was a difficult time and most of it was my fault.

I was thirty years old and I'd never had such a long spell out with injury. I didn't know how to cope. At the back of my mind was the fear I might never get back. The specialist was convinced

I'd be fine if I rested, but a lot of dark thoughts can come into your mind when you're sitting around.

All I wanted to do was play again.

One day I got a phone call from a surgeon in America. He'd heard about my case and said he wanted to help. He said he'd been doing operations on American footballers who were suffering with symphysis pubis injuries. It involved fusing the pelvic bones together and he'd had a lot of success. I didn't like the idea of being a guinea pig, so I told him I wasn't interested. I later heard that another young English footballer had the operation done but that sadly he had failed to make the expected recovery. So I definitely made the right decision.

As days dragged into weeks, I could feel the rest at home doing my body good. Mentally though, I was in bad shape. Cecil Poynton rang a few times, but I never got a call from Bill. I had the definite feeling I was out in the cold. I was cut off from the day-to-day camaraderie of the club and the banter between the players and I missed all that.

None of the players rang me, but I didn't take that personally, not at all. That's the way it is with players. Your main focus is on yourself and playing to the best of your ability. That may sound selfish, but that's the way you have to be if you want to be successful.

I didn't socialise with the other players at Spurs. Quite a few of them were free and single and lived up in Hertfordshire, near our training ground at Cheshunt. So, naturally, they'd all go out together on Saturday night for a few drinks, or to a club. I wasn't part of that. I lived south of the river in Cheam in Surrey and I had a young family. June and I socialised with ex-Fulham team mates including Bobby Robson and George Cohen and their families. We moved in different circles, but it was never a problem.

My relationship with the players at Tottenham was that, when I was working with them, I was one of them. When we were on tour and we went to a bar after a game, I'd join in the fun, of course. I wasn't an isolated figure, or anything like that. A few of the lads felt the lash of my tongue when things went wrong in a game. That may not have gone down too well at the time, but I don't think I had any enemies at the club. I certainly never got that impression. I went my own way, but I don't think anyone held that against me.

Everyone knew how much I hated to lose. I set high standards for myself and expected the same from those around me. But I was no different from players such as Bobby Moore and Bobby Charlton. When you're playing for your country at the highest level, you don't want to let things slip. Average players have average careers. The ones who push themselves to be the very best they can will always stand out.

But when you are out of the first team with a long-term injury, you become a nonentity because you're not doing the job you were put on this earth to do. It may sound harsh, but players know that and understand it. I was the same myself. I didn't ring players when they were injured. So, I didn't expect calls every five minutes from the lads. But I do think Bill Nick should have found time to ring the captain of his club.

It never happened.

Without matches and training, I soon put on half a stone. My ideal playing weight was 12 stone 12 pounds. At that weight, I felt fit and strong. Now I was sitting around getting flabby. In the end, I couldn't stand it any more, and I went back to training a few days before I should have done.

I remember Martin Chivers welcoming me back with a big hug. He'd had a very nasty injury where his knee-cap literally went up into his thigh. Martin was out for almost a year with that, so he knew what I'd been through.

I didn't see much of Bill Nick and the first team. I started jogging on my own, then I trained with the reserves. Things went well and by mid February I felt ready to play. I needed competitive games to build match fitness. I played for the reserves at

Bristol Rovers and I didn't get the run out I wanted. They put a man on me for the whole game.

I'd done a man-to-man marking job on Pelé in the World Cup finals in Mexico in 1970. Now I was on the receiving end. I was an England international making a comeback and young players from other teams saw a chance to make a name for themselves. It all came down to reputation.

The same thing happened when we played Swansea City reserves at White Hart Lane. It was an afternoon match and there were only about a thousand in the ground. As soon as we kicked off, this young lad of about sixteen came and stood next to me. He didn't say a word, just stared at me. I ran upfield and he stuck to me like glue. His manager had obviously told him, 'You pick up Mullery, don't give him a kick.'

I thought I'd have a bit of a laugh with the lad. I ran over to the tunnel at the side of the pitch and, sure enough, he came and stood by me. Then I started to walk down the steps to the dressing rooms. This kid looked very confused. I said, 'Look son, I'm going for a pee, if you want to come you can . . .'

We went on to win the game 7–0 and I scored. Those reserve-team games were a bit of a farce in some ways, but I could feel myself getting fitter. I had a few aches and pains after the games, but my groin was fine. That encouraged me to train harder. I was longing to get back in the first team.

Spurs were still in the UEFA Cup. They had beaten Rapid Bucharest of Romania 5–0 on aggregate in December. Martin Chivers got three of those goals. Now we were up against another Romanian side, UT Arad, in the quarter-finals. The first leg was away and was due to be played on 7 March.

I thought I might get on the trip if I could prove my fitness. I got the chance when a reserve game was arranged at Swindon Town, shortly before the squad flew out to Romania. The match gave Spurs the chance to assess the fitness of several first-team players.

My game was based on being an extremely fit person. I'd spend the whole ninety minutes tackling and passing, running up and down the pitch from box to box. To quote the old cliché, I covered every blade of grass. I didn't lose too many 50–50 tackles. I didn't set out to hurt other players, but I was very powerful and I did expect to win the ball. I could read the game and pass well, but at the heart of everything was this fantastic energy I'd been blessed with.

All the way through my comeback, I'd been holding back a bit. I was afraid of my groin going again. I decided really to test myself at Swindon. The pitch was a quagmire. If I could play well on that, I could play on anything. There was only a handful of people watching, but it was a very big game for me. Everything seemed to fall into place. For the first time in ages, I felt really strong. I kept running on that mud heap for the whole game.

When I walked off at the end, I was absolutely convinced I'd done enough to prove I was fit. Eddie Baily, our manager on the day, phoned Bill Nick to tell him who had played well. We were all sitting on the coach by the time he came back. I was in my usual seat at the front of the bus. Eddie climbed up the steps, stood right beside me and started talking to the players.

'Right lads,' he said, 'all the following will be flying out to Romania with the first-team squad. John Pratt, Terry Naylor, Phil Holder . . .'

I looked at him and said, 'Ed, didn't I get a mention?'

He said, 'No, you never got a mention, mate. Sorry about that.' And with that he sat down in the seat next to me and we were on our way. Eddie made no attempt to take me on one side and tell me what was happening, he just blurted it out in front of all the players, while I sat there like a lemon. What price man management?

I hardly spoke to Eddie on the way back. I thought to myself, 'Something's wrong here. I've just played through a mudbath, I feel absolutely fine, I'm the club captain and Bill still won't pick me.'

I hadn't been near the first team for four months. I wasn't even training with them. Now John, Terry and Phil were going away with the team and I was staying at home. I felt frustrated and angry. I decided to have it out with Bill when the team got back.

Spurs beat UT Arad 2–0, with goals from Mike England and Roger Morgan. Naturally, I was pleased we'd won, but I had to sort out my own situation. Before my groin injury, I'd always got on as well as anyone with Bill Nick, but there was a distance between us now. I believe the best way to deal with a problem is to tackle it head on, so I asked to see Bill after training later that week. It was just me and him in his office at White Hart Lane.

Bill always kept his office door shut, so I knocked and heard his gruff voice. 'Come in.'

It was a bit like going to see the headmaster at school. Bill sat behind a big, old wooden desk at the far end of a long room. He didn't stand up. He just gestured to me to sit down on a hard, upright chair. Bill didn't do anything to make you feel comfortable. No cups of tea, it was straight down to business.

Players always felt a bit of fear and trepidation when they went in to see Bill. But I was determined to stand my ground. I wanted to put him on the spot and give him a piece of my mind about not taking me to Romania.

'How did the game go at Swindon?' he said.

'You know how it went,' I replied. 'Eddie phoned you straight after the game.'

Bill didn't say anything, so I carried on. 'I know you had a good result in Romania, but to be honest I was a bit pissed off I wasn't on the trip.'

'Well, you're not fit,' said Bill.

'I am fit,' I told him. 'I played on a mudbath at Swindon and I came through it no problem. Surely that proves I'm fit again. Anyway, even if you'd just taken me and put me on the bench, I wouldn't have minded that. At least I would have felt I was back in the fold again. I would have felt wanted.'

His face didn't change.

'I'm not in that frame of mind, of making people feel wanted. You're either fit or you're not. And if I say you're not fit, you're not fit.'

'Well, I'm not happy with that.'

'What do you want to do about it, then?'

'Well, to be fair, I think I'd like to go to Fulham on loan.'

I knew Fulham wanted me because their manager, Bill Dodgin, had recently phoned me. I played with Bill for a couple of seasons when he joined Fulham from Arsenal towards the end of my first period at Craven Cottage. He was a big, rangy centre-half. Good player. Now he was the Fulham manager and he had phoned me up at home the day before and asked if I fancied a loan spell with him. He said he could promise me plenty of first-team games.

'I need competitive games,' I told Nick.

'You're getting competitive games in the reserves.'

'No, I'm not. I've got little kids following me around with instructions to "stop Mullery". It's a waste of time. I think I'd be better off at Fulham. At least I'd get first-team football, even if it is in the Second Division.'

'OK,' said Bill. His voice was flat, no emotion at all.

'Well, before you say OK, is there any chance of me getting back in the first team here in the near future?'

'I don't think so,' said Bill. 'Not at the moment anyway.'

Bill picked up the phone and called Bill Dodgin right away, with me sitting there. He told him, 'You can have Mullery for a month, but we can have him back any time we need him.'

And that was that, I was on my way to Fulham. I'd been playing for Bill Nicholson for eight years, over 350 games, but when I walked out of his office that day, I felt like a stranger.

I'm not one to sit around feeling sorry for myself for long and

I arrived at Fulham the next day, determined to prove Nick wrong. To say to him by the way I played, 'Look what you're missing.'

I felt at home at Fulham straight away. After all, I had played there since 1957 and everyone made me welcome. Bill Dodgin showed me some respect, which came as a nice change from what I'd been experiencing.

We travelled up to Hull City the same day and I was ready and raring to go for my first match the following afternoon. But the football fates decided to hit me again. I went over on my ankle in the game and it swelled up like elephantiasis. I was devastated. Just when I wanted to play well, I was injured again.

Bill Dodgin spoke to me after the game, which we lost 4–0. 'Sorry about the ankle,' he said. 'I'll have to tell Bill Nick. You need to go back to Tottenham for treatment.'

'No, I don't want you to do that,' I told him. 'The swelling will go down in a few days. I want to play in the next game.'

'I'm not sure about that, Alan.'

'I am. There are reasons, Bill. I know what I'm doing. I won't let you down.'

Bill stood there looking apprehensive.

'Look, no one at Spurs needs to know about this,' I said. 'We'll just get on with it, all right?'

Bill could see how important it was to me. He knew what it was like to be out with an injury. I was there the day he broke his leg at Aston Villa the season before I left and the sound went round the ground like the crack of a whip. It was a horrible break. His shinbone was literally sticking out through his sock. He tried to make a comeback, but that injury ended his career.

Now my career was the one on the line and I needed his help. There was a pause, while Bill made up his mind what to do. Then he smiled.

'OK, Alan, you know best.'

And I did know best. There was no way I was going back to

Tottenham crocked again. What would Bill Nick have said then? Going back as a loser was not in my plans.

I played on for Fulham. I could kick with both feet, but my right was the strongest and the new injury was to my right ankle. Sod's law. I had a painkilling cortisone injection before every game. Sometimes I needed another at half-time. They were very effective. But later, when the jabs wore off, I felt sick with the pain.

It was not an easy time, but my obsession to prove Bill Nick wrong overcame everything else. The ankle gradually improved and Fulham started to play some decent football. I remember scoring in a good 4–0 win at home to Sheffield Wednesday. I was playing really well. Bill Dodgin said it. The lads in the team said it. The Press said it. I was expecting a call from Tottenham any day to say they wanted me back, but I didn't hear a thing.

Meanwhile, Spurs had drawn 1–1 at home to UT Arad on 21 March. Alan Gilzean scored as the club moved into the semi-finals of the UEFA Cup. It was great news, but I felt a long way from the action.

At different times, both John Pratt and Phil Beal had taken my place at Spurs. They were tremendous servants to the club, but I knew neither of them was as good as me at my best. Then they both got injured. I thought, 'Surely Bill Nick must give me a call now.' But no call came. Instead, I heard Bill had put a young lad called Philip Holder in the team. I'd only just retired from playing for England. I was very disappointed to think Holder was playing in my place, when I knew I was fit again. Even if I was half fit, I should have been playing ahead of Phil.

I felt like fourth choice. It hit my pride and the scars went deep. I began to wonder if Spurs would ever want me back.

All I could do was keep playing well for Fulham. On Easter Saturday 1 April, we beat Millwall 1–0 at home. They were pressing for promotion at the time and it was a really good

London derby. Two days later we lost 1–0 away to Leyton Orient. I was disappointed with the result, but happy to know I'd come through two tough games in three days without any problems. Little did I realise my biggest game of the season was just two days away.

The phone rang at home that night. The conversation went like this:

'How are you, all right?'

'Who's that?'

'Bill.'

'Bill who?'

'Bill Nick.'

'Oh, hello, Bill.'

'You playing well?'

'Yes, I'm enjoying it.'

'We've had Charlie Faulkner [Spurs' chief scout] watching you, home and away. He's come back after every game saying you're the best player Fulham have got and we should get you back here.'

'Is that right? I wasn't aware of that.'

'Yes. We've got AC Milan at home on Wednesday. Pick your boots up tomorrow at Fulham, then get over here and do some training. We've got so many injuries, we need you to play. See you tomorrow.'

And with that, he put the phone down.

I thought, 'Thanks very much for welcoming me back!'

I resented the way I'd been treated. I'd been through the toughest test I'd known as a player. At times I'd felt really down and alone. But there had been no support from Bill Nick. Now I was needed, it was report back tomorrow, business as usual.

If he had called me back to play the Easter games, it wouldn't have been so bad, but calling me now, at the very last minute, made me feel as if he saw me as the last resort. I was being used, taken for granted, but I kept all those feelings well hidden.

I phoned Bill Dodgin who was sorry to see me go. He'd enjoyed me playing for Fulham and I'd enjoyed it, too. But this was something special, going back to Tottenham for a European semi-final. Especially after all the injuries. This was my big chance and I was ready.

It's amazing how quickly things can change in football. On Easter Monday I'd been playing at Brisbane Road in front of a few thousand fans. Now here I was, getting ready to play against AC Milan in the UEFA Cup semi-final at White Hart Lane, in front of a full house of 54,000.

I saw Bill Nick as soon as I walked back into the club the next morning, a day before the game.

'Everything all right?' he asked.

'Yes, fine,' I said.

'Good. Go and get changed for training then.'

And with that he walked off. I didn't expect any more, to be fair.

I felt nervous as I walked down to the dressing rooms. Bill Nick had treated me like a novice. My confidence had been eroded. I didn't know what the players' reaction would be now I was back. I needn't have worried. A big cheer went up as soon as I walked in the door. Lots of handshakes, wisecracks and laughter. A tremendous welcome, which meant a lot to me.

I sat down and started getting changed. I looked round the first-team dressing room and I knew we could beat AC Milan. All the stars who would play in the game were there. Pat Jennings, Joe Kinnear, Cyril Knowles, Mike England, Alan Gilzean, Steve Perryman, Martin Chivers, Martin Peters . . .

Yes, it was good to be back.

European nights have always been special at Tottenham. Glory glory nights when all things are possible. And we won our share of glory that Wednesday night. We wore an all-white kit and we sparkled under the floodlights. I was made captain again, too. I didn't expect that. Martin Peters and Steve Perryman had both done the job while I'd been away.

Eddie Baily held up the armband in the dressing room before the game and said to Bill Nick, 'Who's captain tonight?' Bill didn't hesitate. 'We've only got one captain at this club,' he said. Eddie threw the armband to me.

I think Bill knew exactly what he was doing. It was a terrific boost before the game and just showed how good a manager he was on match days. He and Eddie Baily were at their best then. Eddie would wind everyone up in the dressing room before a game. He'd be swearing and shouting, saying the team you were playing against was rubbish. 'We'll beat these, no trouble at all,' he'd yell. He'd give you a hug and say the player you were marking had no chance against you. 'Let him know you're there early. Don't let him settle.' Eddie was in your face, doing all he could to get you fired up and motivated.

Bill was much quieter, but he'd been captain of Spurs on many occasions and he was a born leader. There was a stealth to everything he did. He'd go round talking to the players one at a time. He would explain exactly what he wanted you to do. The tactics for every game were crystal clear in his mind. Mike England's job was to dominate everything in the air at the back. My job was to win the ball and give it to players such as Martin Peters and Alan Gilzean.

When Dave Mackay left Tottenham, I became Bill's leader on the field. I talked all the way through matches, I never stopped encouraging other players, telling them what to do. I was totally caught up in the action. Nothing else crossed my mind for a second. Ninety minutes would fly by, because I was concentrating so hard.

Bill liked that in me. I wanted to win as much as he did. When players did something wrong, I'd be the first one on their backs.

When they did it right, I'd give them a hug. And I pushed myself as hard as everyone else. I lived every minute of every match, I really did.

AC Milan were riding high in the Italian league and they had some great players in their team on 5 April, the night of the first semi-final. Fabio Cudicini (father of Chelsea's Carlo) was in goal. He was coming towards the end of his career, but he was still a legend in Milan. AC's best player was Gianni Rivera, a very skilful playmaker whom I played against five times in my career. If Rivera gave them style, Romeo Benetti gave them bite. He was the archetypal midfield hatchet man. He could be hard and nasty, but he was a great player, too. Rivera and Benetti were the heartbeat of AC Milan. They were the ones who would give us problems.

I loved the feeling of leading the team out on to the field again that night. As soon as I heard that Tottenham roar, I felt at home. Benetti and I clashed a few times in the match. He could dish it out, but he could take it, too. At corners and free kicks, you had to be careful. He tried all the usual tricks, but there was no way he was going to faze me. I felt on top of my game.

It was such a relief to be free of the pain that had ruled my life over the past few months. I fitted into the team like I'd never been away. We played really well and won 2–1. Steve Perryman scored both our goals with excellent shots from outside the box. We went 2–0 up, but Benetti pulled one back for AC Milan before the end.

The papers made good reading the next morning: 'Mullery's Back!', 'Fairy Tale Return for Spurs Skipper' and all that business.

Two weeks later we flew out to Milan for the return leg. On the coach journey to the San Siro stadium, the AC Milan fans tried to shake us up. We had a police escort, but a few bottles still hit the windows. Then we got stuck in traffic near the ground and a mob started to rock the coach, trying to turn it over.

It was a bit harrowing at the time, but nobody panicked. If anything, the Italian hooligans made us even more determined to go out and get a result. There were some great characters in that Spurs team. Come the hour, they'd stand up to be counted, there was no doubt about that.

I was really fired up for the game and when Martin Chivers knocked a ball square to me in the first half, I crashed it in from about twenty-five yards. There's a photo of me scoring that goal and the ball looks squashed flat with the power of the shot. It flew into the net past Cudicini. Rivera scored a penalty for AC Milan with about half an hour to go and it was all hands to the pumps for a while, but we weren't about to give it all away. We won 3–2 on aggregate.

We couldn't leave the pitch straight away because the Milan fans were throwing bottles and coins, anything they could lay their hands on. We stood in the centre circle for about twenty minutes until the soldiers and police cleared the ground. We weren't bothered, we'd beaten AC Milan and we were on our way to the final.

Those Milan games sparked a fantastic run for the team. We went nine games unbeaten, right through to the end of the season. That included an away win at Highbury where I got one of the goals, as we beat Arsenal 2–0. That gave Spurs fans something extra to savour!

We played Wolves in the UEFA Cup final, the first ever to feature two English teams. Wolves were a strong side with some very good players. Mike Bailey was a good tackler and fine passer of the ball with endless energy. Mike played over four hundred games for Wolves.

Mike Bailey had nearly joined Spurs when I signed in 1964.

When Bill Nick came to Fulham general manager Frank Osborne's house to talk to me about moving to Tottenham, he started with an odd question. 'Can you play full-back?'

'No,' I said. 'Why do you ask?'

'Well, if you could play full-back, there's another wing-half we could go for and he's a very good player, too.'

'Who's that?'

'Mike Bailey.'

'Yes, Mike's good,' I said, 'but I'm not playing full-back. You'll have to make a decision who you want to sign, him or me.'

Bill made that decision and I joined Spurs.

Mike would have probably won a lot more than one England cap if it wasn't for me. He played his best football in the late sixties and early seventies, but I was always ahead of him in Alf's eyes.

As far as Mike Bailey's career was concerned, Alan Mullery was very bad news!

Derek Dougan and John Richards were a terrific partnership up front for Wolves. Dougan was an established international player with Northern Ireland. Richards was a young lad coming through and making a name for himself. 'Doog' was tall, wiry and brave. A mad Irishman who had no fear of going for diving headers when the boots were flying. John Richards was a much more cultured player, with an excellent first touch and a cannonball shot. David Wagstaffe was another dangerous player. I always rated him very highly.

The UEFA final was played over two legs and we knew we were in for two tough games. The first match was away at Wolves on 3 May 1972 and we gave a magnificent performance. Martin Chivers was superb. He got two goals. I made one of them for him. Then Jim McCalliog pulled one back for Wolves with a quick free kick, so we went home with a 2–1 lead.

The second leg came two weeks later. I didn't have the best build-up to the game. Nothing to do with injury this time. I nearly missed the kick-off because I was stuck in traffic!

The players drove themselves to the ground for home games in those days. I used to enjoy it. The streets were always filled with supporters and they'd call out to you as you drove along. Fans would sound their horns and give you a thumbs-up. It was good. It fired you up for the match.

There was no strict control over the build-up for big home games. Getting a good night's sleep the night before and eating the right pre-match meal were left to the individual. The players we had at Spurs were good professionals. They all prepared in the right way.

My routine for an evening game was always the same. I'd have a good lunch, then leave home in Cheam mid-afternoon with June. We'd pick up my dad in Notting Hill, then drive round the North Circular Road to White Hart Lane. On the night of the UEFA Cup final, the roads were solid. I've never seen traffic like it. I started to get really worried. We were sitting in a jam at Henley's Corner on the North Circular and nothing was moving. There was every chance I could miss the match.

I had to do something drastic, so I turned off the main road and started trying to make my way to Tottenham through the side roads. I didn't know where I was going. I kept turning down blind alleys, or hitting more traffic. It was a nightmare. Like one of those dreams where you are desperately trying to get somewhere and you're actually going nowhere.

We were meant to be there an hour and a half before the game. When I finally made it to the ground, I was forty-five minutes late. I rushed into our dressing room and, to be fair, I still had plenty of time to get changed. But all the hassle on the way to White Hart Lane definitely unsettled me. I liked to take my time getting ready for games. That night I was rushed and edgy. I just didn't feel right.

Our dressing room was quieter than usual. I think there was a certain apprehension among the players. Everyone expected us to beat Wolves; we'd get no big accolades if we won. There was no open-topped bus ride around Tottenham planned, or anything like that. But if we lost, it would be an absolute disaster. So we were under pressure. We could hear 50,000 Spurs fans in the ground above the dressing rooms singing their hearts out. They were really up for the match. We didn't want to let them down.

As captain, it was up to me to be positive. I stood up and said, 'We've got every chance of winning this tonight. Let's make sure we do, then we'll give the supporters a lap of honour with the Cup. OK?' Everyone agreed.

We ran out to a huge welcome and in no time I was on the scoresheet again. We won a free kick and Martin Peters curled a beautiful ball into the box. Wolves' giant keeper, Phil Parkes, came for it but I got there first and scored with a header. A split second later, Phil smashed into my leg and spun me round in the air. I fell on my head and it knocked me out. My first words, when I came round, were, 'Did we score?'

We were 3–1 up on aggregate but David Wagstaffe, who was having a fantastic game for Wolves out wide on the left, scored a magnificent goal. It flew past Pat Jennings, who had no chance. After that, Wolves kept battling all the way to the final whistle, but luck was with us. My goal was enough to give us the draw we needed on the night. Spurs had won the UEFA Cup for the first time.

It was the club's first European victory since Danny Blanchflower lifted the Cup Winners' Cup in Rotterdam in 1963, after a superb 5–1 win over Atletico Madrid. Spurs were the first English team to win a European trophy. Now we were following in their footsteps.

The trophy and medals were presented on the pitch. Wolves received their losers' medals, then we went up. These days, big-match presentations are accompanied by fireworks and ticker tape. I received the UEFA trophy off a rickety old table! But when I lifted the Cup into the night sky, the roar from the Spurs fans was unbelievable.

We had some team pictures taken, then started on our lap of honour. Suddenly, thousands of Spurs fans broke through the security and streamed on to the pitch. They lifted me and the Cup shoulder high. The rest of the Spurs players ran down the tunnel to the safety of the dressing rooms. I was left out there on my own. I suppose it could have been dangerous, but after all I'd been through in the last six months, I just wanted to enjoy it.

Those celebrations with the fans must have lasted nearly half an hour. I knew there were more skilful players than me at Tottenham: Martin Peters, Martin Chivers, Alan Gilzean, people like that. But I'd proved I had a lot to give, too. People had been saying the king was dead. Well now the king was back . . . and that felt good. Very good indeed.

But my happiness didn't last long.

When I finally got back to the dressing room, I was glad to put the trophy down. It weighed a ton! It was soon filled with champagne and we all had a drink to celebrate. The mood among the players wasn't euphoric, but it was OK. We knew we hadn't really played well, but we'd won the UEFA Cup for the fans and ourselves and that was all that mattered.

Bill Nicholson came in looking irritated.

'I've just been in the Wolves dressing room,' he announced. 'I told them they were the better team. You lot were lucky. The best team lost tonight.'

It was a tactless thing to say to a team that's just won a European trophy, but that was Bill. Discretion was not one of his strong points. It wasn't enough to win, you had to win playing well. That was at the heart of his philosophy. So, even though we'd won the Cup, Bill wasn't happy and he let us know it there and then.

I found it very strange. He could have waited a few days to make his feelings known. That would have been much better. But Bill could be a hard man to play for. Maybe that caught up with him in the end. He resigned as Spurs manager just two years later and he told me himself he'd lost the support of the players. To be honest, I was not surprised.

Bill didn't do himself any favours the night we won the UEFA

Cup. He had his say, then walked out. You can imagine the atmosphere in the dressing room after he'd gone. Nick had killed the evening stone dead.

The players all trooped up to the boardroom for a reception. There was food and drink, but the mood was subdued. Bill didn't mix with the players. He stood with the directors, who were quite a snooty lot. It was definitely an 'us and them' situation and there was no real sense of celebration at all.

Tottenham had won another trophy, but that was what we were expected to do. The directors were pleased we'd won, but it certainly wasn't a party atmosphere. I stayed for an hour or so, but to be honest I was glad to get away.

There were still plenty of fans outside the ground, singing and dancing. They gave me a big cheer as I drove out. It was good to see a bit of genuine happiness after the stilted atmosphere I'd been in.

I didn't say a lot on the way back. We dropped my dad off and when we got home, June went to bed. I could never sleep after matches, so she wasn't surprised I wanted to stay up. The truth was, I needed some time on my own to think.

I got a bottle of chardonnay out of the fridge. My mind was racing. The next morning there would be pictures of me in the papers, smiling and holding the UEFA Cup. Fans would think I was one of the happiest men alive, yet here I was, sitting alone in the middle of the night, going back over the season in my mind and trying to make some sense of it all.

Earlier in this chapter, I talked about professional football being like a rollercoaster. That 1971–72 season really proved the point. It took me on a mind-spinning ride of extreme highs and lows. Probably the best memory was scoring the goal that beat AC Milan in the semi-final. I still treasure that. One of the sweetest strikes I ever made in my life. The lowest low was feeling abandoned by Tottenham when I was injured.

I sat there for hours turning it all over and over in my mind. Every time I came back to the same conclusion: what hurt most was how I'd been treated by Bill Nicholson.

I think I made a good contribution to Tottenham's history when I finally went back. I scored two crucial goals in the UEFA Cup and lifted the team as captain. I felt I'd done enough to prove to Bill I should have been playing for Tottenham all along. I'd made my point. But the whole thing left a nasty taste in my mouth.

It could have all been so different. If Bill had put his arm round me after the game that night and said, 'Well done, Alan. You've played really well for us since you got back. I'm proud of you.' But Bill Nicholson never spoke to anyone like that. He didn't put an arm round players. He was not a tactile person. It just wasn't his style.

A few hours earlier, I'd been cheered like a hero. Now I was left alone with one big question nagging away at the back of my mind. Was Bill getting ready to unload me? I didn't want to leave Spurs, but I couldn't rule it out. Dave Mackay was Bill's all-time favourite player, but Nick was ruthless when he felt the time was right for Dave to go. It was the same with Jimmy Greaves. Maybe I was due for the same treatment.

If so, Bill would see I could be as stubborn as he was. I wouldn't be going anywhere until the deal was right for me and my family. I still had a year to run on my contract and I was happy to honour that, but maybe Bill had other plans. I had the strong feeling there was trouble ahead.

Whatever happened, Spurs had won the UEFA Cup. Nobody could take that away from me. I looked out of the window and saw dawn was breaking. I got up and went to bed.

But I knew I wouldn't sleep.

2

THE BEST OF TIMES, THE WORST OF TIMES

14 June 1970. León, Mexico
West Germany 3 England 2 (aet)
I was at my peak then as a player.

Despite the heat and the altitude, I felt strong and full of running. I was inspired by the total belief we were fireproof. We were going all the way. England were going to win the World Cup again.

West Germany were a dangerous side, liberally sprinkled with superstars including Beckenbauer, Müller and Seeler. Losing Gordon Banks with food poisoning, on the morning of the game, had robbed us of the best goalkeeper in the world. But we were still supremely confident; we knew we could beat the Germans.

The first half was tight, very keenly contested. Then, after thirty-one minutes, the ball broke to me in midfield and I saw our right back, Keith Newton, making a strong run down the wing. I hit a long cross-field pass straight into his path. It was the kind of pass you'd like to savour, but there was no time for that. My mind was running fast. I made a diagonal run into the German box. I was expecting one of them to block me, close me down. But amazingly, I was free.

Keith's angled pass to the edge of the six-yard box was perfect. The minute I hit it, I knew it was a goal. The ball flew past German keeper Sepp Maier and into the back of the net. Berti Vogts, the future Scotland manager, hit me with a tackle, but he was too late. We were one up and on our way to the semi-finals.

I was swamped by my team mates. That fateful day in León would ultimately turn out to be the most disappointing in my whole career, but I didn't know it then. I just felt a great rush of excitement and happiness.

As we ran back to the halfway line, I glanced across at the England bench. True to form, Alf Ramsey was sitting quietly, showing no emotion. A lot of critics thought Alf was cold and aloof, but I knew better. Without Alf's help and support I would have been thousands of miles from Mexico, watching the game at home on TV.

Two years before, I'd been sure my World Cup dream was over before it had even begun . . .

5 June 1968, Stadio Communale, Florence, Italy

The date is stamped on my memory. That was the dark day I became the first England player ever to be sent off in an international game. We were playing Yugoslavia in the semi-finals of the European Championship. They kicked lumps out of us the whole of the game. The referee really was poor. He gave us no protection at all and we ended up losing 1–0.

I got sent off in the last minute. By then, my frustration had boiled over. Dobrivoje Trivic was one of Yugoslavia's many hard men. We'd already clashed a few times. Then he saw his chance to hit me from behind. His studs slashed down the back of my leg. I looked down at my calf. The sock was ripped and blood was pumping out of the open wound. It was possibly the worst tackle I ever suffered.

I spun round in anger and kicked Trivic straight in his crown jewels. He went down in a heap. The ref came over and sent me off. It was the right decision, of course. I'd lost control and I deserved to go, no doubt about it.

As I walked off, I felt ashamed. I'd let Alf down. I'd let my country down. And I'd let myself and my family down, too. I didn't know Alf well at that stage, but I knew his reputation. There was no way he'd ever pick me again. I could forget playing in the World Cup, that was for sure.

Nobby Stiles was on the bench. He came running round the touchline and shepherded me into the dressing room. When you think I'd taken Nobby's place in the England team, playing the role he filled so well in '66, it was an amazing gesture. But that's the kind of man Nobby is. Very genuine.

The ref blew the final whistle shortly after sending me off. I was still sitting in the dressing room, feeling dazed. I think I was in shock really. Then I heard the stamp of studs out in the corridor as the players started to walk back in.

'Come on, mate,' said Nobby. 'Try and keep out of Alf's way for a few minutes. He's not going to be too happy about this. Let him cool down a bit.'

I knew Nobby was right. I quickly got undressed and jumped in the bath. I heard Alf's voice and ducked my head down under the water. I don't know what I was thinking of. I couldn't hide in there, could I? Just shows you how shaken up I was. I could already imagine Alf saying, 'You're a disgrace, Mullery. You'll never play for England again!' I was dreading looking him in the eye.

I'd only been under the water for a few seconds when I felt a hand grab my hair and lift my head up. Alf was looking down at me. I braced myself; this was it.

But all he said was, 'I'm glad somebody decided to give those bastards a taste of their own medicine.'

And with that, he pushed my head back under the water!

I couldn't believe it. It was such a relief. And Alf had done it in such a good way, man to man with only me and him there. Alf may have kept strangers and the media at arm's length. He hated the Press. But inside the dressing room he was much more accessible and had the total respect of his players. We were loyal to him and he was loyal to us.

He proved it in spades to me that day in Florence.

Just before I left the dressing room, he called me over for a quiet word. 'I don't want you talking to the Press about the sending off,' he said. 'Don't say a word. I'll do all the talking that's necessary, all right?'

'OK, Alf.'

I really appreciated how Alf had dealt with the incident. But as I sat in the coach waiting to go back to the hotel, I still had this terrible feeling that I might never play for my country again. I now knew Alf would back me, but what would the executives at the FA say? They were very 'old school tie' in those days. I couldn't see them forgiving me.

The next day, the papers were full of me walking off the pitch in disgrace. I felt dreadful. But Alf must have been busy working behind the scenes. I got a phone call from him the day after we got back to England.

'How are you, Alan?'

'Well, I've been a bit worried, Alf, to be honest.'

'I thought that would be the case. That's why I'm calling. Your punishment for the sending off will be a fine of £50.'

'Oh . . . right,' I said, feeling relieved.

Then Alf said something I've never told anyone before.

'I'll pay the fine,' said Alf. 'As far as I am concerned, the matter is at an end.'

I thanked him for all his help and put the phone down.

Alf had supported me all the way, which I am sure would not have been the case with my club manager, Bill Nicholson at Tottenham. Bill would have said, 'You got what you deserved. You should have kept your temper.' But Alf saw the bigger picture. He was very protective of his players and he detested teams who came into games wanting to kick us off the park.

It had been a similar scenario two years before, in the World Cup quarter-final against Argentina. Their captain, Antonio Rattin, got sent off in a very tough game and Alf called them 'animals'. George Cohen was about to swap his England shirt for one of their player's at the end of the match, but Alf stepped in and grabbed the shirt back.

'No, George,' Alf told him. 'You will not change your shirt with any of these players. I will not allow that, definitely not.'

I think he felt the same way when I got sent off. We took some terrible stick from Yugoslavia. He realised why I reacted the way I did. Maybe that's why he paid my fine. However you look at it, it was excellent management. After that, I would have done anything for him.

I've never met a player yet who played under Alf Ramsey, who has a bad word to say about him. He was extremely strict but he treated you like men, not little boys. When he was relaxing with the team, he was good company. He'd join in the banter. He had a dry sense of humour and a nice style in one-liners. We had some really great times on those England trips.

But when it was time to get serious, he would talk to you quietly and be very clear about what he wanted from you in the game. His planning was always very thorough. Immaculate, in fact.

He was also careful to guard against complacency among his players. Bobby Moore and Bobby Charlton were always sure of their place in Alf's team, but nobody else knew from one game to the next. It was Alf's way of keeping us on our toes. He never told us who was in the side until the day before.

Even top stars learnt to take nothing for granted. There's the famous story of Alf giving Geoff Hurst a lift after an England game. When Geoff got out of the car he said, 'See you next time, Alf.'

'If selected, Geoffrey,' was Alf's reply.

Alf's prediction that England would win the World Cup in 1966 came true. He was equally certain England would retain the trophy in 1970.

He was determined to leave nothing to chance. It was typical of Alf to start his planning a year in advance, so we flew out to South America in the summer of '69 to get acclimatised to the altitude and temperatures we would face once the tournament proper got under way. The trip also gave Alf and the FA the chance to look at hotels and plan where we'd stay and train.

We played Mexico on 1 June 1969. There were 100,000 there to see the game in Mexico City at the Azteca stadium and we drew 0–0. The venue was up at 7,000 feet and the temperature was over 100°F in the shade. So to go into the game with little physical preparation was a real test. We did well to get a draw, because we were dying on our feet.

The pollution and humidity made it difficult to breathe. Stamina was a big part of my game but it was very hard to run as I wanted to over there. If you sprinted fifty or sixty yards, you were sucking in air for the next two minutes, trying to recover. It was Alf's way of driving home the point that good preparation was going to be vital when we returned to defend the World Cup.

A week later, we defeated Uruguay 2–1 at the Estadio Centenario in Montevideo. The pitch was dry and bumpy and the dressing rooms were dreadful, too. As a national stadium, it left a lot to be desired. But we played extremely well until literally the final minute of the game.

I got the ball just inside our half. I turned and played it back to our keeper, Gordon Banks, to run down the clock. I didn't see their centre-forward behind me. He latched on to the ball and was one-on-one with Banksy. I was sure I'd cost us the win, but Gordon made a magnificent save and saved my blushes, too!

As I walked off the pitch at full-time, Alf stormed up to me. He was fuming. 'What the hell do you think you were doing?' he snapped. 'Knocking the ball back like that, you could have cost us the game.'

'Alf, I didn't see him.'

'Well, open your bloody eyes then! Why the hell did you pass back anyway? Why didn't you just knock it upfield?'

'I thought it was safe to play it back to Banksy.'

'Well, it wasn't safe, you stupid sod. You're lucky Gordon saved you, that's all I can say. Bloody lucky.'

I'd seen the understanding side of Alf. Now he was letting me know, in no uncertain terms, that, when it came to playing for England, sloppy mistakes would not be tolerated.

I thought, 'Blimey, I'm out of the next game.' But Alf didn't operate like that. He'd marked my card and left it there. Unless I was dumb, I wouldn't make the same mistake again in a hurry.

The last game of the '69 tour was against Brazil, at the Maracana stadium in Rio de Janeiro. I still remember the thrill of flying in across a clear-blue summer sky. The huge statue of Christ looked out across Rio from a mountain high above the city. It was stunning. Then I caught my first glimpse of those beautiful sandy beaches, beside a turquoise sea. All along the coast there were big modern hotels. I couldn't wait to land.

It felt really good to be in Rio. We were world champions and we were taking on Brazil in their own backyard. They had a brilliant team, with world-class stars like Pelé, Jairzinho, Tostao and

Carlos Alberto and I was really looking forward to the challenge.

It was only a short coach journey from the airport to our hotel, which was five minutes' walk from Copacabana beach. As soon as we arrived, Alf gathered all the players together.

'I don't want you sunbathing,' he told us. 'The sun is extremely fierce, so don't lie out in it. You can go for a walk if you like, but please remember we have an extremely important game here in two days' time.'

We all nodded and went off to find our rooms.

As usual, I was sharing with Bobby Moore. As soon as we got to the room, Bobby started to get undressed. He grabbed a pair of shorts from his case and put them on under his tracksuit.

'What you doing?' I asked.

'I'm going on the beach.'

'Hold on,' I said. 'Alf's just told us no sunbathing.'

'It'll be all right,' Bobby said. 'We can have half an hour down there, no problem.'

I didn't want to stay in the room on my own, so I did the same as Mooro and off we went.

The Copacabana is stunning. A curving sandy beach, with lovely cafés and restaurants all around. It's where the beautiful people go to be seen. Crystal-clear water, waves rolling in, a gorgeous place to be.

Mooro and I walked on to the beach. We took our tracksuits off and lay back on the sand. There were some local kids playing football and they seemed to know who we were. One of the lads came over and picked up Bobby's tracksuit top. He stared at the three lions on the crest.

'*Inglaterra?*' he asked.

'Yes . . . sí,' said Bobby.

The boy used sign language to ask Mooro if he could have his tracksuit top.

'No, no,' Bobby laughed. 'Sorry, mate, can't do that.'

Demon fast bowler! I loved cricket, but football always came first

Notting Hill's finest. My first team photo, in the early 50s (that's me, top right). Five of the Rugby Boys' Club missed this moment of glory

Fulham have new star in Mullery

By DAVID WILLIAMS

West Brom. 2, Fulham 4

MORE than one name in this West Bromwich line-up will be down for consideration before England's selectors today.

After this second successive home tanning the obvious query is—WHY?

This is not just an assessment after one match.

If I heard manager Gordon Clarke aright, it's something that's been creeping up on Albion for quite a while.

It's, according to the Albion boss, a feeling of "We are it" among some of the Albion stars.

If that's so, it's time someone around the Hawthorns slapped them down and reminded them who doles out their pay packets and who around the terraces makes them possible.

I exempt only one Albion man—Setters.

Not because of his two goals in the last quarter of an hour, but for his non-stop effort to rally a flagging side.

Fulham were that all-too-rare pleasure these days—a down to earth club side.

It baffles me how veterans like Roy Bentley and thinly-thatched Eddie Lowe keep it up.

At the other end of the age-scale I here and now predict a great future for Fulham's 17-year-old right-half Alan Mullery.

Seventeen years old and I'm a star!

Don't all laugh at once! Sipping tea after training with my hero Johnny Haynes (*left*) and 'Budgie' Byrne at an England get-together. We look shattered

Pinch me, I'm dreaming! In the Fulham first team at seventeen, next to my mentor Roy Bentley who is top row left

A brand new world. My first day at Tottenham Hotspur, March 1964

It takes two. Spurs' keeper John Hollowbread and I deal with the threat of Manchester United's brilliant Denis Law

Kissing the captain Dave Mackay after beating Chelsea in the 1967 FA Cup final at Wembley

Trudging off in shame. I was the first senior England player ever to be sent off. The darkest day of my career

BBC

Mullers the pop star! Singing on *Top of the Pops* with the 1970 England World Cup squad

Take that. I put England 1–0 up against West Germany in the 1970 World Cup quarter-final. People still ask me about this goal

Back home. A lovely airport welcome from my wife June and daughter Samantha

POPPERFOTO

EMPICS

The goal that won the UEFA Cup for Spurs in 1972 and my last for the club. I was knocked out in this clash with Wolves' giant 'keeper Phil Parkes

If I look knackered as I lift the UEFA Cup, it's because I was

One of the best football photos ever. Billy Bremner learns a lesson – don't mess with Mackay!

GETTY IMAGES

MIRROR PIX

A memory to treasure. Mooro and I leave Wembley for the last time

EMPICS

Glory Glory Tottenham Hotspur. Lifting the 1971 League Cup with two greats, Martin Chivers and Bill Nicholson

Listening intently to the England manager. I always respected Sir Alf

You can't help laughing. Peter Mellor gives Alec Stock an extra pair of ears at the photo call for Fulham's 1975 FA Cup final

TOPFOTO

EMPICS

'This Is Your Life,' says Eamonn Andrews. I'm in shock!

Mum never thought she'd be on TV. Here she is in her Dame Edna Everage glasses

I'm glad my dad was there to enjoy the show. He died just a couple of months later

MIRROPIX

First Division here we come. Victory parade with the Seagulls

COLORSPORT

Mullery the manager. Making my point to the Brighton players

SURREY STUDIOS

June and I relax at our dream home in Banstead, Surrey, with children Samantha and Neal and our dog Pelé. You couldn't get the ball off him either!

The young lad grinned. He gestured towards the pitch.

'You want play football?'

'No, thanks,' smiled Bobby. 'We watch.'

The boy ran back to his mates and the game started again. We realised they were very good little players. The ball hardly touched the sand. They were flicking it to each other with real skill. When they got near goal, they hit some terrific volleys.

Gradually, more of the England lads came down and joined us. Jeff Astle, Alan Ball, Martin Peters, Geoff Hurst. The Brazilian kids came over again and asked us to play. Jeff who, bless him, was as daft as a brush, didn't need asking twice. He joined in, so Bally went over, too.

Soon we were all playing. Inside fifteen minutes, the Brazilian kids were beating us 3–0. We got the feeling we could have a problem when we played the full national side in two days' time!

After the kickabout, most of us went back to the hotel, but Jeff Astle decided to stay a bit longer. Of course, he fell asleep in the sun and came back looking as red as a tomato. Alan Ball was Jeff's best mate, so he smuggled him up to their room and told him to get some kip.

When we all went down for dinner that night, Alf realised Jeff was missing.

'He's in bed, Alf,' said Bally. 'He's not feeling too good.'

Alf turned to England trainer, Harold Shepherdson. 'Harold, can you go up and make sure Jeff is all right?'

'I'll come with you,' said Bally.

Alan got to their room just in time to warn Jeff. When Harold walked in, Jeff had pulled the sheet up to his chin to hide his sunburn. But, of course, his face was bright red. Harold soon worked out what was going on. Alf went up and gave Jeff a terrible rollicking, then stormed back to the rest of us.

'Was anyone else down on the beach sunbathing this afternoon?' he snapped.

'Don't be silly, Alf. On the beach? You must be joking.'

We played Brazil on 12 June at the famous Maracana stadium. There were 135,000 fans there and the atmosphere was electric. Not only were the stands packed with excited fans, there were photographers, reporters and TV crews all round the pitch. I'd never seen anything like it.

Alf talked to me before the game. 'I want you to mark Pelé. Follow him everywhere he goes.'

I didn't say anything, just nodded.

'You don't look too happy, Alan,' said Alf.

'Well, if I follow him everywhere and don't give him a kick, it's going to spoil the game for me. I'd much rather be free to enjoy it.'

That may sound naïve, but that's how I felt. Playing in stadiums like the Maracana was what I'd dreamed of all my life. I wanted to go out there and show what I could do. I didn't want to be shackled in a negative role. But Alf was having none of it.

'You just do what you're told,' said Alf, 'because if we lose you and they lose Pelé, we've got a much better chance of winning this game, haven't we?'

I thought, 'Thanks very much!' So much for my creative contribution! But, of course he was right.

When the game started, I literally followed Pelé all over the pitch. Every time he got the ball, I was with him. I tried not to give him any space at all. After a while, he seemed to get dispirited. I'd succeeded in minimising Pelé's threat. I can't say I enjoyed it, but I'd done the job Alf asked me to do.

Pelé did score with a penalty, about ten minutes from time. That gave them a 2–1 win. But we played well and, although I hated losing to any team at any time, I felt we'd learn from this experience.

Pelé was very sporting after the game. We shook hands and he gave me his shirt with the famous number 10 on the back. I'd done a good job closing Pelé down, but I knew we would see a very different player at the World Cup. The great players always raise their game when the stakes are highest. There was a lot more to come from Edson Arantes do Nascimento!

Pelé's yellow and green Brazil shirt was one of the most treasured possessions from my playing career. Swapping shirts with probably the greatest footballer of all time was a very special moment for me. Some years ago, when June and I were moving house I realised that the Pelé shirt was missing. I've never seen it again. So, if anyone out there reading this book can help me get it back, please get in touch. It would mean a great deal to me.

Overall, Alf was happy with our South America tour. We'd drawn with Mexico, the hosts of the next World Cup, beaten Uruguay and narrowly lost to Brazil, the favourites for 1970. The players in the squad knew that, as long as they kept their form, they had every chance of being on the plane to Mexico in a year's time. And that was very reassuring.

My last memory of that trip is of Bally and Jeff Astle standing on a table in the restaurant at Rio airport, leading a big sing-song of Del Shannon's 'Swiss Maid'. If you know the song, Jeff was doing the yodelling part!

Alf looked embarrassed, as you might expect.

'Jeffrey, I think you should get down now,' he said, when they finished the song to loud cheers.

Jeff looked at him with a big grin. 'We can't stop now, Alf. They love us!'

And Jeff and Bally went straight into their encore . . .

England went unbeaten through seven matches in the 1969–70 season. So we were in confident mood when we flew out to Mexico on 4 May 1970, for a month's preparation before the

World Cup. We even had a hit record to send us on our way. We all appeared on *Top of the Pops* and 'Back Home' went on to top the UK charts for three weeks.

Alf Ramsey is on record as saying the overall quality of the 1970 England squad was higher than in '66. We certainly had a really good blend of players. Some of the World Cup winners were still there, along with younger stars who had come through in the last four years. Alf took twenty-eight players to Mexico. The six who did not make the final cut at the end of the month were Peter Shilton, Ralph Coates, David Sadler, Brian Kidd, Bob McNab and Peter Thompson.

England's twenty-two-man squad for the 1970 World Cup finals was:-

Goalkeepers: Gordon Banks, Peter Bonetti, Alex Stepney.

Defence: Keith Newton, Terry Cooper, Brian Labone, Bobby Moore, Tommy Wright, Jackie Charlton, Norman Hunter.

Midfield: Francis Lee, Alan Ball, Martin Peters, Nobby Stiles, Emlyn Hughes, Colin Bell, Alan Mullery.

Forwards: Bobby Charlton, Geoff Hurst, Peter Osgood, Allan Clarke, Jeff Astle.

When we arrived in Mexico, we were driven to a comfortable low-rise hotel on the outskirts of Mexico City. The hotel was in a very wealthy suburb of the city with beautiful properties all around. Alf allowed us a few days to relax and get used to the altitude and temperatures before we started training in earnest. Once again, he warned the players about the sun. He said we could have five minutes sunbathing on our front, five minutes on our back and five minutes in the pool. Then we had to put our tracksuits back on and sit in the shade. This time we paid attention.

The threat of kidnapping was taken very seriously. The England players could only leave the hotel if accompanied by a bodyguard. Most of us didn't bother to go out much. It was a case of filling the time the best you could. There were no videos, DVDs or video games then. Some players read a lot, others relaxed in their rooms and some of the lads played cards. Alf didn't mind that, but he said he didn't want any cash on the table. We could play for money, but debts were to be paid later in private.

Geoff Hurst and Alan Ball enjoyed a game of cards. They only played for pennies but when Jeff Astle came to watch, Bally saw the chance for a wind-up. He pretended to bet fifty quid here, a hundred quid there. Geoff played along with the gag. Jeff Astle was gullible and he took it all in. He kept saying, 'Don't be daft, Bally. You can't do that.'

Alan said he could afford it. After all, he was on a thousand pounds a week at Everton. So the money was no problem. Jeff was stunned – he was only on about a hundred quid a week at West Brom at the time. The truth was, most of us were on about two hundred a week at our clubs, but Bally told us to tell Jeff we were on much more.

Jeff came up to me one evening.

'Alan, can I ask you a personal question?'

'Of course, Jeff.'

'How much do they pay you at Spurs?'

'Well, the basic is eight hundred a week,' I said. 'But, of course, it's more than that with bonuses.'

'Eight hundred a week?' said Jeff. 'I can't believe it.'

'Why?' I said, managing to keep a straight face. 'Most of the lads are on that sort of money, aren't they?'

'Well, I'm not,' he said and stalked off.

We kept the joke going the whole time we were away. When Jeff got back to West Brom, he said he wouldn't sign a new contract for less than a thousand pounds a week. It made the papers. 'Astle Wants Parity with England Stars'. Finally the penny dropped and Jeff realised we'd been winding him up all along. Being the lovely lad he was, he took it all with a smile.

There was a good atmosphere in Mexico from the start, but when the time came to get serious, we were ready to go. Although we'd had a few days to acclimatise, training at over 7,000 feet was still very tough. A lot of players were physically sick on the first day.

Alf Ramsey, Harold Shepherdson and the rest of the coaching staff worked us hard from the start and they knew exactly what they were doing. Alf felt we had to go through the pain to come out the other side. It was the only way to get ready for the big games ahead.

Alf had arranged for the coach we travelled in at home to be shipped out to Mexico. Sid Brown, our regular driver, was there, too. Every morning we drove out to the Reformer Club, which was a sports and social club where ex-pats could enjoy a little slice of England. They even played cricket there!

The football pitches were immaculate, like manicured lawns, with perfect playing surfaces. But Mexico was a land of stark contrasts. Just a few yards from the side of the main pitch, there was a steep slope down to a filthy stream. There were tin shacks just the other side, where people lived in dreadful conditions. The stream filled the air with the stench of pollution, but I saw the locals washing their clothes in it.

Every day we saw the contrast between rich and poor. We were training in a top-class sports club with its beautiful clubhouse and facilities. Next door was a shanty town. You couldn't help feeling sorry for the people in those tin huts, but we had to stay focused on the job we had come to do. And that was to get fit for the World Cup.

Inside a fortnight, we'd cracked it. Our bodies adjusted to the local conditions. I found I could run again, like I did in England, without gasping for air. Mind you, after training, every bone in your body ached. We'd go back to the hotel and lie on our beds and drink endless bottles of water to recover from the dehydration.

Training was never easy in Mexico, but Alf's carefully planned schedule got us to the point where we knew we could keep running for ninety minutes. That was a major boost to our confidence.

The spirit in the squad was excellent. The players were always up for a laugh and joke. We were quite close to the Press in those days. I always trusted journalists Steve Curry, Jeff Powell, Desmond Hackett, Brian Woolnough and Peter Batt. They were good football writers who loved the game. They lived in the same hotel as us and we got on well.

But there was a feeling among the players that the gentlemen of the Press didn't realise just how hard we'd had to work to acclimatise to the heat and altitude. So we asked them if they would like to play us in a friendly game. Just a bit of fun, ten minutes each way.

The journalists were keen to take us on and we had our tactics all worked out. From the first whistle, we passed the ball to feet and made sure they did the maximum amount of running and chasing. After ten minutes four of them had collapsed, and the rest were all gasping for water. At one stage it looked like we'd have to bring the oxygen on!

I think it's fair to say we made our point, but the Press lads took it well. It was all part of the excellent atmosphere that surrounded the England squad, going into the most important tournament of our lives.

When Alf heard the Italian team was about to book into our hotel, he gave us all the day off. He told us we could do what we liked. Have a couple of beers and go in the pool for as long as we wanted. All rules were off for the day.

When the Italians arrived, they saw us swigging beers by the pool and thought that's what we'd been doing all along. We were superfit, but they didn't realise that. It was just one of Alf's mind games. He was into mind games long before Wenger, Ferguson or Mourinho.

We got on well with the Italians. It's amazing now to think how many of them smoked. A lot of England players did, too. The Italians always had wine with their meals, but we weren't allowed to do that. After our day off, we were back to a 'no alcohol' regime. Mind you, the Italians went on to reach the final, so maybe we should have carried on drinking!

England's build-up to the World Cup was going very well indeed. Next stop was Bogotá. We arrived on Monday 18 May for our friendly against Colombia. The Tequendama Hotel was said to be the best in town. The mood in the squad was relaxed; nobody could have guessed the drama that was about to unfold.

It was early evening when we reached the hotel. Mooro and I took our bags up to our room, then came downstairs to wait for dinner. We sat with Bobby Charlton and a couple of other players.

The hotel had a huge reception area with various shops. Bobby Charlton wanted to look for a present for his wife, Norma, and Bobby Moore said he'd go with him. They both strolled over to the Green Fire jewellers.

I didn't go with them, but I saw them look in the window then go into the shop. They came back a few minutes later. They hadn't bought anything and we carried on chatting. There was nothing to it.

Five minutes later, we were surrounded by armed police shouting at us in Spanish. The shop owner was there with the girl who had been behind the counter. She pointed at Mooro. He was told to get up from his seat and the cushions were lifted up. The police also felt down the back of the chair.

Alf arrived and demanded to know what was going on. The hotel manager explained that an emerald bracelet (worth £600) had gone missing from the jewellery shop. Mooro and Bobby Charlton denied all knowledge of the incident. Police took statements from them both then left. The situation calmed down.

Alf had been quick to defend his players. He knew Bobby Moore and Bobby Charlton were totally trustworthy and honest. They were, after all, the gentlemen of English football. There was no way they would steal from a shop. Alf dismissed the accusations out of hand. He was sure it was a misunderstanding and everyone in the England squad felt the same.

But Alf remained wary. When we went in for dinner shortly after, he laid down some new ground rules. He told us not to use any of the shops in the hotel and not to go anywhere on our own. He wanted us to stay in groups at all times.

There was tension in the air at the Tequendama Hotel. But it didn't affect our performance two days later, when we beat Colombia at the Stadium El Campin in Bogotá. We played very well and beat them 4–0. Bobby Charlton and Alan Ball both scored and Martin Peters got the other two. The match was played at an altitude of 8,660 feet, which was even higher than Mexico City, but we all coped well with the conditions.

After the game, the *Daily Mirror* journalist Ken Jones (cousin of Cliff Jones, the Spurs winger) said to me, 'I can't believe the way you kept running today. How can you do that at this altitude? You never stopped.' That was a compliment, coming from Ken who was also a former player. Our altitude training had really worked for me. I felt fit and strong.

Another reason for feeling good was that I was now firmly established in the team. As late as 1969, Nobby Stiles was still the man challenging me for my position. Everyone remembered him dancing round Wembley with his socks down round his ankles, when England won the '66 World Cup. He was still very popular with the fans and rightly so. But Alf gave me my chance on the South America tour in '69 and I took it. I played consistently in all three games and adapted well to the conditions. I think that swung the balance in my favour.

Now I was number one going into the World Cup, not Nobby. Jack Charlton was in the opposite situation to me. He had lost his place in the team to Brian Labone and he was like a bear with a sore head. He sat on his own, reading newspapers and magazines that had been flown in from England. He didn't want to be disturbed. If you tried to talk to him, you soon got the message. He was a proud man who loved playing for his country, but he was no longer number one and that tore him apart. Being in the team was everything.

Beating Colombia so convincingly was a fantastic result. It sent shockwaves through all the World Cup teams. Our 4–0 win told them England were ready to defend their trophy.

We flew to Ecuador the next morning. It was an incident-free trip and we went on to beat the national team 2–0 at the Estadio Olimpico Atahualpa in Quito on 24 May. Francis Lee and Brian Kidd got our goals. It was another very professional performance, this time at the towering altitude of 9,300 feet. Quito is just twenty-two miles south of the equator and very humid; the mountains around the city were engulfed in thick, low clouds. But we emerged unscathed.

Everything was going well on the football side of things, but the off-field tensions returned the next morning at the airport. Our tour schedule had been set months before. There were no direct flights from Quito to Mexico. We had to fly back into Bogotá, then catch a flight to Mexico.

Alf had arranged for us to go to the Tequendama Hotel to have a meal and watch a film, rather than hanging around at Bogotá airport waiting for our connection. I'm sure it seemed a good idea at the time, but in the light of recent events it was far from ideal.

I think we were all apprehensive about going back to Bogotá, although nobody spoke openly about it. We hoped the incident with the bracelet was behind us, but Colombia was such a volatile place, you could not be sure.

Bobby Moore looked calm as we waited for the flight. The pressure just seemed to roll off him. But I remember seeing Bobby Charlton smoking a cigarette and looking far from happy. Bobby was always a very quiet man and he was never keen on flying, after the Munich tragedy. But on that morning he looked more nervous than usual and who can blame him?

When we got to Bogotá, our worst fears came true. Some reports say Bobby Moore was questioned by police at the airport. I don't recall that, but I do remember what happened at the hotel.

We were all put in a basement room and told not to go anywhere. We started watching an old James Stewart film called *Shenandoah*. Alf liked westerns, so we watched a lot of them.

Suddenly the doors burst open. A group of armed police rushed in, grabbed Bobby Moore and took him away. Alf jumped to his feet and tried to protest, but the police pushed him away. Bobby Charlton was visibly shaken. He must have wondered if he'd also be dragged off for questioning as a witness to the incident.

The rest of us sat there, shell-shocked.

Why didn't the England players do more to defend Bobby Moore? The answer is simple: the police were all armed and we were left in no doubt that, if things got out of hand, they would use those weapons. It was a very dangerous, life-threatening situation. Anything could have happened.

As soon as the police left the room, Alf rushed out to see what was happening.

He told us all to stay where we were and do nothing. Two hours dragged by with no news of Mooro. The situation was still very unclear when the police eventually came in and told the rest of us we could go to the airport. Alf came with us, but FA Chairman Dr Andrew Stephen and FA Secretary Denis Follows stayed in Bogotá.

On the way to the airport I was dreading the sound of police sirens screaming up the road and Bobby Charlton being pulled out of the coach and driven away. At the airport, I was still frightened they'd grab Bobby at customs. None of us could relax until we were safely in the air again and on our way to Mexico.

But, of course, we'd left our captain behind and that was a terrible feeling . . .

We were in low spirits when we arrived in Guadalajara, our base for the start of the World Cup. I was as close to Bobby Moore as anyone in the England team. We always roomed together. I still couldn't believe what had happened to him. Now my shock was turning to anger. How dare they treat Mooro like that? I knew I wouldn't relax until he was safely back with us, but there was nothing I could do. Just wait.

The England team was staying at the Hilton. We had booked the whole of the fourteenth floor. There were a lot of England fans in the hotel and, of course, the Press. They had been with us through the whole build-up period. We saw them every day and it was never a problem.

They started out writing about our training sessions in Mexico City. Now they had a much bigger story, one for the front page. Bobby Moore was under arrest for allegedly stealing a bracelet.

Would he go to jail?

Would he be released in time for the World Cup?

Nobody knew.

Meanwhile, back in Bogotá, the FA executives were working closely with Keith Morris, the First Secretary at the British embassy in Bogotá. They managed to persuade the local authorities not to put Mooro in jail. Instead, he was placed under house arrest at the home of Alfonso Senior, Director of Colombian Football. He was to be accompanied by two armed guards at all times.

At the time, the England squad didn't realise the extent of the top-level diplomatic moves taking place behind the scenes. Documents released in 2001 revealed that British Prime Minister,

Harold Wilson, was personally involved in the fight to free Bobby Moore.

On 27 May, there was a reconstruction of the alleged crime at the Green Fire jewellery shop. A new witness said he had been looking in through the shop window at the time and had seen Bobby take the bracelet. (His testimony was later discredited.) Moore's main accuser was the female assistant from the shop, Clara Padilla.

Under Colombian law, Moore had the chance to question Padilla face to face. The little shop was hot and crowded and, by all accounts, Padilla looked very nervous. Bobby was ice cool. Padilla said she had seen Bobby take the bracelet from a display cabinet, then put it in his pocket. Bobby asked which pocket he had put the bracelet in. Padilla said the left. She was very clear about that.

Bobby Moore was wearing the same England tracksuit he'd worn on the day of the incident. He turned to the judge and the police and raised his arms to show that the tracksuit jacket had only one pocket – on the right. Bobby smiled at his accuser, who was nervously puffing on a cigarette. Mooro had made his point. Padilla was mistaken.

The next day, Thursday 28 May, Judge Pedro Dorado ruled that there was no evidence to warrant sending Bobby Moore to jail. He was free to rejoin the England team in Mexico, but the case was left open.

(In the aftermath of the incident, various conspiracy theories abounded as to why Moore had been accused. One theory suggested the whole affair must have been a deliberate attempt to disrupt England's preparations for the 1970 World Cup. This has never been substantiated.

In December 1975 the Foreign Office wrote to Bobby Moore to tell him the case against him in Colombia had been officially closed.

In 2003, ten years after Bobby Moore's death, the Public Records Office released documents revealing that the head of the Colombian police had been convinced of Moore's innocence. He believed the main suspect to be an unnamed woman who allegedly offered to sell the stolen bracelet to members of the Colombian underworld. The exact truth remains a mystery . . .)

Bobby had a first-class ticket out of Bogotá on Friday 29 May. He flew to Mexico City where he stayed at the home of Eric Vines, a member of the British embassy staff. The overnight location was supposed to be secret but Jimmy Greaves, who had just completed the World Cup saloon car rally, arrived during the evening for a drink and a chat!

When I finally saw Mooro again, on Saturday 30 May, it came as a complete surprise. I'd just come out of my room at the Hilton in Guadalajara and I was waiting for the lift. The lift doors opened and Mooro walked out. He was still wearing his England tracksuit and I could see he'd lost weight. He looked tired and drawn, but it was wonderful to see him again.

I instinctively hugged him and took him to the room we were sharing with Alex Stepney and Peter Thompson. While they were greeting Mooro, I rang Alf.

'Alf, Bobby's back.'

'Order a bottle of champagne and five glasses,' he said. 'I'll be along directly.'

While I was phoning room service, Mooro took off his tracksuit and threw it out of the window. I looked out and saw a crowd of Mexican boys fighting over the tracksuit down in the street. Bobby was always very particular about what he wore and how he looked. He must have hated being in the same clothes for days on end. So the first chance he got, that tracksuit had to go.

Apart from that little flash of temper, Bobby was his usual cool self. Alf wanted to know exactly how Bobby was feeling and how he had been treated. Mooro said he was fine and made it clear he wanted to play in our first Group 3 game in three days' time.

Alf told him he would have to attend a major press conference that afternoon. Bobby must have felt exhausted, but he took it all in his stride. I can't think of any other person in the England squad, including myself, who would have taken these extraordinary events half as well as Mooro did. He stayed cool, calm and collected. He was exceptional.

It was the same when we went down to dinner with the squad that night. Mooro strolled in as if he'd been with us all along. The players were delighted to see him. They gathered round and wanted to know what had happened in Bogotá, but Bobby played it all down. You could see the strain of what he'd been through in his face and I'm sure he'd had his share of sleepless nights, but he kept all the tension and anger inside.

Bobby didn't need to spell things out for the other players. It was obvious he wanted to forget the events of the past few days. What had happened in Bogotá was history. His focus was now firmly on the tournament ahead and that's what he expected from the rest of us, too.

There's no doubt in my mind that Alf saw Bobby Moore and Bobby Charlton as his two star players. There was a close bond between them. Mooro was a leader and so was Bobby Charlton. Everyone looked up to Mooro. Bobby Charlton was extremely fit and, although he only played about sixty minutes in each match, seeing his name in the starting line-up was always a boost psychologically.

If we'd lost Moore and Charlton in Bogotá, I'm sure Alf would have been devastated. He would have seen England as a ship without a sail.

England went into the 1970 finals using very similar tactics to those used four years earlier. Alf Ramsey had won the World Cup and we were happy to be guided by him. We played 4-4-2 and it suited the players Alf had at his disposal.

We all knew our job within the team. I was very fit and could do the running needed in midfield. Bally was full of energy, too. Bobby Moore was brilliant at marshalling things at the back. Martin Peters was very consistent and excellent at drifting into the box late. Geoff Hurst still led the line very well indeed.

Unlike some England players in recent years, for example, Wayne Rooney in the 2006 World Cup, we all played in our best positions. Alf picked you to do the job you did for your own club. Simple logic tells you that has to be the best way to select a side. We all took great pride in being the best in our particular position. I'd taken over from Nobby and I knew he'd love his place back, so I had to play well to stay in the team. It was good, honest competition.

I flew to Mexico thinking, 'Nobby's not going to take my place. Colin Harvey's not going to take my place, Colin Bell's not going to take my place. It's mine. I'm number one and that's where I'm going to stay until we win the World Cup.'

There was fierce competition for places in that squad, but I never once saw it flare up or get nasty. We had some very strong characters, but the spirit was excellent. Alf deserves credit for that.

Our opening match was against Romania on 2 June 1970 at the Jalisco stadium in Guadalajara, the venue for all three of our qualifying games in Group 3.

The England team that day was Gordon Banks, Keith Newton (sub Tommy Wright 51), Terry Cooper, Alan Mullery, Brian Labone, Bobby Moore, Francis Lee (sub Peter Osgood 75), Alan Ball, Bobby Charlton, Geoff Hurst, Martin Peters.

We'd played Romania twice in the past two years, drawing 0–0 in Bucharest in '68, and 1–1 at Wembley in '69. Romania were a very tough side, so we knew what to expect. We had dossiers on them and Alf showed us film clips from their recent matches and talked about individual players. The preparation for all our games was handled with great care and precision.

We beat Romania 1–0 in front of over 50,000 fans. Geoff Hurst had scored the last goal in the 1966 tournament; now he got the first in 1970. Bobby Moore had a great game and lifted the whole team. His return definitely gave us a boost at just the right time. The match may have been short on excitement, but we were on our way and getting a win in our first game was vital.

Back at our hotel, we were weighed to see how much weight we had lost. Then we were given bottles of mineral water to drink and told to lie down for a few hours. When you are dehydrated, your whole body aches. It took me thirty-six hours to recover fully.

The day after our win over Romania, there was a training session for all the squad players who hadn't taken part. The rest of us just strolled around and had a massage to loosen our muscles. We needed that rest, but the following day we were back in full training with the rest of the lads. Everyone was looking forward to the next game . . . Brazil!

Alf Ramsey was a brilliant manager in many ways, but his public relations skills left a lot to be desired. His relationship with the Mexican Press was frosty, to say the least. Alf had insisted on bringing our own provisions and even, as I've said, our own coach from England. The local journalists took umbrage and made sure their readers got the message that the England manager thought Mexican food was not good enough for his team.

In fact, all our food was impounded at customs on arrival. We never saw our Angus steaks, the Mexicans had them! It's true we had our own chef, but for a long time all he could cook us was fish fingers and chips. We got sick of it. I've never eaten a fish finger since! Alf would not let us touch the local food. And that definitely also applied to the local water. As ever, Alf wanted what was best for his team, but it turned into a PR nightmare.

There was a lot of bad feeling towards the England team by the time we played Brazil on 7 June. The night before the game, Brazilian and Mexican fans got together to make sure we didn't get a wink of sleep. There were Mexican bands playing outside the hotel. Samba rhythms filled the night. Hundreds of cars drove up and down the street, sounding their horns for hours on end. People were shouting and screaming. Fireworks were going off.

The noise was unbelievable, but the Mexican police did nothing to stop it. It was impossible to sleep. We had to move rooms at about 3 a.m., going to the back of the hotel, where we did manage to get some rest.

We all felt a bit bleary the next morning, but we were determined not to let it affect us. If anything, the events of the night made us even more focused on the game ahead. And, to be honest, the adrenalin that flooded through me on the way to the stadium more than made up for a bad night's sleep.

We were not overawed by Brazil. They had great players, including Pelé, Rivelino, and Gerson, but we had world-class stars, too – Gordon Banks, Bobby Moore, Geoff Hurst and Bobby Charlton. We wanted to win our qualifying group. That meant beating Brazil and we were confident we could do it.

Over 70,000 fans crammed into the Jalisco stadium, in the afternoon heat.

The England team was Gordon Banks, Tommy Wright, Terry Cooper, Alan Mullery, Brian Labone, Bobby Moore, Francis Lee (sub Colin Bell 63), Alan Ball, Bobby Charlton (sub Jeff Astle 63), Geoff Hurst, Martin Peters.

It was the game everyone had been waiting for. The current world champions against the former world champions and the match surpassed all expectations. I still watch the tape from time to time. There is so much to enjoy; individual skills and great end-to-end team play. It was probably the best game I ever played in and many observers have said I gave my best performance for England that day.

Alf again asked me to man-mark Pelé, as I'd done a year before. He was a different prospect this time. His level of performance rose to the occasion. Now I could see why they called Pelé the best in the world. But, after the game, Alf told me I'd done a terrific job. I followed Pelé all over the field, winning tackles and closing him down. He had very few opportunities. When he ran into the box, I was there. When he dropped short, I was there.

The one time I let Pelé go, in the fifty-ninth minute, Brazil scored. I had to move across to cover their centre-forward Tostao, who had the ball in our box. I thought he was going to shoot with his powerful left foot, but instead he turned and hit a cross with his right. Pelé controlled the ball with a perfect first touch, then flicked it right to Jairzinho, who smashed the ball into the net. That was the only time I was more than five yards from Pelé during the whole game.

His best scoring chance came in the first half and is now part of football folklore. I was goal-side of Pelé, but he climbed high to beat Tommy Wright in the air and powered a superb header down towards the corner of our net. I heard Pelé scream, 'Goal!' and it did look a goal all the way. Then Gordon Banks threw himself to the right and somehow pushed the ball up over the bar. I was the first to congratulate Banksy.

It was one of the greatest saves of all time. No doubt about it.

A lot of England players gave great displays that day. Mooro was simply magnificent. Bobby Charlton played well before Alf took him off after an hour, as he had against Romania. Geoff Hurst was outstanding, but missed a terrific chance. Francis Lee could have scored, too.

The best chance of all fell to Jeff Astle, when he came on as sub for Bobby Charlton in the second half. The ball broke free to Jeff by the penalty spot. All he had to do was roll the ball into the corner of the net, but poor old Jeff stabbed it wide with his left foot.

We were disappointed to lose 1–0. A draw would have been a fair result, but we just could not score on the day. Still, we knew we had played very well and I was confident we would meet Brazil again . . . in the World Cup final.

I hugged Pelé at the final whistle. There was a real sense of mutual respect between us.

'You are the cleanest player I have ever played against,' he told me. I didn't know what to say. It was a wonderful accolade from a brilliant player.

Then Pelé walked across to greet Bobby Moore and the famous photograph of them smiling and swapping shirts was taken. Mooro and Pelé were the two best players on the field that day and the sporting way they congratulated each other summed up a great day for football.

A few years later, Pelé toured the UK with Santos. I had the chance to talk to him again and he told me England were the only team Brazil feared in 1970. After the game in Guadalajara, they knew we would be a real threat if we met again in the final. Sadly, that was not to be.

Back in the dressing rooms, I was chosen for a routine drug test. That held no fears for me, but I was so dehydrated I could not pee. I'd been so engrossed in my duel with Pelé, I hadn't noticed the damage I was doing to my body.

Before the match, I had been out on the pitch with our doctor, Neil Phillips, and he told me the temperature was 100°F in the shade and the humidity was 110. Those conditions were bound to take their toll, even after all our training and acclimatisation.

So, when the drug testers asked me to pee in a little cup after the game, I could not go. They gave me some mineral water and that did not help. They put me in a room and I drank six bottles of Coca-Cola but still nothing. I sat there for two hours drinking water. The rest of the team were already back at the hotel.

Finally, I went into the bathroom again and managed to produce a tiny amount of pee in the cup. I decided to top it up with the local tap water, which was a really stupid thing to do. Nobody in their right mind should muck about with a drug test. But I was so tired and depressed, I just had to get out of there. I'd put myself at risk, but to my amazement the sample passed and I was free to leave.

I went to bed and my body ached from head to toe. All I could do was sip water and wait for the pain to pass. I had to rest for over six hours before I felt strong enough to get up and move about. Even then, I didn't feel like eating and I slept badly that night. I was still wound up after the game; we'd come away with nothing.

Our final Group 3 match with Czechoslovakia, four days later, was now vital. We had to win to go through to the quarter-finals. Our team for the game was Gordon Banks, Keith Newton, Terry Cooper, Alan Mullery, Jack Charlton, Bobby Moore, Colin Bell, Bobby Charlton (sub Peter Osgood 65), Allan Clarke, Jeff Astle (sub Alan Ball 65), Martin Peters.

Over 49,000 fans came to the game, but it was a real anticlimax. We won a dour, defensive match with a penalty by Allan Clarke early in the second half. As soon as the ref blew for the penalty, Allan grabbed the ball and put it on the spot. He was confident and he wanted to take it. That goal put us in the quarter-finals.

We finished second in Group 3, two points behind Brazil. Now we faced our arch rivals, West Germany, in the quarter-finals.

We drove down to León in the team bus, with a police escort. León itself was a fairly nondescript industrial city. The accommodation was OK: a motel in a guarded complex and we stayed in chalets in the grounds. It had an open-air swimming pool and was only a short drive from the Nou Camp stadium, where the match would be played.

We arrived the day before the game and went to see the stadium, which was not very impressive. It was smaller than the Jalisco stadium in Guadalajara and you felt it would lack atmosphere, even on a match day. There was no big sense of excitement about the game in León, the locals didn't seem interested. That was a bonus in one way. At least we got a good night's sleep.

We had to be up early the next morning, 14 June, because our match was a midday kick-off. We all had breakfast and were sitting on the coach by 10.30 a.m., ready to be driven to the ground. Everything seemed normal.

I was sitting next to Alf Ramsey in the front seat. He looked behind him and asked Harold Shepherdson, 'Is everyone on board, Harold?'

'Hold on, Alf, I'll just have a count.'

Harold counted all the players and said, 'We're missing one.'

'Well, who's that?' said Alf, sounding irritated.

Harold looked round the coach again. 'It's Banksy.'

'Go and get him, please. Tell him we're all waiting.'

Harold jumped off the coach and jogged off across the grounds to get Banksy from his room. Two minutes later, Harold was back, looking a bit shaken. He stood on the steps of the coach and spoke quietly to Alf. I heard every word.

'Banksy can't get off the loo,' said Harold. 'He's got Montezuma's revenge. Every time he tries to move from the toilet, he has to run straight back again. I hate to say this, Alf, but I don't think he can play today.'

Alf did not say a word. He got off and went to see for himself. By now, there was a buzz of conversation around the coach. The players were all wondering what was wrong. When Alf came back, he looked very serious, but he kept the emotion out of his voice. He stood at the front.

'Catty, you're playing,' he said to Peter Bonetti. 'Gordon's not fit, so you are in goal.'

With that, Alf turned to our driver. 'Come on, Sid, let's go.'

Alf sat down next to me and off we went. He didn't say a word, all the way to the ground.

When Peter Bonetti heard the news, he looked shocked. He was expecting to sit on the bench. Now, suddenly, he had to deputise for the best goalkeeper in the world.

I would have picked Stepney for the game ahead of Bonetti. Alex was a very strong character, nothing fazed him. He had won the European Cup with Manchester United two years before and his big-match temperament was excellent. Don't get me wrong, Peter Bonetti was a first-class keeper, but I don't think he was the right choice on the day.

The England team against West Germany was Peter Bonetti, Keith Newton, Terry Cooper, Alan Mullery, Brian Labone, Bobby Moore, Francis Lee, Alan Ball, Bobby Charlton (sub Colin Bell 70), Geoff Hurst, Martin Peters (sub Norman Hunter 81).

We started well and were full of running. I put us 1–0 up after twenty-two minutes. Martin Peters added a second after forty-nine minutes and, for over an hour, things were looking good.

Franz Beckenbauer pulled one back after sixty-seven minutes. It was a fairly weak shot, but the ball slipped in under Bonetti's body. A soft goal, a real sickener that definitely shook our confidence.

Some have since criticised Alf, saying that by taking Bobby Charlton off, he freed Beckenbauer to score that vital goal. The fact is that Bobby was still on the field when Germany scored. Alf took Bobby Charlton off a couple of minutes later and sent Colin Bell on to give us a fresh pair of legs in midfield. To be fair to Alf, he was only following the pattern of all our previous games in Mexico. Bobby played for just over an hour in each of them. But this time, things went badly wrong.

With Bobby Charlton gone, Beckenbauer found more time and space to push forward and influence the game. In the seventy-sixth minute, the Germans were level at 2–2 with an extremely lucky backwards looping header from Uwe Seeler. We'd been on a high for most of the game. Now we felt the tiredness and dehydration setting in. The sun seemed hotter, it was harder to breathe. Norman Hunter came on for Martin Peters to help us through the last ten minutes of the game.

Alf got us together at full-time and said what he'd said in '66. 'You've won it once, now go out and win it again.' But it was less convincing this time. It was 100°F the shade and the England players were physically drained. All the momentum was with the Germans. Some critics still attack Alf for not freshening up the team for extra time. They forget that sides were allowed only two substitutions per match in the 1970 World Cup finals and we'd used both of our changes. We had to play with what we had and as everyone knows, we lost 3–2 in extra time to Gerd Müller's close range volley in the one hundred and eighth minute.

After the game, we all sat in the dressing room in silence. Alan Ball had tears in his eyes and he wasn't the only one. There were no recriminations. Nobody had a go at Catty, or anything like that. The truth was that we had been 2–0 up and, as a team, we should have held on to that. I was in a state of shock. I'd been so sure we'd go all the way. Now it was over. It was the worst feeling I ever had in football.

We had cold showers, put our tracksuits on and went back to the hotel. We sat by the pool and Alf ordered champagne. We all had a glass and Alf thanked us for what we had done in the tournament. He said he was very proud to be our manager. I felt sorry for him. He was obviously bitterly disappointed, but carried it with dignity as always. It was all very sad.

Would we have won if Gordon Banks had been in goal?

That's the question I'm still asked to this day. Well, I'm sure Banksy would have saved Beckenbauer's first goal. I don't blame Cat for the other two, but if he'd kept Beckenbauer's shot out we would have still been 2–0 up and playing well, with only about twenty minutes to play. And, yes, I believe we would have gone on to win from there.

There have been various conspiracy theories about Banksy's illness. To be honest, I don't believe any of them. I think it was just a fluke. A stomach bug that laid him low at a vital time. I don't think anyone tampered with his food or spiked his drink. It was just bad luck.

Afternoon faded into evening at the hotel. Banksy was still in his room. The rest of us sat around having a few beers and trying to work out where it had all gone wrong. The journalists who had been following the England team for the past six weeks were having a meal together at a restaurant down the road. They invited us to join them for a few drinks, so a crowd of us went down there.

It was a huge restaurant with a stage and, as the evening wore on, Peter Batt of the *Sun* decided to get up and entertain us all. Peter was a real character, a Cockney who later became one of the original scriptwriters on *EastEnders*. Anyway, we'd all had a few drinks by this time, so why not?

Peter got up on the stage and started his one-man show. We were all laughing and cheering him on. It was a bit of light relief at the end of an awful day. Then the door at the back of the restaurant flew open and in walked – make that staggered – the drunkest German fan in León.

He peered at us through bleary eyes.

He didn't realise we were the England team, but he knew we were English so he lifted his German scarf in the air and started shouting.

'Deutschland! Deutschland!'

Peter Batt said, 'Excuse me. You might have won the game, but this is our evening, so bugger off!'

Peter started again. The German fan was not impressed.

'Deutschland! Deutschland!'

'Look, I've told you,' said Batty. 'I've had enough. I don't want any more, right?'

I don't think the German understood a word of what Batty was saying.

'Deutschland! Deutschland!'

This time Peter jumped off the stage, walked straight over to the German fan and in the ensuing mêlée the fan was knocked over. He went down like a sack of potatoes. He was out cold. Batty jumped back on the stage and finished his party piece. We couldn't stop laughing. It was like something out of an old slap-stick film. We were lucky the drunken fan was on his own or the Press might have had some new headlines to write.

'England Team in World Cup Riot!'

We left shortly after. It was definitely time to get back to the hotel!

I often wonder what that German fan thought when he finally came round.

The FA gave us all the opportunity to stay on and watch the semi-finals and final, but I had been away for six weeks and I was missing June and our little girl, Samantha. Inside two days I was on my way home.

Brazil went on to beat Italy 4–1 in the final, with goals from Pelé, Gerson, Jairzinho and Carlos Alberto. They were arguably the best team the world has ever seen, but I still believe we could have given them a much closer game than Italy did.

Losing in the 1970 World Cup was shattering, but overall the tournament was a marvellous experience, a real adventure. I lived through every emotion on that trip and made friendships that have lasted a lifetime. There was a wonderful camaraderie between Alf and all his players. It was like a club team. We all got on so well together. It was a special time in all our lives.

Even today, people ask me about the 1970 World Cup finals. They still remember the great games and players, the sheer thrill and spectacle of it all.

I know those memories will live with me for ever.

3

OUR NAME WAS ON THE CUP

Friday 2 May 1975

The eve of the FA Cup final. The papers were full of stories of Moore and Mullery going to Wembley for one last chance of glory. Second Division Fulham against First Division West Ham United. We were sure we could beat them. Our name was on the Cup.

Fulham were staying at the West Park Lodge Hotel, set in thirty-five acres of parkland in Hertfordshire. It was the perfect place to get away from it all and prepare for the game. The players all had dinner together in a private dining room, then settled down to watch a film called *Paper Tiger*, starring David Niven, before getting an early night. We had our own projector so we could relax away from the public.

The film had just started when the door flew open and a little man in a suit walked in, holding a huge bundle of papers.

'Fulham Football Club?' he said.

'This is a private room,' shouted one of the lads. 'Get out!'

But the little fella would not be put off. He peered through his glasses. 'Bobby Moore?'

'Yes?'

'I've got a writ for you,' said the man and served him with a writ. 'Now, Alan Mullery? Alec Stock?' He had writs for everyone. By this time someone had turned the film off and all the lights were back on. The players were fuming. What the hell was going on?

'Well,' said the little man, 'we understand you're not going to wear the boots tomorrow.'

'Boots? What boots?'

'Our client's boots. They've got a contract saying you'll all wear them in the final.'

'We didn't sign any contract.'

'Well, your manager did! So, we'll see you in court tomorrow morning. Thank you.'

And with that, he walked out.

Everyone turned to Alec Stock, who looked very embarrassed. He admitted he had done a deal with the manufacturer at the start of the season, never dreaming we would actually get to Wembley. He'd kept quiet about the whole thing. Now we were in trouble. The manufacturer was threatening to call off one of the biggest games in the club's history.

On the night before a Cup final, you want your players to go to bed feeling confident and relaxed. We went to bed wondering if the game would even be played. Luck had been on our side all the way to Wembley. Maybe now, at the last minute, our luck had run out . . .

The full story of Fulham's amazing Cup run really began the day Bobby Moore signed from West Ham United. I played my part in that.

When I rejoined Fulham from Spurs in 1972, Alec Stock promised I'd succeed him as Fulham's manager. He gave me his word on it. So, when he called me into his office one day in March 1974, I was keen to help in any way I could.

'How well do you know Bobby Moore?' asked Alec.

'Well, I slept with him for five years.'

Alec looked quizzical. 'What d'you mean "slept with him"?'

'With the England team.' I laughed. 'We roomed together for five years.'

'So how would you feel if he joined Fulham?'

'As a player?'

'Yes. Not coaching, playing.'

'I'd be delighted.'

'You wouldn't feel overawed or anything?'

'Don't be daft,' I said. 'If you've got a chance to bring him here, do it. He'd be a great addition to the club, on and off the field.'

Alec paused for a moment.

'The thing is, Alan, I don't know Bobby that well. But the word is he's had a falling out with Ron Greenwood and he's thinking of leaving West Ham. Would you go over and see if you can talk him into signing for us? We've got a contract ready to offer him. See if you can persuade him to join us.'

So my first job as a trainee manager was to sign England's World Cup-winning captain! The prospect of playing in the same side as Bobby in our twilight years really appealed to me. So I jumped into a minicab with the Fulham club secretary, Graham Hortop, and in no time at all we were at Upton Park talking to Mooro.

I knew Bobby too well to go into a big rose-tinted sales pitch. I just said, 'If you want a bit of fun for the next four years of your life, come and join Fulham. It's a lovely club to play for. The lads are friendly. We've got a great team spirit. Nobody expects us to win every week. As long as you try your best, that's all anyone asks. It'll be a nice place to play out the last few years of your career and you'll really enjoy your football.'

I'm sure Bobby could have gone to any one of a dozen clubs, but what I'd said must have struck a chord because he chose Fulham. I didn't talk money with him. It didn't even enter my head. I left all that side of things to Graham Hortop. I was on £150 a week and Mooro probably got double. That didn't bother me at all. Good luck to him. We were getting one of the world's greatest players. That was the only thing on my mind.

Mooro made his debut at Craven Cottage against Middlesbrough on 19 March 1974. After twenty minutes we were 4–0 down. Bobby ran over to me and said with a rueful smile, 'I might have made a mistake coming here!'

What a way to welcome an England hero. It could only happen at Fulham.

Bobby and I had known each other for nearly twenty years. He joined West Ham as a midfield player, but they turned him into the cultured central defender who led England to World Cup glory in '66. The only possible chinks in his game were his pace and heading. But his magnificent football brain put him so far ahead of situations, he was never exposed in those areas.

I have never met a man with so much style; he had a real presence about him. He would walk into the dressing room before a match, looking like he'd just stepped out of Burton's window. He'd wear a smart jacket, with a collar and tie. The creases in his trousers were always razor sharp. His shoes were never scuffed, his hair was never out of place.

He was always immaculate.

He'd get changed for the game and look just as good in his football kit. Then he'd come back in at the end of the match looking just the same. No sweat on his shirt, no mud on his shorts. Mooro was a class act all round.

Nothing ruffled him. I remember his first away game for Fulham at Bristol City. The players had their own private coach on a special train taking fans to the game. When we got on the train at Paddington, Bobby and I settled down in a block of four seats with a table. We fancied a game of cards to pass the time. I started shuffling the pack. Bobby got up and said he'd be right back.

I saw him go over to the steward. Bobby had a quiet word with him.

'OK, Mr Moore,' I heard the steward say, 'that'll be fine.'

Bobby slipped the steward some money, came back and sat down. The whole thing only took a few seconds. Bobby smiled at me.

'Cut to deal?' he said.

And that was it, until we got back on the train after the game, which we had won 1–0. Mooro led the way and sat down in exactly the same seat he'd used on the journey from London. The steward smiled and Bobby nodded. No words were spoken.

The train pulled out of the station and we started playing cards. Bobby leaned to his right and pulled a can of lager out from under his seat. He drank it down and the steward took the empty tin. Then Bobby pulled out another can and started on that. I suppose the journey took about two and a half hours. Mooro had twelve lagers in that time, but it was all done in such a stylish way, like a scene from a Steve McQueen film. Mooro would never have been seen surrounded by a pile of empty cans. He was far too cool for that.

When we got back to London, he thanked the steward and walked off up the platform looking as smart as ever. You would never have guessed he'd had one beer, let alone twelve.

Mooro had been excellent in our defence that day. I could see the influence he was already having on the players around him. Bobby was like me, he still loved playing football. His passion for the game was still there. And when the action was over, he liked to relax. As with everything else, he did that his way.

I was still slightly in awe of Mooro even though we'd played together for England, so you can imagine how the other Fulham players felt. We were just an ordinary Second Division side and suddenly Mooro was in the team. It gave everyone a lift. Bobby was so modest, he never played the big star. He was quite quiet in the dressing room, but everyone was thrilled to have him there.

So who were the players Bobby found himself playing alongside at Craven Cottage? The goalkeeper was Peter Mellor, whom Fulham signed from Burnley. I remember how shocked Mooro was when he saw Peter's hands for the first time. I think Peter had literally broken every finger on both hands. They looked a real mess, to be fair.

'Are you sure he can catch the ball with those things?' Bobby asked me later. I told him not to worry. Peter was a good keeper. And he proved me right on the way to Wembley, that's for sure.

John Cutbush was right back. Very quick going forward, with a nice touch on the ball. The left back was Les Strong, a smashing lad and the comedian of the team, but he could really play. When people ask how much influence Bobby Moore had on the other players at Fulham, I always cite Les Strong. He was an unknown kid when Mooro joined Fulham. Within two years he was very close to the England Under-23 side.

Centre-half John Lacy was another who benefited from playing alongside Bobby. He joined Fulham direct from London University and went on to join Spurs for £250,000. John was strong in the air and hard in the tackle. Barry Lloyd and Alan Slough were in midfield. Barry had a very strong left foot and Alan never stopped running. He was a good, steady player who could also play at the back. He joined Fulham from Luton with Viv Busby, a powerful forward who scored some vital goals.

Irish international Jimmy Conway played out wide on the right. Not very brave, Jimmy, but very quick. John Mitchell, the centre-forward, on the other hand, was a strong lad and as brave as they come. His control wasn't the best, but he scored goals regularly. Finally, Les Barrett played out wide on the left, a good crosser of the ball.

And that was our team. A very genuine bunch of players who always gave one hundred per cent. It was a happy dressing room and Mooro soon felt at home. We both enjoyed working with the younger players. They really listened to what we had to say. Everything we wanted them to do in games they did, to the best of their ability.

Bobby and I just wanted to enjoy our last few years as players. So, when the 1974–75 season rolled around, we had no great expectations. A nice little run in the Cup would be a bonus. That's the way I saw it. But walking out at Wembley in May?

Everyone at Fulham knew that would never happen.

In the third round we drew Hull City at home. We were quite happy with that. Hull were in the same division as us. They were a good footballing side, not a bunch of cloggers. They had some good players, like forwards Chris Chilton and Ken Wagstaff who scored literally hundreds of goals for the club. But we felt we had enough to beat them. It didn't work out that way. We played them on 4 January 1975 and they held us to a 1–1 draw at Craven Cottage. Jimmy Conway scored for us.

We were still feeling confident for the replay three days later. Hull City's pitch was always magnificent and we knew it would suit us. The stadium itself was pretty dour in those days, but there was a decent crowd and they saw a good game, which ended 2–2 after thirty minutes' extra time. Viv Busby got both our goals.

In those days, after two draws in the Cup, the teams would usually spin a coin to see at whose ground the third match would be played. If both teams did not agree to spinning a coin, the FA would stage the match at a neutral ground. That's what happened with Hull City and we finally saw them off with a 1–0 win at Filbert Street, Leicester, on 13 January. Alan Slough hit our winner.

We had battled hard to get through to the fourth round. Our prize was a home game against Nottingham Forest, who were also in the Second Division. Brian Clough had just taken over as manager and he was full of drive and ambition.

Craven Cottage was packed for the match on 28 January. Unfortunately, it turned out to be a boring 0–0 draw. We had to go up to their place six days later and held them 1–1, with a goal from John Dowie, who was not a regular in our team. On this occasion we spun a coin and won, so it was back to the Cottage for another 1–1 draw on 5 February. Alan Slough got the goal that kept us in the tie. We finally beat Forest 2–1 on 10 February, in the third replay at Nottingham. Viv Busby got both our goals and we deserved our win. We played very well on the night.

Brian Clough didn't give us any praise, but it didn't bother me; that was Cloughie, wasn't it? He'd do all he could to wind up the other team. I thought he was an absolute out and out character. We needed him in football. They say he was the best manager England never had and I would go along with that.

I used to love watching Cloughie on TV in the 1970s. He was on the first-ever panel of football experts with Brian Moore, one of football's best-ever commentators and presenters. They did some terrific shows together and Cloughie was a natural in front of the cameras. I suppose he was a bit like José Mourinho is today. José can be very outspoken. Cloughie was the same. Some of the things he said about people in the game were quite outrageous, but nine times out of ten he was right. He said the things other people were thinking. He was very honest and I liked him for it.

He had a good sense of humour, too. I remember Brian Moore asking him if he ever talked to his players about tactics and how the team should play.

'Yes,' said Cloughie. 'We sit down and talk and they tell me what they think . . . then we agree I was right all along!'

But Cloughie was not smiling the night we beat Forest. A good Cup run would have suited him as the new manager. He was not happy.

'See Cloughie's face?' said Mooro, after the game.

'Glad I wasn't in their dressing room,' I said.

'Might have been a bit lively.' Bobby smiled.

'Not bad though, Bob.'

'What's that?'

'Everton next. We've got nothing to lose, have we?'

'We'll give them a game,' said Mooro.

That fifth-round tie, away at Goodison Park, was sure to be our toughest test yet. Everton were riding high in the First Division. Their centre-forward, Bob Latchford, was a real threat. Nobody gave us a chance, as we drove up to Liverpool on the eve of the match. But we'd already played seven Cup games. Some teams win the Cup playing fewer games than that. We were not in the mood to lay down and give it all away.

We stayed in the Adelphi Hotel. After dinner, we all went out for a stroll, before going to bed. I can remember some Everton fans slagging us off and saying what their team was going to do to us the following day. It was done in good humour, but it wound me up a bit. I thought, 'I'd love us to go out there and win it.' My competitive instinct was as strong as ever. Still crazy after all these years!

A bit farther down the road, we saw a bloke stagger out of a pub. He wanted to start a fight with a policeman. The next thing we knew, the policeman was beating him up. We all had the same idea. That's enough excitement for one night. Let's get back to the hotel.

I shared a room with Mooro, as usual. Bobby never wanted to go to sleep early. I'd go to bed and he'd watch TV. He always had it on quietly, so it was never a problem. The next morning in Liverpool, we were both up early and went down to breakfast together. Bobby said he'd slept well. We were ready for the Everton game.

We ran out at Goodison Park in front of 45,000 fans, on 15 February. Bobby and I were used to big games. But we got a kick out of seeing the thrill it gave some of the other Fulham lads, who were doing it all for the first time. My only worry was that some of them might freeze on the day, but the atmosphere seemed to lift the team.

We were absolutely fantastic, unbelievable. We completely outplayed Everton and beat them 2–1 with two more goals from Viv Busby. It was our best performance of the whole Cup run and Bobby Moore was brilliant on the day. He seemed to have so much time at the back. Everton came at us hard towards the end of the game, but Mooro kept our defence calm and focused. I was pleased with the way I played, too. It was a great game to be part of and a dream result.

Some cities have a tradition of great sportsmanship in football. Liverpool is one of them. Everton and Liverpool fans have always been the same. If your team plays well against them, they will show their respect. Fulham walked off that day with the applause of the crowd ringing in our ears. When you think how disappointed those Everton supporters must have been, it was a magnificent sporting gesture.

We crowded back into the dressing room on a high. We were all singing at the tops of our voices in the showers. Then we all gathered round the radio to hear the draw for the next round, which was due to be made at five o'clock. We were dreaming of a big team at home. Then our number came out of the bag. Away to Carlisle United, the draw nobody wanted. Carlisle were struggling in the First Division and went on to be relegated that year. There was no glamour in going to Carlisle. We knew it would be tough.

In twenty minutes we'd gone from the high of beating Everton, which was absolutely fantastic, to the biggest low you could think of, because of the draw. Carlisle were our bogey team. We got beaten every time we went to Brunton Park. The one bonus was their playing surface. It was Cumberland grass, the same as Wembley. So it was always a beautiful pitch to play on.

Chris Balderstone was their captain, a very fit man who played football and cricket. He once got a first-class century for Leicestershire in a county match, then played football for Darlington in the evening. John Gorman was in that side, too, at left back. He went on to play for Tottenham for many years, then did a lot of coaching with Glenn Hoddle before becoming a manager in his own right.

Thousands of Fulham supporters made the long 700-mile round trip for that sixth-round tie on 8 March. The ground was full, and what it came down to really was Carlisle United against our keeper, Peter Mellor. He gave one of the best goalkeeping performances I have ever seen. We were never in the game. They ran us daft. Peter played them on his own. When they were through one-on-one he stopped them. He was tipping shots over the bar, making full-length saves. Fantastic.

This is absolutely true; we only had one shot at goal in the whole game. It was a very weak effort from Les Barrett's wrong foot that bounced before it got to the goalkeeper and somehow went in the net. We won 1–0. It was wonderful to be in the semi-finals, but it was embarrassing given how we'd played. Bobby Moore was smiling and shaking his head in the dressing room after the game. He couldn't believe it either. It had to be the luckiest win either of us had ever had.

We were starting to believe our name really was on the Cup. We listened to the draw for the semi-final and we got Birmingham City, who were in the First Division, but not the best side left in the competition. We'd avoided Ipswich Town and West Ham United, which suited us. Birmingham had good players, including Kenny Burns and Trevor Francis, but we felt we were in with a chance, as long as we played better than we had at Carlisle.

The semi-final was played at Hillsborough, Sheffield, on 5 April. We were outstanding. John Mitchell scored and we totally outplayed City. I was sure we were on our way to Wembley. Then their big centre-half, Joe Gallagher, headed an equaliser. We had been the better side, but it didn't change the score: 1–1.

The replay was under lights at Maine Road, Manchester, four days later. It was probably one of the most boring games anyone had seen for years. Both teams were determined to give nothing away and defences were on top. Birmingham did manage a few attacks, but Peter Mellor kept them out. So we went into extra time.

Fulham never really looked like breaking the stalemate. Then, with only thirty seconds to go, Jimmy Conway hit a great cross from the right. John Mitchell and their keeper both lunged for the ball. John got there first. His shot hit the keeper on the chest, bounced back and hit John on the knee, then bounced over the keeper and into the back of the net.

There was barely time to get back to the halfway line. Birmingham kicked off and the ref blew for full-time. Fulham had to be one of the luckiest teams ever to reach the Cup final, but we didn't care. We were on our way to Wembley!

The enthusiasm back in the dressing room was wonderful. I can see them all now. Les Strong, who was so happy that night but would miss the final through injury. Peter Mellor, the keeper who got us there. John Lacy, the university boy, justifying turning to football. Jimmy Conway, who would have dreamed of all this as a kid in Ireland. Les Barrett, a lad from South London, now playing in the Cup final. John Mitchell, who'd scored in both our semi-finals. Alan Slough, Viv Busby, John Cutbush, John Fraser, all now going to Wembley. Unbelievable!

Mooro and I just sat there. We'd played two hours of football and we were absolutely knackered. Bobby was thirty-four and I was thirty-three. Now we were going back to Wembley one last time. Bobby was his usual laid-back self. He wasn't jumping up and down with the rest of them, but his smile told me he was thinking the same as me: 'Good for you, lads. Make the most of it. Enjoy it!'

Alec Stock was holding court and trying to stay very cool. He had one hand in his blazer pocket and looked like Captain Mainwaring out of *Dad's Army*. 'Well done, lads,' he was saying. 'Now slow down, slow down. I've got a few things to say . . .' But everyone was too excited to listen.

Then Tommy Trinder, our chairman, came bouncing in. Tommy was a top comedian, who made his name in the old music halls. He was Fulham through and through and this was his finest hour. He had tears of joy in his eyes and was hugging all the players. I've never seen a man look happier. Tommy's big catchphrase was, 'You lucky people!' It was certainly true that night.

The other semi-final had also gone to a replay. The news came through that West Ham had beaten Ipswich 2–1 at Stamford Bridge, with two goals from Alan Taylor. That made our result even more special for Mooro. A Cup final against his old club. As my mate Jimmy Greaves used to say on TV, 'It's a funny old game!'

I'd already won one Cockney Cup final when Spurs beat Chelsea 2–1 in 1967. Now I felt I could win another with Fulham. West Ham were a First Division side and would start as favourites. But we'd already played them in the League Cup that season and won 2–1. I scored the winner with a free kick. So we could beat them again at Wembley. Our name *is* written on the Cup, we thought. It's there.

We had a great night out in Manchester. The players all had their wives and girlfriends with them. We started with a champagne buffet at the hotel, then we decided to go out on the town and go clubbing. We really let our hair down and got back to the hotel at about four in the morning.

A lot of the Fulham staff had come up for the game. They were planning to go home by train that night, but when we won they all stayed on. They didn't have anywhere to go, so the players had extra people in their rooms sleeping on the floor, on chairs, anywhere they could find a space. It was bedlam.

Somehow, we all managed to catch the train back to London the following morning. We had to go back to the Cottage to pick up our cars. Crowds of people were there to see us come home. We weren't expecting it. Fulham had never seen anything like it before, but then the club had never been in the Cup final before.

My good-time feeling during that Cup run was boosted even further by receiving an MBE from Her Majesty The Queen for 'services to football'. One of the directors at Fulham, Eric Miller, was a very good friend of Harold Wilson, the British Prime Minister. He used to lend the PM his helicopter to travel around the country. I think Eric put me forward for my award.

June and I got dressed up for the big day at Buckingham Palace. We took little Samantha with us, too. When I met the Queen, she complimented me on my playing career. I thanked her and said I had enjoyed every minute, but I would be retiring soon.

She took at step back and looked at me, then smiled, 'You're too young to retire.'

Another very happy day.

The atmosphere at the club was amazing in the build-up to the final. I did all I could to help Alec Stock in the office and he let me listen in when he was giving Press interviews over the phone. He used to say, 'Never give them a hundred per cent of the story. Always hold something back.' He was that way as a person, too. I'd been working closely with Alec for almost three years, but I still didn't feel I really knew him.

He had a major surprise waiting for me when he called me to his office on the Monday before the final and said, 'Do you know anybody who wants some Cup final tickets?'

'Not really,' I said. 'All the lads have had their allocation from the club for their families and friends. I think everyone's sorted.' I thought he was talking about a dozen spare tickets or something, but there was more to it than that.

'How many tickets have you got then?' I asked.

He took a plastic carrier bag out of a drawer and put it on his desk. It was full of Cup final tickets.

'Can you help me sell these?' he asked.

I was amazed. In those days, each team in the final got 15,000 tickets for their fans. The other 70,000 tickets were distributed by the FA. Obviously, the demand at the clubs far outstripped the supply. Tickets were like gold dust. How Alec had a carrier bag full of spare tickets was a complete mystery.

I didn't ask him where they came from. In fact, I didn't know what to say at first. I thought of walking out. My profile was pretty high at that time and, if I got found out, it could end my career. But Alec was building me up to take over from him as manager and I suppose I felt an obligation.

I wasn't naïve. Everyone knew there was a black market in Cup final tickets. Players were not on huge wages. If they sold the fifteen or twenty tickets they were allocated for the final, they could make a killing. Those tickets would never be sold on the street. They would go for corporate and business use. There was a risk element to selling tickets, but no major stigma was attached to it. It was seen as no great crime. Everyone knew it was going on. What was astonishing was the sheer number of tickets Alec had to sell. I took the plastic bag off his desk.

'Let me make a few calls,' I said.

I only needed to make one. I knew someone who was in that line of business. He told me it was a bit strong asking him to get rid of so many Cup final tickets five days before the game, but he'd have them for a fiver over face value. I didn't stop to ask Alec if the price was right. I drove straight down to the tout's flat in South London. I gave him the tickets and he gave me a pile of cash. I put the money in the plastic bag and drove back to Fulham.

I emptied the carrier bag on to Stocky's desk. I can't remember exactly how much was there, but it ran into thousands of pounds.

'Thanks very much,' he said. 'You've done a terrific job.'

I stood there staring at this pile of readies. If Alec had offered me a cut, would I have taken it? The honest answer is I don't know. I didn't get the chance to find out!

'Thanks again,' said Alec. 'See you later.'

I turned round and walked out. That was it. I'd taken all the chances and he'd pocketed all the money. Looking back, I must have been crazy to take a chance like that. It just shows how much the promise of becoming Fulham's future manager meant to me. It had been a bizarre afternoon. I decided to put the whole thing out of my mind.

Cup final week was special. Something new was happening every day. I have to give Alec credit for being a good PR man. One of his best ideas was a walkabout by the players in the streets around Craven Cottage, on the Wednesday before the game. All the houses had black-and-white scarves and banners. It looked fantastic, it really did. People were running up to us for autographs, or just to shake us by the hand and wish us luck. It was a lovely experience.

Then we got the coach out to the West Park Lodge Hotel in Hertfordshire, where we would be staying until the final. On the Thursday night, I was driven back into London with Alec Stock and Bobby Moore, for the Football Writers' Association dinner at Lancaster Gate. I'd been voted the 1975 Footballer of the Year and

I wanted to be there to receive the award in person. It was wonderful to win an award like that. It meant a lot.

All the top names in football were there that night, but I was not nervous about giving a speech. It was a forerunner to all the public speaking I'd do in later life. I told some funny stories from my career and they went down well. I had my last line worked out.

'I'd like to thank everyone who voted for me,' I said. 'As for the rest of you . . . bollocks!'

Back in Hertfordshire, we did some light training on the Friday and our minds were really on the game. Then we had that surprise visit from the little man with the writs and our world was turned upside down. Could the FA Cup final really be cancelled? Surely not, but we couldn't totally rule it out.

Most of the players were amazed by what Alec had done. They could not believe he had done a secret deal with a boot manufacturer. It didn't surprise me, of course, after the business with the tickets, but I kept that all to myself.

Nobody slept well that night.

Les Strong was injured, so we sent him to the court the next morning. He didn't get back until nearly lunchtime. Les said, 'I've got good news and bad news. The final's on, but you've got to wear the boots.'

There was no way we were going to do that. We all had our favourite boots we were used to playing in. The ones we were being told to wear looked like Aladdin's boots to me, and I wasn't going on a magic-carpet ride. This was the FA Cup final at Wembley.

All the lads who were not playing in the game had to sit and paint white stripes along the side of our boots, so they looked like the ones we were supposed to be wearing. And thats how we walked out at Wembley for the biggest game of the season. It's hard to say how much the farce over the boots affected us on the day, but we never got into the match.

West Ham grew stronger as the game went on and deserved their 2–0 win. Unfortunately, after playing so well in the Cup run, Peter Mellor was at fault for both the goals Alan Taylor scored in the second half. We were well beaten.

If you ask me what happened after the final whistle in 1967, when Spurs won the FA Cup at Wembley, I can tell you everything in extreme detail. Magnificent memories like hugging Dave Mackay and seeing tears in the great man's eyes; the cheers when Dave lifted the Cup; running round the pitch barefoot, with the Cup on my head; seeing Bill Nicholson dripping wet in the dressing room, when the lads threw champagne all over him; hearing Terry Venables leading one of the greatest sing-songs of all time. I can see it all now, as clear as day.

But when I think about 1975, my mind goes blank. A terrible feeling of anticlimax filled my whole body the second the game was over. Fulham's Cup run to Wembley had been magical, but now our dreams were in tatters. I must have gone up to collect my loser's medal, but I don't remember it. It's all a blur. Wembley is a place for winners, not losers.

But one important memory has stayed with me over all these years.

I was walking off the pitch. All I wanted to do was get down the tunnel into the dressing rooms. I felt terrible. Suddenly I felt an arm round my shoulder.

'All right, Al?' said Bobby Moore.

'Not really, Bob,' I said. 'We just lost.'

'Yes, we lost,' said Mooro, 'but we were there . . .'

I didn't say anything. There was nothing to say. I didn't feel the same way as Mooro. I just felt devastated. The Press had written a lot about Bobby and me before the final. Would the two former England captains lead Fulham to glory? Could we write one last glorious page in our scrapbook of memories? The answer was no; we never even came close.

Bobby and I walked off the Wembley pitch together for the last time, in silence . . .

That memory came back to me very clearly eighteen years later, when I heard Bobby Moore had died on 24 February 1993, at the age of fifty-one. The same age as me.

I was on a business trip to Kuala Lumpur in Malaysia. A young cleaner at the hotel stopped me in the foyer.

'Bobby Moore dead,' he said.

I thought he was asking a question.

'No,' I told him, 'Bobby Moore's not dead. I saw him not long ago.'

'Sorry,' said the lad. 'Bobby Moore dead. You wait please.'

He hurried off and came back with a local paper. There was Bobby's picture. My heart went cold. It was awful. This was Friday evening in Kuala Lumpur. I was just getting ready to go to the airport for the overnight flight home. Bobby had died on Wednesday, back in London.

I'd seen him only a couple of weeks before. I knew he was very ill, of course. He had just made a public announcement that he was battling with bowel cancer. He'd lost a lot of weight and looked very pale. But he was still working on the radio for Capital Gold and, in himself, he seemed the same old Mooro. He said he was doing all right.

I remember pulling his leg about the beret he was wearing and he laughed. That's my last memory, Bobby smiling and saying he'd see me soon. He must have known he didn't have much time left, but he didn't want a lot of fuss. That was so typical of the man.

When we parted that day, I never dreamed I'd just seen my dear friend for the last time . . .

I left the hotel and was driven to Kuala Lumpur airport in a daze. It was a thirteen-hour flight back to London. All I could think about was Mooro. He was such a gentleman. Everyone who met him felt they'd made a new friend. He was always very laid back, but he loved meeting new people, having a drink with friends, going to clubs. He knew film stars, pop stars – everyone loved Bobby.

Sadly, his life had been cut tragically short. I could still see him in my mind, with that warm smile and lovely dry sense of humour. It was hard to believe he was gone. The only consolation was that he had really enjoyed his life and lived it to the full.

I thought about what he'd said to me when we walked off Wembley together, for the last time.

'Yes, we lost, but we were there . . .'

Those simple words summed up his philosophy of life.

I couldn't get on his wavelength at the time. I was too wrapped up in my own disappointment. But I understood now. He was saying enjoy life as it happens. Live for the day. Bobby Moore lived every day to the full. He valued all the good times that came his way.

Pelé said Mooro was the best defender he ever played against.

Alf Ramsey said, 'Bobby Moore was my captain, my leader, my right-hand man. He was the spirit and the heartbeat of the team. A cool, calculating footballer I could trust with my life. He was the supreme professional, the best I ever worked with. Without him, England would never have won the World Cup.'

Now Bobby was gone. I don't mind admitting a few tears were shed on that long, lonely flight home. Mooro's death put my own life into context. I thought how much I had to be grateful for. So many amazing things had happened to the little boy who grew up in the wartime streets of West London.

4

THE ONE THAT GOT AWAY

I was born on 23 November 1941, at 14 St Mary's Place in Notting Hill. My mum had me in the little two-up, two-down terraced house in West London that was to be my home for the next twenty years.

My dad was Charles Patrick Mullery. His nickname was Obo but, for the life of me, I don't know why. My mother was Elizabeth Maude. They already had two children, Kathy who was twelve and nine-year-old Teddy.

Nine months earlier, my dad had been home on leave. Now he was back fighting in France as a private in the army and my mum was left to raise three kids on her own. It was a tough time. German bombers were pounding London night after night and we got our share.

It was a lot for a young woman to take on and, when I was just a few days old, my mum made a mistake she didn't tell me about until years later. There was an air-raid siren on the roof of the police station down the end of our road. One night it went off and she grabbed Teddy and Kathy, like she had so many time before, then rushed over the road to shelter in a block of flats. Everyone knew the corner ground-floor flat was the safest place to be in a raid. There were five storeys above it and a stairwell ran to the top, giving good stability if the building was hit. It may sound dangerous now, but it was the best option they had at the time. If a bomb hit one of the houses, it would be flattened. At least you had a chance in the bottom corner flat.

On the night in question, my mum was crowded in there with about forty neighbours, mums and children mainly, of course. All the young men were away fighting the war. Suddenly, my mother realised she'd left me upstairs on the bed in our house. She went hysterical and wanted to run across and fetch me, but the bombs were already falling, so the other women held her back. The second the raid was over, she ran home and found me none the worse for wear. It must have scared the life out of her though, especially as the nearest bomb that night dropped just two streets away from our house. The Alan Mullery story could have ended there and then.

But, if Mum made a mistake that night, she made up for it during the rest of the war. In fact, for the rest of her life. She always encouraged and supported me and I thought the world of her.

As a little boy, I got used to being woken in the middle of the night. Mum would wrap me up in a blanket and quickly carry me to the 'safety' of the flats. I can still remember the sirens echoing down the street. During the raids, we could hear explosions all around us, but I wasn't frightened. As long as Mum was there, I knew I'd be OK. My mum was my rock of stability in the middle of all that madness.

It's amazing now to think of all the neighbours crammed into that little ground-floor flat. You'd think the kids would have been screaming and crying, but it wasn't like that at all. The worst time was when the bombs stopped falling. It was almost silent as we waited for the all-clear to sound. Then we ran out into the streets to see if our homes were still standing. I saw houses that had been flattened by bombs, but I took it in my stride because I didn't know any different. Thankfully, I never saw any dead bodies, although many people did die round Notting Hill.

My mum and her friends were incredible people. If you think of the fear they must have lived with on a daily basis, yet they kept it all from their kids and just got on with life. My mum was totally unselfish. She'd be up at five every morning to go office cleaning, then back home to get my brother and sister off to school.

London was living through a nightmare, but Saint Mary's Place was like a cocoon. I felt safe there and I hardly ever left it. Even as a young boy, I was free to go out and play. The mothers took it in turns to keep an eye on the kids. In the summer, Mum would put a chair out on the pavement and talk to the neighbours. Another favourite place for a chat was a low wall by the little recreation ground. The mothers would meet there while their kids played.

If you've seen the actress Imelda Staunton in Mike Leigh's film, *Vera Drake*, then you know what my mum looked like. 'Dressing up' for her meant having a wash and putting on a clean floral pinafore dress. She was without vanity.

It was a small world and we all knew and trusted each other. The front doors of the terraced houses were never locked. It was quite tribal. If a stranger walked down our street, everyone would stop and stare at them. Who were they? What did they want? Strangers soon got moved on, unless they had a good reason to be there. It was like something out of an old western film, chasing the bad guy out of town. Our own style of Neighbourhood Watch.

We didn't have much in the way of money or food. My biggest

treat was having an egg every day for my tea. My friends would have bread and jam, or bread and dripping, but I always had a boiled egg and soldiers. So I was privileged in that way.

My mum kept chickens in the backyard and they were free to run where they wanted. Most of them were no trouble, but we had a cockerel that was as big as a turkey and he was vicious. I was about three by this time and this cockerel was nearly as big as me. I was really frightened of him. He'd fly up and try to peck you. He'd attack the rest of the family, too, but I was the smallest so he went for me most of all.

The problem was the only toilet we had was out in the backyard. I'd stand nervously at the back door, looking for the cockerel. It was only a small concrete yard, so I'd wait until he was down the far end, then run into the toilet and slam the door shut. It's ironic that a future Spurs player should have so much trouble with a cockerel, but I hated that bird!

Winter was the worst time, because sometimes the water in the toilet would freeze and you'd have to take a kettle of hot water out there to melt it. After all these years, I can still remember how cold it was sitting on that loo seat. There were strips of newspaper on a string on the wall. We didn't have any toilet paper.

There was a tin bath hanging on the wall in the yard. Every Saturday night, my mum would bring it in and fill it up with hot water. It took ages. I was the youngest, so I got the last bath. I think I sometimes came out dirtier than I went in! Life was pretty basic, but I thought that was the way everyone lived.

I can actually put a date on my first football memory: 8 May 1945, VE Day, and I was three years old. The war in Europe was over and the whole country was celebrating. There was a street party in Saint Mary's Place, Union Jacks flying everywhere and tables in the middle of the road loaded with food and drink. The neighbours all pooled what they had. Someone wheeled out a piano and the grown-ups had a sing-song. I remember playing football in the street. I was wearing a pair of dungarees and I looked like Huckleberry Finn! I was running along with a tennis ball at my feet. I beat two or three of the other lads and whacked the ball into the goal, between two jumpers. It felt the most natural thing in the world. I didn't realise then, of course, but I'd found my future.

The war was over and my young life was about to change for ever.

I was playing football in the street on another day a few months later, when I saw three soldiers walking down the road, with big kit-bags on their shoulders. We all stopped and stared: we weren't used to seeing grown men in our road. We'd grown up surrounded by women.

A woman rushed past me, shouting and crying, and fell into her husband's arms. Another woman ran across the street and did the same. The last soldier walked straight past me and into our house. That was my dad and I didn't know him from Adam; I'd never seen him before. I didn't know what to do. I went to the front door and looked in. There was my dad kissing and hugging my mum. She told me to come and say hello to my dad, but I just stood there staring at him. Mum came and took me gently by the hand, trying to encourage me, but I kept pulling away. Dad didn't come and give me a hug, or anything like that. It was a strange feeling. I was very wary. It can't have been easy for him either, away fighting all those years then feeling like a stranger in his own home. I'm sure the war left its mark on him.

We all had to get used to a new way of life, but there was one big bonus about Dad coming back – he hated the cockerel in the backyard as much as I did and, if it came anywhere near him, he'd give it a kick and send it flying.

One morning, near Christmas, I came out of the toilet and the cockerel flew at me and slashed me with its claws. I met a few hard tacklers later in life, but none of them could compare to that bird. I ran into the house with blood streaming down my legs.

When Mum told my dad what had happened, he was very angry. He was worried next time it might be my eyes. So, two weeks later we all sat down to a very nice Christmas dinner. That cockerel had had his chips, or should I say roast potatoes? My dad did the carving and he gave me a leg. I never enjoyed a meal more.

Yes, that crazy cockerel was history, but I was soon facing a new test of nerve. Saint Clement's Junior School was just down the road from our house, but when Mum left me there on my first morning, it felt like a whole new world. I was used to running free, but suddenly, I had to sit at a desk and keep quiet. I felt trapped.

In the afternoon, we had to go in the school hall and lie down on mattresses for a little nap. I'd never been to sleep in the afternoon in my life. I hated it and made such a fuss that I was sent home. Mum calmed me down, but when Dad came home he soon made it clear I was going back to school the next day and I'd better get used to it. And he was right, of course. Going to school was like anything else in life, you had to find your own way of dealing with it. Over the next few years I settled down and did well in the subjects I liked, such as history and geography. Other subjects, especially maths, left me cold. I couldn't wait to get out of the classroom. I enjoyed cricket and used to play for hours in the playground. I could bat and bowl well. (When I was older, I would even play at Lord's!)

Yes, I enjoyed cricket from an early age, but football was always my first love. It didn't take me long once I moved to the Junior school to get in the first team, although the other boys were about three years older than me. The sports master, Mr Bush, saw I was a good little player and gave me the encouragement I needed. I played on what we used to call the right wing, so being small wasn't a problem. I was quick and I never pulled out of a tackle. I hated losing, even in a five-a-side game in the street. The only player I ever met who hated losing more than I did was Dave Mackay, but that was some years in the future.

I was growing up fast and I got used to the way life had changed in our street. But I never got used to my dad's drinking and what it did to him. When Dad wasn't drunk, he was quiet and easy-going. But once he'd had a few drinks, everything changed. He became loud and abusive and wanted to take on the world.

He wasn't the only one. There were plenty of heavy drinkers down our road. In the war, our mums used to sit chatting on that little wall by the rec. Now, on the weekends, the men would sit there. I can picture them still with their scarves and cravats, these men who'd come home from the war. As soon as they heard the shutters go up at the pub, they'd be straight in there for the lunchtime session. Then, in the afternoon, you'd see them staggering back down the road to their houses.

My dad would come in drunk, shouting at my mum. He'd eat his meal, then go up to bed to sleep it off. In the evening he'd wake up, have a wash and go back to the pub again for the evening session. Nobody talked about it in those days, but my dad was an alcoholic. He spent every lunchtime and evening in the pub, seven days a week.

I tried to keep away from him, but it wasn't easy. Me and my brother Teddy slept in a double bed in my parents' room. We had to climb over their bed to get into ours. The lack of privacy hadn't bothered me before, as sharing a room with Mum had been re-assuring in the war, but now Dad was home it felt awkward.

In time, my sister Kathy got married and left home. Then Teddy went off at eighteen to the army to do his National Service, so I was the only one left with Mum and Dad. One advantage was that I got my own little bedroom, but the walls were so thin, you could still hear everything anyway. When my dad came home drunk at night, I'd hide under the covers and pretend to be asleep. I dreaded hearing him yelling at my mum.

One night, I woke up and heard Dad shouting. The noise was worse than ever, so I crept downstairs to see what was happening. Dad was so drunk, he couldn't make it outside to the toilet. He'd messed himself. I saw my mum helping him out of his stinking trousers and pants and washing him down. It was traumatic. I just sat there in the shadows, watching it all.

Finally, Mum saw me. She didn't show any emotion. She just quietly said, 'Go back to bed, son.' I went upstairs feeling confused, upset and angry. The time would come when I'd pin my dad against the wall and warn him to lay off my mum or I'd sort him out. But that was in the future. For now, I was just a kid. What could I do? I hardly slept that night.

The next morning, I waited until I heard Dad go to work. When I came downstairs, the house was neat and tidy. The only thing that told me I hadn't dreamt the whole thing was the smell of antiseptic in the air. I got used to that smell over the years. My mum didn't say a word about what had happened. I never heard her complain once. Maybe she was too frightened, or maybe she still loved my dad despite it all. I'm sure she never once thought of leaving. She was loyal to him until his dying day.

Dad wasn't a big man, but when he was drunk he liked a fight. He'd often come back from the pub covered with blood. Mum would wash him down and treat the cuts. Once, when I was about nine or ten, Dad got me involved with a fight he'd had with a man at the pub. I think it was a bit of a running feud and Dad wanted to sort it out, once and for all. He went up to the pub with me to get this man. He told me to wait outside the pub door with my cricket bat. If the man ran out, it was my job to whack him across the shins. I did what I was told and sure enough the man ran out. I belted him with my bat, then Dad caught him and gave him a hiding.

It seems incredible now, but life was like that. Notting Hill was nothing like the Hugh Grant film. You had to learn to look after yourself. If you didn't, you were in trouble. I remember going home and telling my dad that some big kids at school were picking on me. He said, 'Get some boxing lessons, then.' I did and it helped, especially when I came up against a couple of tough characters called the Brooks Twins.

They stood out, even in an area like Notting Hill. They were always together and they always backed each other up in a fight. You didn't want to get on the wrong side of them. One day they decided to pick on me. I was climbing a rope in the school gym. Suddenly, the rope started to twist round in a circle, slowly at first, then faster and faster. I looked down and saw the Brooks Twins swinging the rope and laughing at me. I held on as long as I could, then I fell and hit the hard wooden floor.

I didn't have to think what to do next, it was pure instinct. I jumped to my feet and punched the nearest twin in the face. Next thing I knew, they were both on top of me. Luckily, the sports master ran over and pulled them off. He asked what had happened. I didn't want to split on the other kids; that was something you never did. So he said if we wanted to fight we could do it the proper way, with gloves on. He got some boxing gloves and I had to fight the twins, one at a time. I took a fair few punches, but I gave as good as I got. The Brooks Twins respected me after that.

One of my assets as a footballer was my will to win. I never knew when I was beaten. That all came from the hard lessons I learnt as a kid. Not in the classroom, but on the streets – and in the school gym.

I was captain of the school football team in my last year at Saint Clement's. I was about ten. We were all really excited when Mr Bush said he was planning to take us on tour to the Isle of Wight. The Isle of Wight! It was like going abroad. Trouble was the trip cost £5 and my dad's drinking meant he never had any spare cash.

I took home the letter about the tour and Mum said I'd have to ask Dad. I was really nervous waiting for him to come home from work. I was almost sure he wouldn't let me go. He took one look at the letter and said, 'I'm not spending a fiver on that.' So, no tour for me.

I went into school the next day and told Mr Bush what Dad had said. I didn't cry, that wasn't my style, but he could see how disappointed I was. We stood there in silence for a few seconds, then Mr Bush said, 'Don't worry, Alan, I'll pay for you.' I couldn't believe it. It was the most generous thing anyone had ever done for me.

I've been on a lot of football tours in my life, but that first trip is etched in my memory. I was away for five days with all my mates and, of course, I loved it. I can still remember the excitement when we all crowded on to the coach and headed off to the south coast.

The tour was a real eye-opener for me. Up to that point, I'd lived most of my life in our road. I'd seen the sea a few times, but only on day trips in my aunt and uncle's car. On the ferry, one of the kids started a rumour that you needed a passport to land on the Isle of Wight. I wasn't that naïve, but some of the lads weren't too sure.

The next big thrill was checking in at our hotel in Sandown. Our school team in a hotel. Amazing! I don't remember very much about the actual matches, but I do remember coming home with a little glass lighthouse, filled with layers of coloured sand I'd collected from Alum Bay. I was really pleased with that.

My family had never had holidays, but the following summer Dad told us we were going hop-picking in Kent for six weeks. We went every year after that. Lots of families from down my street went. We'd pile in the back of a lorry and drive down to Kent. Once we got to the farm, we unloaded our stuff into the huts where we'd be living, one family per hut. Our first job was to get fresh straw to fill the big mattress. There was a curtain down the middle. Parents one side, kids the other, that's the way it worked. The huts had tin roofs so, when it rained at night, you couldn't sleep for the noise.

There was no running water. You had to get your water in a bucket from a pump in the farmyard. As for the toilets, they were just holes in the ground and . . . well, as they say now, don't even go there!

It sounds rough and ready, but I had a lot of fun in Kent. My mum was out all day, picking the hops with her friends. A lot of the men just came down for the weekends, but my dad stayed for the full six weeks, because he had a good job. He was what they called a poll man. He would clear any hops that were left on the top of the vines, then load them up on the lorries.

He probably made good money, but of course he spent all his spare time in the boozer. He regularly borrowed money from the farmer. When it was time to go back to London there was nothing left. He'd spent it all on drink.

It didn't matter to me. I was just happy to be out in the country with my mates. We'd go off for hours at a time, no problem. I can remember walking down the dusty country lanes and hardly ever seeing a car. I loved it, because it was all such a big adventure.

You often hear stories about hop pickers having fights with the locals, but my little gang wasn't like that. We got on well with the local kids. They showed us the best places to play. They knew where you could dam a local stream and make yourself a pool deep enough to swim in. Best of all, they knew where to go scrumping to get the juiciest apples.

The farmer, Mr Lux, had two lovely golden retrievers. My dad had a scruffy little mongrel called Sandy that followed him everywhere. Sandy was only small, but every time he saw the farmer with his two great big dogs, he'd go for them. They'd grab him by the neck and throw him up in the air, but he never learnt. He kept picking fights and coming off worst, just like my dad.

Many years later, I went back to the farm with June. The old huts were still there.

June couldn't believe we'd lived in such a dump for six weeks every year. And she was right, it was a dump, but to us kids it was a holiday and looking back, I only hear the sound of laughter. The camaraderie was incredible. That's what made it so special.

Back in Notting Hill it was time to leave Saint Clement's and move on. I failed my 11-plus exam, so I didn't have far to travel. St John's Secondary School was down the other end of our road.

As soon as I arrived, they put me in the senior football team. Most of the lads were four years older than me. It was the same when the cricket season came round – I was straight in the first team. I've got an old team picture. All the other lads are twice my size. I'm sitting on a chair and my feet don't even reach the ground.

I played at Lord's twice for the Federation of London Boys' Clubs against the Middlesex Young Professionals. That all stemmed from playing for Rugby Boys' Club in Notting Hill. One of our former members was already a player at Lord's. John Murray kept wicket for Middlesex and England.

I made fifty in my first innings at Lord's and a golden duck in my second. I know which memory I prefer. I got the chance to go for trials with Middlesex, but there was some confusion over the arrangements and I turned up on the wrong day. I remember standing outside the famous Grace Gates feeling totally frustrated. My dreams of following in John Murray's footsteps were not to be. But I soon got over it.

Football filled my life. Some Saturdays I'd play on the wing for the school in the morning, then in goal for Rugby Boys' Club in the afternoon. There were no showers then, so I'd turn up for the second game with my legs already caked in mud.

I remember scoring two goals in a match, when I was playing in goal. The other team weren't much good. We won 37–0. I got bored in goal, so a couple of times I ran the length of the field and scored.

I started watching QPR around that time, too. Sometimes I went with friends, but I often walked to Loftus Road alone; nobody gave it a second thought. I liked to get there about two hours before kick-off. There was a good café near the ground where I'd get a bag of chips for sixpence and sit eating them on the terraces. I always stood right at the front, behind one of the goals.

My first hero was QPR's goalkeeper, Reg Allen. He eventually signed for Manchester United for £10,000, which was a fortune in those days. He wore one of those old roll-neck jumpers and always looked immaculate, with a parting straight down the middle of his Brylcreemed hair.

I saw Reg make some great saves, but the match I remember best was against Notts County, when Tommy Lawton scored a couple of perfect powerful headers. Reg didn't make any mistakes that day, Tommy was just too good for him. People talk glibly about legends in the game, but Tommy Lawton really deserves the tag.

I enjoyed watching QPR but, of course, I preferred playing. As I got bigger and stronger, my game improved. I can give you the exact date when I first thought about making it as a professional. It was just two days after my twelfth birthday.

25 November 1953. England 3 Hungary 6

I'd never been to Wembley stadium. I'd never even considered it a possibility, even though it was only a few miles across London. My mum and dad could never afford treats like that. But the match was on TV and I wasn't going to miss it.

I should have won an Oscar at school that morning. I was bent double with chronic stomach cramps. Every time the imaginary stabbing pains hit me, I moaned and groaned. My teacher was so worried, she sent me home.

A couple of hours later I was over the road at Aunt Rose's flat – she was the only one in the family with a telly – watching the grainy black-and-white pictures that were to give English football the major shake-up it so desperately needed.

I stared at the screen in wonder. I loved the way Ferenc Puskás and his team played the game. I'd never seen football like that before. What stood out was their pace and their superb ball control.

Hungary played in a 4-2-4 formation and Hidegkuti scored a hat-trick from midfield.

They were in a totally different class from England, light years ahead. And on 23 May 1954, Hungary proved the Wembley result was no fluke by beating England 7–1 in Budapest. That still ranks as England's worst-ever defeat.

I hated seeing England lose, but I was excited by the brilliant football Hungary had played. For the first time in my young life, I had a dream to chase. I wanted to be out there, playing for England against the best in the world, in fabulous stadiums like Wembley. That match shaped my future. From that day on I knew what I wanted to be: a professional footballer.

Nobody in my family had ever been the least bit sporty, apart from my brother who was a good cross-country runner at school. No football stars had ever emerged from our area, so people were naturally sceptical about my chances.

I remember a teacher asking us to do a composition about what we wanted to be when we left school. I just wrote one sentence: 'I want to be a professional footballer.' He read it and said, 'I don't know any footballers, do you? Maybe you should think of something else.' But I didn't want to think of something else. I wanted to be a footballer and I was determined to make it happen. It didn't matter what anyone else thought. If you're chasing a dream like that as a kid, you need to believe it yourself. If not, you've got no chance.

A lot of the lads I grew up with turned to a life of crime because of the lack of education and job opportunities in our area, but I was different. I knew football was my passport to the future. I've been very critical about my dad and his drinking, which doesn't mean I didn't love him, but I didn't want to turn out like him. Even as a kid, I knew there must be more to life than that.

One of the toughest men from my childhood was called Joey Cannon. He was a few years older than I was. He has subsequently become an accomplished writer, but at that time he seemed like a scary customer to me. He was, though, always very good with local people, the people he knew. That was the code. Later on, Joey wrote about me in one of his books. He said I was the one who broke free of that tough environment. The one who got away.

Things didn't happen by chance. I knew my next big step was to get into the West London Boys' team. It took a while. I went for my first trial as a right winger. The man running the team asked me if we'd got a phone at home. When I said we hadn't, he told me not to worry, they'd be in touch, but I never heard from him.

The next year I went to the trials as a centre-forward and the manager asked, 'Has your family got a phone yet?' I said no. He said he'd be in touch, but again nothing happened. My junior football career just wasn't happening the way I'd hoped.

Then I made one of the most important decisions of my life: I decided to play in midfield or, as we used to say then, wing-half. Nobody told me to do it, I made the switch myself. I wanted to be in the heart of the action of every game. I enjoyed tackling and pushing forward, so right-half was perfect for me.

The next time I went for a trial for West London Boys, at the start of the 1956–57 season, I got picked. In fact, I was soon made captain of the team. I got picked for Middlesex Boys, too. Things were moving fast, but I didn't let it go to my head, I just concentrated on making the most of every chance that came my way.

I got my first ever pair of new boots that season. Aunt Rose came round one day when I was cleaning my old ones. She saw what a state they were in and gave me £5 to buy a new pair. It was a lot of money, but she could afford it because she was running a pub at the time. Rose was very good, she always looked after me.

I caught the tube up to Great Portland Street and bought the boots from a big sports shop called W.G. Gross on Euston Road. When I got home, I took the studs off and wore the boots for the rest of the day. I kept walking up and down the stairs, trying to break them in. I played for West London Boys the next day and ended up with blisters all over my feet. But, overall, those boots definitely helped my game. I was playing better than ever.

Proof of my progress came when I was selected for London Boys against Manchester Boys. The home leg was played on 29 October and it was memorable for three reasons. First, we played it at Tottenham, so I got my first visit to White Hart Lane. Second, I came up against Nobby Stiles, who was a tough little player even then. Third, my hero Johnny Haynes was at the game with Fulham's general manager, Frank Osborne. Apparently, I made a good impression on them both and they marked me down as one to watch for the future.

When we arrived in Manchester for the away leg, the day before the game, a tour of Old Trafford was arranged for us. As luck would have it, the first team were training there that day, so we saw all those great players – Duncan Edwards, Tommy Taylor, Roger Byrne, Harry Gregg, Eddie Colman and Bobby Charlton. Matt Busby was taking the training out on the pitch. I remember Tommy Taylor chatting to us about our match, then he did a couple of warm-up laps, before practising his shooting. Roger Byrne was pinging crosses into the box from the right wing. Tommy had to run into the box and hit them first time on the volley. He caught the first one perfectly. The ball flew into the net. Harry Gregg was a great keeper but he had no chance. I'd never seen a ball hit with that sort of power.

Everyone at Old Trafford was friendly that day. So you can imagine how I felt on 6 February 1958, when I heard the terrible news about the Munich air crash. I couldn't believe so many of the stars I'd seen that day were dead. They were heroes to thousands of people and now they were gone. It was so sad. The news sent a chill right through me . . .

I went into 1957 knowing it was make-or-break time for me. I was in my last year at school and if I was going to sign for a professional club, it had to happen in the next few months.

West London Boys trained at QPR. Their trainer, Alec Farmer, used to tap me up all the time. He said QPR was the club for me and they'd sign me when I left school. Playing for my favourite team would have been brilliant. If QPR had asked me, I would have signed like a shot, but they never got round to offering me a contract.

They say God has a plan for all of us and my life changed for ever in one day. West London Boys were through to the quarter-finals of the English Schools' Trophy. We were expecting to play the match at Loftus Road, but it got switched to the Harrods sports ground in Hammersmith.

After the game, a man called Mick Simmons introduced himself. He was a scout for Fulham. I knew they'd shown some interest in me but, if the match that morning had been at QPR, Mick would not have been there to see me play. Fate had taken a hand and Mick asked me straight out how I'd feel about signing for Fulham. I'd always dreamed of playing for QPR, but this was a definite offer so, of course, I was interested. Mick asked me to think about it and gave me a ticket for Fulham's match that afternoon. When I got to Craven Cottage, there were 30,000 fans in the ground and I had one of the best seats in the house. I found myself on a bench on the track, right beside the pitch. I was only about twenty yards from the dugouts, where the managers were sitting.

The match started and I was really wrapped up in the action. Time seemed to fly by. Imagine my surprise when Fulham's number 11 suddenly walked off the pitch and sat down on the bench beside me. Someone from the crowd offered him a fag and he took it. He sat there with his legs crossed and a big smile on his face, smoking a cigarette and watching the game. The fans behind us were all laughing.

Back on the pitch, Johnny Haynes won the ball and hit a fifty-yard pass to where his left winger should have been. The ball ran harmlessly out of play. When Johnny saw what was going on, the air turned blue. He was screaming at the number 11, everyone could hear what he was saying.

The player on the bench waited until Johnny had finished, then shouted back, 'When I'm out here waiting, you never pass to me. Then, when I'm having a fag, you decide to give me the ball!'

Even Johnny Haynes had to laugh.

The player on the bench was Tosh Chamberlain. I thought to myself, 'I've got to join this club! I'll have some fun here.' And I was right. Two years later I was playing for the first team and a whole new world lay ahead.

5

STARRY EYED: THE BOY BECOMES A MAN

The white Sunbeam Alpine drove slowly down St Mary's Place, looking for number 14. Heads turned and people stared. You didn't often see a flash sports car down my road.

It stopped outside my house and a tall, well-built man in a smart sports jacket climbed out. It was Frank Osborne, general manager of Fulham football club. He was a larger-than-life character who drank a bottle of whisky and smoked eighty cigarettes a day and would live to the age of ninety-one. In his youth he'd been the first Fulham player to be capped by England. He knew the game inside out and he was determined to make Craven Cottage my new home.

Frank had heard on the grapevine that a few London clubs were after me. QPR, Brentford, Charlton and West Ham United had all shown interest. There was talk of Chelsea, too.

Frank made sure he was first in the queue. It was April 1957, just a couple of weeks after my memorable trip to see Fulham play. I'd left school the previous Friday. Now it was Monday morning and Frank was knocking on my door.

I'd had a letter from the club, setting up the meeting. That in itself was an event. We hardly ever got letters at our house, apart from bills. I can still remember the thrill of opening it and seeing the Fulham club crest. It was a moment I had dreamed about. Signing for a top club. Now it was coming true.

Frank arrived at our house early. My mum had just got back from her cleaning job. We all sat at the table in our small kitchen. I tried to look calm, but inside I felt excited. Mum made us all a cup of tea and we started talking.

'I saw you play for London Boys at Spurs, a few months ago,' Frank told me.

'I heard you were there,' I said.

'Did they tell you who was with me?'

'Johnny Haynes.'

'That's right and he reckons you can play, son. What d'you think of that?'

'Johnny Haynes is his hero.' My mum was pleased for me and she meant well, but what she said was a bit embarrassing. Made me feel like a kid in front of Frank.

'Is that right, Alan, Johnny's your hero?'

'He's a great player,' I said. 'I hope to be like him one day.'

'Well, join Fulham and it might just happen.'

I nodded and waited to see what else he had to say. 'If your son signs for Fulham, Mrs Mullery,' said Frank, 'he can concentrate on his football, or we can help him to get a trade. For example, we have close links with a fruit and vegetable company in Covent Garden. We could get him a job in the offices there.'

'What do you think, Alan?' asked Mum.

The thought of trailing up to Covent Garden every morning didn't appeal to me at all. 'I'd rather just learn about football,' I said.

'In that case you can be one of our ground staff boys.' Frank smiled. 'Come and see me with your dad on Thursday and we'll get it all sorted out.'

'OK, Mr Osborne,' I said. 'Thanks very much.'

When he had gone, Mum poured us both another cup of tea. 'What's a ground staff boy?'

'I haven't got a clue,' I said.

But I knew I would soon find out . . .

My dad took the morning off work on the following Thursday. He didn't say much on the tube ride from Latimer Road station to Hammersmith, but he was wearing his suit and a tie, so I knew he saw this as a special occasion. I was dressed up, too. From Hammersmith we took a trolleybus for the short ride down Fulham Palace Road to Craven Cottage. We sat downstairs on one of the long seats just inside the door. There was another long seat opposite. I looked across and couldn't believe my eyes: Johnny Haynes was sitting there. He was wearing a beige trench coat and his hair was neatly combed.

I caught his eye for a moment, then whispered to my dad.

'Over there, it's Johnny Haynes.'

'Johnny who?' he asked in a loud voice.

Dad didn't know the first thing about football, none of my family did. So I let the subject drop. I was too embarrassed to look at Johnny again, but it was still a thrill to see him. My mum was right, Haynes was my hero. He was one of the main reasons I wanted to join Fulham.

Looking back now, I have to smile. The England captain riding to work on a bus. It would never happen now, would it?

When we got to Craven Cottage, we were shown into the boardroom. It was very impressive, with a long table and polished wooden chairs. My dad and I sat there feeling a bit overawed; we were certainly getting the VIP treatment. Frank Osborne came in, with a cigarette hanging out of his mouth. He was wearing a shirt and tie and had a trilby hat on his head. He got straight down to business.

'As you know, Mr Mullery, we are keen to sign Alan as a ground staff boy. How does that sound to you?'

'Well, what sort of money is he going to earn?'

'It's five pounds a week, but he'll have to pay tax on that.'

My dad was earning about twelve quid a week at that time, as a skilled electrician, so the money they were offering me as a school leaver wasn't bad. I was quite happy.

'That sounds fair enough,' said my dad. 'What do you want to do, Alan?'

'I want to sign,' I said.

'That's what I like to hear,' smiled Frank. 'We've got the contract ready for you. I'll go and get it and you can sign it now.'

And that's what I did. No solicitors, no agents. Just the club and its newest employee. Frank gave me the contract and I signed it without even reading the small print. I think that's the way most people did things then. And as far as my football prospects were concerned, my dad and I had already agreed Fulham were my best bet.

As I've said, Dad was no football expert but I must give him his due. Before that meeting, he found out all he could about the various clubs that wanted to sign me. He worked out that, although Fulham had some great players, many of them were getting towards the end of their careers. Not Johnny Haynes, naturally, but others – Jimmy Hill, Tosh Chamberlain, Roy Bentley, Eddie Lowe and Jimmy Langley, for instance. There were only two young players. Tony Macedo, a nineteen-year-old goalkeeper and right back George Cohen, who had just broken into the first team at the age of seventeen.

'Fulham will need some new blood in a couple of years,' Dad told me. 'By then you'll be bigger and stronger. I reckon you'll get your chance. It'll be up to you to take it.'

My dad's reading of the situation was spot on. It was sensible advice and I knew he was right. I also knew that when my chance came I would make the most of it. I had a very strong inner belief. I knew I could make it as a player. It felt like my destiny.

After I'd signed for Fulham, we all shook hands.

'When do you want to start then?' Frank asked me.

'Any time, Mr Osborne.'

He smiled. 'No time like the present. Go and introduce yourself to our groundsman. He's out there working on the pitch. He'll tell you what to do.'

I left my dad and Frank Osborne talking together. I would see a lot more of Frank over the next couple of years. I regularly washed his car for him and acted as his caddy when he played golf. I never saw him without his famous trilby, even on the course. He loved his golf. When I went to see him in his office, he was often standing there practising his swing. Frank was definitely eccentric, but very shrewd, too.

I walked out of the offices into the deserted ground. I was about to meet another of Fulham's offbeat characters, Albert Purdy, groundsman.

Albert Purdy was dedicated to his job. Fulham's pitch was his pride and joy. He hated anyone going on it . . . even the players. He lived in the Cottage, with his wife Maude. They had a flat above the offices. Maude used to put her Monday morning washing out on the line, including her underwear. The players used to call out to her when they were running round the pitch at training. 'Oi, Maude, we can see your bloomers!' She was quite a plump lady with glasses and when the players wolf-whistled at her she'd turn round and laugh. 'Cheeky buggers!' she'd say.

Albert was out on the pitch, cutting the grass. I walked across and introduced myself, still dressed in my best clothes. Albert told me to go and find something different to wear.

I walked into the deserted home-team dressing room and sat down on a bench. So much had happened so quickly, I needed a minute to gather my thoughts. I imagined what it would be like getting changed in there for a first-team game, then running out to play in the same side as Johnny Haynes. I couldn't wait to get started. I don't know what I was expecting to do as a ground staff boy. Play football all day, I suppose. How wrong I was.

Nowadays, when a young player joins a top club, he is looked after by the academy. He gets all the coaching and guidance he needs to develop his skills as a future professional footballer. In many ways, young players today are treated the same as senior pros. It wasn't like that at Fulham in 1957. I was about to get a three-day baptism of fire.

I found some football kit and went back to Albert Purdy. By this time he'd cut two-thirds of the pitch with his heavy petrol mower, but on the far side the first-team squad were having a practice game. I could see Albert was annoyed. He wanted the players to clear off, so he could get on and finish his job. He didn't like little things like training to get in his way.

Fulham didn't have a training ground as such, so they used Bishop's Park, beside the ground. The players would have practice games on the park pitches, until the park keeper threw them off, then they'd come back and use the pitch at Craven Cottage, which drove Albert Purdy berserk.

Albert told me to find a couple of boxes and pick up litter from the parts of the pitch he'd already cut. Back then, there was no stand on the far side of the ground beside the Thames, and the wind used to whip up off the water blowing the match-day rubbish everywhere. I did what I was told.

When I got back to Albert, the first team were still training. By now he was fuming.

'Go and pick up the rubbish from where they're playing,' he told me.

It was my first day and I didn't want to argue with him, so I walked into the seven-a-side game and started picking up the litter. Fulham's giant South African goalkeeper, Ken Hewkins, told me to get off the pitch, so I did.

'What are you doing?' shouted Albert.

'He threw me off,' I said, starting to wish I was somewhere else.

Albert told me to get back out there. The minute I walked on to the pitch, Ken Hewkins grabbed me by the scruff of the neck and threw me off. Albert came over and started giving me a rollicking. Hewkins realised Albert was behind it all and told him to bugger off. Albert argued back and Hewkins hit him – wallop! – straight on the chin.

Albert went down in a heap and his petrol mower swerved off across his beautiful pitch, carving a zigzag pattern across the neat lines he'd cut earlier. I ran after the mower, but didn't know how to switch it off. It was like something out of an Ealing comedy. Welcome to Fulham football club.

My second day was just as bizarre. When I arrived at Craven Cottage on the Friday morning, the first person I met was Albert whose face was all bruised. Of course, I had to make out I hadn't noticed. I was relieved when he told me I'd be working with another member of the ground staff.

Jack Gordon was a tiny man. He was so small, he should have been a jockey. He had a bald head and must have been seventy if he was a day. His overalls looked like they'd never been washed. He seemed a bit odd, but friendly enough; a nice old boy really.

'Right,' said Jack, 'we need a wheelbarrow and a couple of spades from the storeroom.'

It was dark and dusty under the grandstand. There was a gym the players used for five-a-sides. That was OK, but the rest was empty corridors and storerooms. We went into one of them. Jack threw a couple of brushes and two big, heavy spades into a wheelbarrow and told me to push it. Then he got a pair of old gloves and a heavy tin down from a shelf and we went back out into the corridor.

Some of the rooms had been turned into little snack shops where you could buy food and drink on a match day, things like burgers, cheese rolls and pies. All the mess from the last home game was still all over the floor. Jack and I got busy sweeping it up.

Every time Jack found a bit of old roll or half a pie, he'd put his gloves on and spread some of the sticky stuff from the tin all over it. Then he'd put it back on the floor. I asked him what he was doing, but for some reason he didn't want to tell me. He was concentrating on what he was doing, so I kept quiet. It took us ages to clean the corridor.

'Right,' said Jack, after a couple of hours. 'Tea break!'

We went into his little cubby-hole and he made the tea. I can remember staring at the mugs in disbelief. They were cracked, stained and filthy. I took the tea Jack offered me, but I had no intention of drinking it. Jack sat down in a battered old armchair and began reading the *Daily Mirror*. After about an hour, he started dozing off and I was thinking, 'What am I doing here?' Another half an hour dragged past, then Jack suddenly sat up.

'Time to get to work,' he said.

By now, all the players had gone home after training and it was deathly quiet under the grandstand. I was glad to get up and start moving. As I walked out of the cramped little room, I saw something crawl past my feet. It was a rat, swaying around as if it was drunk.

'Rat!' I shouted.

'I've got it,' said Jack, in a calm voice.

He picked up a spade and flattened the rat, then shovelled it up and threw it into the wheelbarrow. I stood there in shock. This was even stranger than the punch-up the day before. Then another rat ran over my foot.

'You get that one,' shouted Jack. I grabbed the other spade and tried to hit the rat, but I kept missing. It was weaving around all over the place.

'Kill it! Kill it!' Jack was shouting. 'Smash the bastard.'

In the end I clouted the rat and threw it in the wheelbarrow. I didn't like killing it.

'What's this all about, Jack?'

'Got to kill the rats,' he said. 'There's hundreds of them. Got to keep them down. That stuff I was spreading was rat poison. You've got to know how much to put down. Just enough so they look pissed; it's easy to smash them then. Hang on . . . there's another one.'

And with that, he hurried off with his spade and whacked another rat.

If my first day at Fulham felt like an Ealing comedy, this was more like being in the dungeons of the Hammer House of Horror. Luckily, Albert Purdy came along and told me to go and clean the dressing rooms for the first-team game the next day. You never saw me move so fast.

I remember twitching every time I heard a noise in the dressing rooms while I was washing the floors. I was expecting a rat attack any minute. Mick Simmons, the scout who took me to Fulham, banged the door open and I nearly jumped out of my skin.

Mick said he wanted me to come in early the next morning to light the boiler for the first-team match. When he showed me the boiler, my heart sank. It was a massive old thing; it had a big metal grate where you shovelled the coal and various pressure gauges to tell you when it was just the right heat. It provided all the hot water for the home and away dressing rooms.

After a game, players want plenty of hot water and, if it's not there, someone's in trouble. And that someone would be me. I could see it coming.

'I'm not being awkward,' I said to Mick, 'but I haven't got a clue how to work this thing.'

'All right, don't worry, I'll come in and help you get it started, but you'll have to keep it topped up with coal all day.'

So, nine o'clock Saturday morning I was there with Mick lighting the boiler. Even he had a struggle with it and we both ended up covered with coal dust. By midday it was roaring away and all I had to do was keep it going for the rest of the afternoon. Mick said I could watch the first-team game and I was looking forward to it. It would be nice to relax for a change.

I went out to look at the pitch and thought how great it must be to play in front of a full house at Craven Cottage.

'Alan! Over here, quick!'

It was Mick Simmons hurrying towards me, looking a bit rattled.

'Have you got your boots at the club?'

'Yes, I brought them in yesterday.'

'Good,' said Mick. 'You're playing for the reserves at Tottenham this afternoon!'

I was fifteen years old.

'We're one short,' Mick explained. 'Get your stuff quick. The bus is waiting.'

Five minutes later I was on the team bus with a group of reserve-team players I'd never met before. I could see them thinking, 'Who's the kid?'

The coach stopped at a big block of council flats near Chelsea football club. The driver started tooting his horn and a face appeared at a window on the third floor. It was Maurice Pratt, our missing left winger.

'Give me two minutes and I'll be down,' he shouted.

When Maurice finally made it on to the coach, he got a lot of stick from the other players and a telling-off from the reserve-team manager, Joe Bacuzzi. Joe had played over three hundred games for Fulham himself and was very loyal to the club, so he was not impressed.

'Sorry, Joe,' said Pratt. 'Bit of a late night last night.'

Was I surprised by all this? No, not really. I was getting used to crazy things happening at Fulham, so I took it all in my stride. I'd started the day lighting the boiler, then Mick told me I was going to play at Spurs. I finally ended up laying out the kit and sitting in the crowd at White Hart Lane watching the match. Ted Ditchburn was in goal for Tottenham and there were 11,000 people there to see an exciting reserve-team game.

It had been a very strange week, but at least it ended on a high.

1957–58 was my first full season at Fulham.

Having a few weeks there at the end of the previous season had been good for me. At least I knew what to expect, which was plenty of hard work and very little football. There was no point moaning. That was the system and you just had to get on with it.

Ground staff boys were just general dogsbodies. On the Monday after a Saturday home game, we would have to sweep the terraces, which formed three-quarters of the ground. Home crowds were often up around 30,000, so you can imagine how much rubbish they left behind. It took us all day to clean up. The litter was piled up at the foot of the terraces. We had to burn it all before we went home at night.

One bonus of sweeping the terraces was that it gave me the chance to see the first team train. Johnny Haynes was the most skilful player, yet he was the one who always came back for extra training on his own. He'd put a bath towel down in the corner of the pitch, near the Cottage. Then he'd take a bag of footballs to the halfway line on the far side of the pitch and hit them one by one to land on the towel. It must have been seventy yards and the accuracy was amazing. Don't forget I'm talking about the old leather footballs that weighed a ton when they were wet. Johnny was the best player at Fulham, the England captain, but he worked the hardest. I never forgot that.

Other menial jobs included cleaning the toilets, keeping the dressing rooms neat and tidy and getting down on our hands and knees to wash the office floors. These days, clubs have cleaners to do all that, but in my day it was done by the ground staff. There were about nine of us and we all got on well. We were all the same, working-class London boys. We made our own fun and had a laugh.

In the summer we'd spend a couple of weeks digging the pitch with garden forks to aerate it and get it ready for the groundsman to sow new seed. If the weather was good, we'd be out there in our shorts and end up as brown as berries. Fulham always had a fantastic pitch and we played our part in that.

Once the seed was planted, we had to help Albert spread fish manure all over the pitch using heavy shovels. We'd carry the manure across the pitch in wheelbarrows on wooden planks, to avoid cutting up the surface. We did a lot of hard physical work. At times it felt like labouring on a building site, but it did me good. Helped me to fill out and develop the body strength that was to be an important attribute in the years to come.

The worst thing about working with fish manure was that by the end of the day you were covered in the stinking stuff from head to toe. The dressing rooms were locked by the time the ground staff boys finished work, so there was no way we could get a shower.

The first time this happened, I got on a trolleybus to Hammersmith as usual. The minute I sat down, people started sniffing and looking at me.

'Is that you?' said the conductor.

'What?'

'That 'orrible smell.'

'No,' I lied.

'It is him!' said an old lady. 'Chuck 'im off.'

'That's just what I'm about to do, madam,' said the conductor. 'Come on, son, 'op it!'

I had to walk to the tube and when I got there I had a carriage almost to myself. I wonder why that was! It was embarrassing. I told the lads all about it the next morning. Most of them had a similar tale to tell. We asked Albert if we could have a shower before we went home that night, but he didn't want us messing up the dressing rooms. Anyway, the big boiler was never lit in the summer, so the water was freezing cold.

Nobody wanted to help, so we came up with our own idea. There was a row of old metal railings along the top of the open terracing that backed on to the River Thames. Some of the railings were broken, so it was easy to get through to the river. At the end of the day, when we were covered with fish manure, we'd go in the filthy river water for a wash.

We had a big rope and we took it in turns to tie it round our chest and under our arms, before climbing down the bank and jumping into the water. Three or four of the other lads held on to the other end of the rope. The current would drag you downstream, then they'd pull you back up. Looking back, it was reckless and dangerous. People caught polio by swimming in the Thames in the fifties. But we were just kids and we didn't give it a second thought.

Ground staff boys got a raw deal, but it was the same at every club. We were like little chimney-sweeps. We had to do every job going and we never questioned it. Society has come a long way in fifty years. Kids today would speak up for themselves, but we did what we were told. The only chance we got to do any training was late afternoon, when we'd done all our work for the day. Then we'd finally get a ball out and have a kickabout.

I started playing for the youth team in the South East Counties league and I enjoyed the games, but we never got any coaching. Duggie Livingstone, the Fulham first-team manager, was a very distant figure to us kids. So we were surprised when Duggie said he'd give us a training session one afternoon. He took us up to the far end of the pitch and started us on some passing drills. We were all keen to impress. Things were going well, then we heard an announcement over the Tannoy.

'Telephone call for Mr Livingstone.'

Duggie told us to keep working, then ran over to the Cottage to take his call. Half an hour later he still wasn't back and it was getting dark. We went over to the Cottage to see what was going on. The offices were locked and in darkness. Duggie Livingstone had forgotten all about us. He'd had a shower and buggered off. Worse than that, the big iron gates at the entrance had been closed and we were locked in.

We had to stand there in our football kit and boots, waiting for Albert Purdy and Maude to come home so we could get changed. We were freezing by the time they came back. That sums up how we were treated.

Every youth-team game I played in that first season was a special event. That's the way I approached it. Every time I pulled on a Fulham shirt, I was determined to make my mark. At the start of the season I was still only fifteen, but I was playing in the Under-18s league. We played every Saturday morning.

I went straight into the team at right half and immediately felt at home. I was very vocal in matches, encouraging other players, telling them who to mark at corners, things like that. That was the way I'd been at school and I didn't change. I couldn't have if I'd tried, I always played the game with that kind of commitment.

I didn't get any special treatment at Fulham. I knew the club thought I had a chance of making it, but I was just one of a very talented group of young players. The boy the club were really pinning their hopes on was Brian Sullivan, who'd played for Edmonton Boys, just as Johnny Haynes had a few years before. Brian had tremendous skill and ability and the club really looked after him. They gave him a cushy job in the office licking stamps, which was a lot better than shovelling fish manure!

Brian trained with the first team, right from the start, but he never made the grade. None of the young players I started out with achieved as much as I did in the game. Did I want success more? Maybe. It's difficult to say. I didn't think about it at the time and I wasn't trying to get one over on the others. I just focused on my own game and stuck to a simple philosophy: 'Try your best in every match.' And it worked.

I was picked for the reserve team early in 1958 and kept my place for the rest of the season. I was playing with senior pros now and it was a big jump. Ken Craggs, who became my assistant manager at Brighton many years later, gave me a lot of good advice when I needed it most.

Ken Craggs came down to Fulham from Durham with Bobby Robson. They shared digs together, two young Geordie lads who, before they were married, had a roving eye and enjoyed getting to know the pretty girls they met in London. Ken never won a first-team place, but he was a powerful centre-half for the reserves.

Ken says I came into the side brimming with confidence. My reserve-team debut was against Birmingham City and they had a very good player called Eddie Brown. He was about six inches taller than me and had a reputation as a real hard man. Ken says I hit Brown with a crunching tackle in the first five minutes. It wasn't a foul and I won the ball. When Eddie picked himself up off the ground, he looked at me with real respect. He wasn't expecting that kind of treatment from an unknown kid.

Ken Craggs often talked about that game when we were working together at Brighton. 'From that day on,' he'd say, 'I knew you were going to be some footballer. Suddenly, there was this sixteen-year-old lad telling senior pros what to do in the game. It was amazing. I'd never seen anything like that before. You looked at home immediately and that won the respect of the other players. I didn't say anything to you at the time, but I thought to myself "This kid will play for England one day." And I was right.'

I hardly ever played for the youth team after that, just in key games and competitions like the FA Youth Cup. I was making decent progress, even without any coaching.

The atmosphere around the club was upbeat. The first team were playing well and pushing for promotion from the old Second Division to the top level. They had a terrific FA Cup run too, disposing of Yeovil, Charlton, West Ham and Bristol Rovers on their way to the semi-final at Villa Park. There were 70,000 fans at the game and it was a very emotional occasion. Fulham were playing Manchester United, less than two months after the Munich air disaster.

As I have already mentioned, I met many of the United stars who died at Munich when I visited Old Trafford with the London Boys side in 1956. When I heard the news of the plane crash in Germany, it came as a terrible shock.

Most of the crowd at Villa Park were supporting United. That was understandable, but Fulham had to put sentiment to one side and try to win the game. I didn't go, I listened to it on the radio. It was a hard-fought encounter and it ended all square at 2–2.

The replay, the following Wednesday afternoon, was at Arsenal, which didn't seem very fair on United. All the staff at Fulham went. We piled on to coaches for the trip across London to join the big crowd of 33,000. The match was also televised live on the BBC, which was very unusual at the time.

Johnny Haynes, Tosh Chamberlain, Tony Macedo, George Cohen, Roy Bentley, Jimmy Hill. I watched them train every day, now I was seeing them play on the big stage. Fulham lost 5–3, in a real thriller. I was disappointed, but it was still a fantastic day out and it made a huge impression on me. It was the biggest match I'd ever been to and it really fired my imagination.

I started the 1958–59 season with high hopes. I was still a ground staff boy, and I held on to my place in the reserve team from the first game of the season. We went on a good run and I felt I was playing well, so I was puzzled when reserve-team manager Joe Bacuzzi said he wanted to see me. I thought he was thinking of dropping me, but it wasn't that.

'Ken Collins is injured,' Joe told me. 'He'll be out for a couple of games.'

Ken was our captain. A tough defender whose nickname was 'Killer'. Killer Collins.

'I don't mind playing full-back,' I said.

'It's not that, Alan,' said Joe. 'How would you feel about being captain?'

I was amazed. I was still only sixteen, a boy in a man's world and there were some really good old pros in that side. For once, I didn't know what to say.

'The way I see it, you shout at all the other players anyway, so you may as well be captain,' Joe smiled.

Joe Bacuzzi was a good judge of players. He knew I'd respond to the faith he'd shown in me and wouldn't let him down. I was a bit nervous before my first game as captain and I got a bit of leg-pulling from the older players, but as soon as the game started, everything settled down and I was fine. In later years, Joe told me he always saw me as a natural leader.

I turned seventeen on 23 November 1958. It was a Sunday, so I could have a lie-in. I was still living at home. When I went downstairs, my mum gave me a card and a present. Then she cooked a really nice Sunday lunch, which we had when my dad came home from the pub.

I went out for a walk in the afternoon and thought about my career. I smiled at the memory of Ken Hewkins throwing me off the pitch on my first day at Fulham. It seemed like yesterday. Time had flown past and now I was in the reserves and had even captained the side. My main ambition was the same as it had always been: I wanted to be like Johnny Haynes. I knew I would never have his silky skills, but I wanted to match his achievements. Johnny had got into the Fulham first team at seventeen. I aimed to do the same.

I was old enough now to sign for the club as a full-time professional. Frank Osborne said he wanted to see me to talk about a new contract. Before the meeting, Roy Bentley offered me some advice.

Roy was one of the most famous footballers of the fifties. A fearless centre-forward, who was nearing the end of his playing career. Roy was an England international and captained Chelsea to their first League championship in 1955. He was also Chelsea's top scorer for an amazing eight seasons in a row. He dropped back to centre-half at Fulham. I admired him as a man and I was always keen to listen to what he had to say.

'As you know, the most any player can earn is twenty pounds a week,' said Roy. 'Read the contract and see what they are offering you. Make sure you think it's fair, then tell them you want a thousand pounds signing-on fee. They can't pay that to you officially, but they'll give it to you under the counter.'

At that time, a thousand pounds could buy you a house. The thought of asking for all that money made me nervous.

'A thousand pounds, are you sure?' I asked Roy.

'Yes, you stand up for yourself. Tell them you want that money, or you won't sign.'

Roy was like a father figure to me, so I decided to do what he said.

I can see it so plainly now. I was given the day off from my ground staff duties, so I arrived at Craven Cottage suited and booted. I walked into the boardroom and there was Tommy Trinder, the famous comedian and Fulham chairman. Next to him was Frank Osborne, smoking a cigarette and with a glass of whisky at his side. They both had their trilby hats on and sat at the far end of the long, highly polished wooden table. Frank gestured for me to sit at the other end.

'Son, this is a big day for you,' said Frank. 'You've come of age now and we want you to sign full-time for Fulham.'

And with that he slid the contract the full length of the table to where I was sitting. I looked at it. I didn't understand all the legal stuff, all I wanted to know was what they were offering me. It was twelve pounds a week in the playing season and eight pounds a week in the summer. That was good money, as far as I was concerned, but the signing-on fee was only ten pounds.

So I slid the contract back down the table.

'No, I'm not signing that, Mr Osborne,' I said.

'What?'

'I want a thousand pounds to sign on.'

Frank nearly choked on his whisky. There was an inch of ash on the end of his cigarette and it fell into his glass. He looked furious. Tommy Trinder was aghast.

'How dare you?' Frank yelled. 'I'll report you to the Football Association for demanding under-the-counter payments. Now get your arse out of this room immediately!'

I left without a word.

I met Roy Bentley down the corridor and he asked me how I'd got on.

'They threw me out,' I said.

'Don't worry,' said Roy. 'They'll come round, you'll get your money.'

I didn't share his confidence.

I'd been quite close to Frank Osborne since joining the club, but for the next two weeks he completely ignored me. I kept thinking, 'Why did I do it?' Maybe I'd blown my big chance. Would Fulham would kick me out? What if they reported me to the FA, I might never get another club. I was worried sick. Then, one cold morning in December, I was working on the ground and Frank shouted across to me.

'I want to see you in the boardroom . . . now!'

My blood ran cold. This was it, he was going to sack me.

When I got to the boardroom, the door was open.

'Come in and sit down,' said Frank. He was pacing around and he lit a fresh cigarette off the one he'd just smoked. Then he sat down. Not at the far end of the table this time, but next to me.

'Look, I'll tell you what I'm going to do with you,' he said. 'I want you to sign this contract for twelve pounds a week and ten pounds signing-on fee. It's no different from the one Johnny Haynes signed when he was your age.'

He paused and smiled, knowing he had saved the best news until last.

'Sign this contract and I promise you, if you're not in the first team in the next three months, I'll give you the thousand pounds myself.'

That sounded good to me. If things went well I would be in the first team at seventeen. If not, I would get a thousand pounds in cash. A fortune in my eyes.

'OK, Mr Osborne,' I said. 'I'll sign it now, if you like.'

'Your dad has to sign it, too, son. We'll do it in the next couple of days. Don't worry, I've got your word. That's good enough for me.'

I came out of there feeling heady with the excitement of it all. Ten minutes earlier I'd been in a deep depression. Now I felt relieved, excited, amazed . . . and very happy. I was signing full-time for Fulham and I'd be training with the first team from now on. No more scrubbing toilets. No more killing rats. It was Christmas time and the world was a beautiful place.

The boy was becoming a man . . .

6

CARRY ON, FULHAM!

I walked out of Craven Cottage alone.

It was a bitterly cold February afternoon, but I hardly noticed. The same question kept twisting in my mind. *Why*? I was in trouble again, but this time I didn't understand it. What had I done wrong? I'd been training with the first team and playing for the reserves for a couple of months, since signing professional forms. Nobody could have tried harder, but now I was out in the cold. Why? It was a mystery.

The date was ironic, Friday the thirteenth. As usual, the team sheets for the weekend had been pinned up in the dressing room. I wasn't on any of them. I went to see the first-team manager, Bedford Jezzard, but he'd gone home. Nobody else at the club seemed to know anything about it. I got the bus down to Hammersmith feeling confused and depressed.

I bought an evening paper at the tube station. Inside it said a seventeen-year-old unknown kid called Mullery was in line to make his debut at home for Fulham against Leyton Orient the following day. I've mentioned the rollercoaster of emotions players can go through at times. Well, this was a classic example.

Was the story in the *Standard* right or wrong? I had no way of knowing. I finally got a call that evening from the club secretary, Charlie Read. He was a gruff character.

'You've got to be at the ground tomorrow at two,' he said.

'Am I playing for the first team?'

'I don't know, do I?' he snapped and put the phone down.

Not the best way to be told you might be making your debut, but I didn't care. I was in with a chance and I felt the excitement race through my body.

When I walked into the dressing room the following afternoon, Bedford Jezzard came over and shook me by the hand.

'Congratulations, Alan,' he said. 'You're playing today.'

Ex-England international Eddie Lowe had failed a late fitness test, so I was in. Jezzard was a former Fulham player. He knew how nervous I'd be, but he handled things well. He played it all down.

'Just relax, son,' said Beddy, 'you'll be fine.' Bedford Jezzard had joined Fulham in 1948 and played for the club until 1957. He scored thirty-eight goals in the 1953–54 season. He formed a very effective striking partnership with Bobby Robson and Johnny Haynes. Jezzard also won two England caps. He became Fulham manager in 1958.

Of course, I was very nervous, despite what the manager had said. It was less than two years since I'd sat daydreaming in that changing room on my first day at the club. Now those dreams were coming true. I was about to play with Johnny Haynes, Roy Bentley, George Cohen, Jimmy Hill and Graham Leggat. I was amazed it had all happened so quickly.

Most of the players were busy following their own pre-match routines, but Roy Bentley took the time to come and have a quiet word with me. I'd be playing alongside him in the game.

'You're marking Eddie Brown today,' Roy said. 'He's a powerful player and he'll test you out, but I'll talk you through the game. I know all his tricks. You'll be OK.'

That was reassuring.

I felt very proud when I ran out with the team on 14 February 1959. A silly incident before the kick-off helped me to settle down. I was knocking a ball around near the centre circle when I heard Eddie Baily, the future Spurs assistant manager, talking to the referee. Eddie was playing for Orient and he was known for his colourful language.

'Any swearing allowed today, ref?' asked Eddie.

'No, none at all. If you swear at the opposition, you'll be sent off.'

'What about swearing at our own players?'

'I'll send you off for that as well,' said the ref.

'Oh, fuck me,' said Eddie.

I cracked up laughing. I think it did me good.

When the game started, Roy Bentley kept his promise and talked to me non-stop.

'Pick him up, Alan . . . don't let him go . . . push him wide . . . stay with him. Outside left . . . he's free . . . hit him with the ball . . . good pass, son!'

I usually did my share of shouting on the pitch, but this time I had the sense to keep my mouth shut and listen. I had one nasty moment, when I lost sight of the ball in the crowd and remembered how many people were watching. But overall, I couldn't have wished for a better debut. We won 5–2 and Johnny Haynes scored a hat-trick. I was one of the first to run over and give him a hug when the third goal went in. Most fans can only dream of playing alongside their hero, but this was for real.

We all went to the players' room in the Cottage after the game. Right from the start, I loved the feeling of being part of that team. Everyone made me feel welcome, although I was just a kid. The players all had a few beers and I stuck to shandy. Nobody was in a rush to leave.

I found myself talking to Michael Craig and Janette Scott, who were big film stars in the fifties. I'd never met anyone like that before. Then a smiling Frank Osborne came over and quietly reminded me I wouldn't be getting my thousand pounds off him now. It was the first time I'd thought about the money. I didn't care and Frank knew it.

We stayed at the Cottage until about eight in the evening and I loved every minute. Then it was back to reality. I got on a trolley-bus to Hammersmith and bought the evening paper to read on the Tube going home. What Bernard Joy wrote in the *Evening Standard* that night gave me the perfect end to a perfect day. 'Mullery, the dark-haired wing-half making his debut, is surely an England star of the future.'

(Bernard Joy was one of Britain's top football writers and his high opinion of the young Alan Mullery was echoed by every leading newspaper of the time. I was hailed as Fulham's 'find of the season', instantly linked with those other home-grown stars, George Cohen and Johnny Haynes. The Press headlined Fulham's 5–2 win as the 'St Valentine's Day Massacre', and I was instant 'star of the future'.)

When I got home to Notting Hill, I popped in the pub at the end of our road. My dad was already in there. He'd been at the game and it must have been a rush for him to get to the ground because he only heard I was playing at the last minute. But if he was proud of me, he didn't show it. I didn't stay in the pub long.

My mum gave me a hug and kiss when I got home, but she always did that. It had nothing to do with playing for Fulham. She heated my dinner up and, while I was I eating, I told her all about my day. She was pleased I'd done well, but didn't really grasp what a breakthrough I had made. With a family like mine, success was never likely to go to my head. A hero's return? You must be joking.

I kept my place in the side for the rest of the season. I played fourteen games during the crucial run-in, when we won promotion to the First Division. I slotted into the team well. The Press started calling me 'No Nerves' Mullery, but it would have been a different story without Roy Bentley guiding me through virtually every game.

Our pre-match routine never changed. Roy would sit me down and tell me about the player I'd be marking that day. Roy knew them all. He'd played against them many times. I had no idea. The media coverage was so different then. You hardly ever saw football on TV, just Cup finals and internationals. *Match of the Day* was first screened on Saturday 22 August 1964.

Later in my career, dossiers on opposing players became fashionable. Managers like Alf Ramsey gave their players as much information as possible. Roy did that for me, just when I needed it most. He helped George Cohen, too; he was a father figure to us both.

Roy saw that heading was a weakness in my game. He taught me how to jump and attack the ball. Today, players are often criticised for raising their arms when they go up for headers. Roy told me you have to raise your arms to get the height you need, just like a high jumper. You may hit other players with your leading arm, but it's not deliberate. It's just part of the game.

Roy was the epitome of what I wanted to be. He would never back down from a challenge. I saw that a few weeks after getting into the first team. We were playing a seven-a-side on the pitch at the Cottage one morning. We all enjoyed those games. They were keenly contested, but there was no heavy tackling. It was all about good movement and sharp, accurate passing.

Suddenly, an Irish player called John 'Paddy' Doherty went over the top in a 50–50 tackle with Roy Bentley. Everyone knew he was out of order. Over-the-top tackles can break legs and end careers. You should never do that to a fellow professional. If you do, you have to expect to face the consequences.

Roy Bentley was livid. He didn't say a word, but we all knew what was coming. The first chance he got he went in hard on Paddy. It was 'law of the jungle' stuff. Roy was determined not to lose face in front of his team-mates. Paddy got to his feet and the two of them started fighting. Frank Penn, our physio, jumped in between them.

'Game's over!' he shouted. 'Let's get this sorted out.'

He led Frank and Paddy to the gym under the main stand, then went to get some boxing gloves from his treatment room. We all wanted to see the fight, so we piled into the gym. Paddy was snarling and shouting about what he was going to do. Roy stood calmly waiting.

When Frank Penn got back with the gloves, he threw us all out, so we stood outside listening. We could hear Frank talking to them, then the sound of a few punches being thrown. It was over in no time, then silence. We all looked at each other, wondering what had happened.

The gym door opened and out came Roy Bentley looking cool and relaxed. He took off his boxing gloves, threw them back through the door and walked off to the showers. We looked in the gym and there was John Doherty flat on his back. He was out cold.

Roy's impressive display reminded me of my fight with the Brooks Twins at school. Different time and different gym, but the same rules applied. If someone takes you on, you've got to stand up for yourself.

I soon had to face my own test of nerve at Fulham.

Around the club Johnny Haynes was modest and quietly spoken, but in matches he had a wicked temper. He would shout and scream at his team-mates for making mistakes, or not reading his passes. He expected them to be as good as him and, of course, they never were. He'd put his hands on his hips and stare at them with disgust. Some players suffered more than others. Johnny's tantrums definitely had an effect on them. They felt intimidated.

It didn't take long for Johnny to turn on me in a game. I'd won the ball and heard Johnny screaming for it. I looked up and saw defenders all round him, so I passed to an unmarked Fulham player instead. Johnny ran at me, breathing fire.

'Give me the bloody ball when I tell you to!' he shouted. He was an inch from my face.

'There were three of them marking you,' I said.

'Don't argue,' he snapped. 'Who the hell do you think you are anyway? Just do what I say.'

Johnny Haynes was the club captain and I'd played only six games for the first team, but I knew I hadn't done anything wrong. I felt angry and grabbed him by the shirt.

'Don't you talk to me like that,' I told him. 'I play the game the way I see it. You'd better get used to it. Right?'

I shoved him away and I could see the surprise in his eyes. He wasn't expecting me to answer him back, but I think he respected me for it. We played many more games for Fulham together, but Johnny never spoke to me like that again. The flare-up was an isolated incident and it didn't change my respect for the man, but I would not stand for any bullying, not even from my hero.

I got another telling-off later in the season. This time I was with George Cohen and I did back down.

George was nineteen, two years older than me. He'd been in the first team for over a year when I made my debut. We were the youngest, so it made sense for us to share a room on away trips. We got on well from the start and have become lifelong friends.

Our temperaments were different. I could be fiery, but George always stayed cool. I can't remember him ever losing his temper. If he got caught by a hard tackle, he'd take it and get on with the game.

(In 1966, Alf Ramsey's full-backs were Ray Wilson and George Cohen. They both had pace and boundless energy. They slotted perfectly into the 4–4–2 system that won England the World Cup. Ramsey's plan called for great mobility from his full-backs and that is exactly what Wilson and Cohen supplied.)

Travelling to away games and staying in hotels was still a novelty to me. We went to play Cardiff City in early April '59. George and I decided to go to the pictures on the Friday night, so we went down to the restaurant early. We were the first customers and the waiter said we were too early for the set meal the team would be having later. We didn't know what to do, then the waiter suggested the à la carte. He didn't show us the menu, but said we could have steak and chips and a nice dessert. We said OK and had a lovely meal, then went off to the cinema.

The following morning, Bedford Jezzard went to reception to settle the club's bill for the night and saw two expensive meals charged to our room. He came and banged on our door and gave us the biggest bollocking ever, threatening to throw us out of the team and cancel our contracts. He was furious because he thought we'd gone behind his back to have the best food in the place.

George and I were mortified.

'We didn't see the menu,' I said.

'He didn't tell us it cost more,' added George.

Beddy stared at us for a moment, then I saw a smile flicker in his eyes. He could see we were telling the truth. We weren't greedy, just naïve.

'Don't you ever do that again, you cheeky little bastards,' he said, but his voice had lost its anger. 'The next time you ask for the fancy menu, it comes out of your wages. Right?'

'Right, boss,' we said.

We never did that again.

Every game that season was a major event for me, especially my first trip to Liverpool. I walked into Anfield and saw Bill Shankly, one of the greatest managers ever, at the far end of a long corridor. He had close-cropped hair and his hands were buried deep in the pockets of a smart trench coat. He looked like James Cagney. He was standing outside the Liverpool dressing room and shouted in through the door.

'You'll have to get changed lads, they've turned up!'

I got to know Bill very well in later years. He was a wonderful man and a great manager, but we held Liverpool to a goalless draw that afternoon. I loved playing in front of 'The Kop', with their songs, chants and passion. I had to cover my ears when Liverpool won their first corner. I'd never heard noise like that in my life.

Fulham finally won promotion with Sheffield Wednesday, who were champions by just two points. To celebrate we went to Fulham town hall for a reception with the mayor. There were crowds of supporters outside and we stood on the steps waving to them. It was a great way to end the season. I'd been under extreme pressure and come through it well.

Now I was looking forward to my next big test. Playing in the First Division . . .

I had over two months off that summer and I settled back into life in Notting Hill. I still saw all my old mates and went to the boys' club with them for a game of snooker or table tennis. They still treated me the same, which is exactly what I wanted. The only difference between us was that when they went to the pub, I'd go home. I didn't want to be seen out drinking. It was important not to get the wrong reputation.

There was plenty of petty crime going on in the area. My uncle was a street bookie, for instance. He'd stand on the street corner taking the bets and paying out when punters won. The police often nicked him for loitering, but he'd just pay the fine and carry on regardless.

You could get most things you wanted on the black market. There were plenty of crooks with holdalls full of transistor radios.

People were poor round my way, so there was a market for knocked-off stuff. If you wanted a TV and had the money, someone would go and steal one for you. That went on all the time. I wasn't judgemental, but people knew me well enough not to bring it to my door. I'd got my big chance at Fulham football club and nothing was going to get in the way of that.

I didn't sit around that summer. I played a lot of cricket, batting and bowling, and went out running regularly, too, so I was very fit when we reported back for pre-season training in July. We all got weighed on the first morning. It was a long close season in those days and most of the senior players had put on a few pounds. Even Johnny Haynes was half a stone overweight.

Bedford Jezzard made it clear the holidays were over. He sent us off on a long run over Hammersmith Bridge, all the way down the towpath to Putney Bridge, over the river and back to the club. Being young and keen, I set off in the lead and soon heard the other players shouting at me.

'Mullers, get back here. Don't you show us up!'

I dropped back into the main group and we plodded round the streets. It was hot work, but Tosh Chamberlain had an idea up his sleeve. One of his mates was a milkman and he was waiting on Hammersmith Bridge. Tosh jumped on his float and they drove off, with Tosh swigging from a nice cold bottle of milk. He waved to us as he went.

'See you later,' he grinned.

The milkman's round took him up by Putney Bridge. Tosh jumped off the float, splashed himself with river water to make it look like he was sweating, then jogged back to the ground through Bishop's Park. When we all staggered back, he was already there. We had to do that run every day for a week and Tosh never missed his milk-float. He was so popular, nobody would have dreamed of telling Beddy Jezzard what was going on.

Tosh Chamberlain was the most outrageous footballer I ever

played with. I've never known a player generate so much laughter during a game. He was a talented winger with a left foot to die for, but he was totally unpredictable.

Fulham folklore is full of Tosh Chamberlain stories.

Like the time . . . he walked off the pitch and had a fag, the first time I ever saw him play.

Like the time . . . he was knocked flat by a reckless tackle and refused to get up again until the referee apologised for not protecting him.

Like the time . . . he took a corner, missed the ball, kicked the flag and broke it in two.

Like the time . . . he hit a back pass to Tony Macedo with such wicked power he broke his ribs. (True story!)

Like the time . . . he ran off the pitch, kissed a pretty girl in the crowd, then ran back on and carried on playing.

I still see Tosh regularly and he is one of the most genuine people I've ever met. He hated violence, especially when it was happening to him. He once thought he heard burglars in his house and shouted down the stairs, 'Take what you like, but don't come up here!'

Self-preservation was behind one of Tosh's greatest goals, too. Fulham were away to Liverpool and Tosh got the ball around the halfway line. He started to run at the Liverpool defence, with Ronnie Moran closing in fast. Tosh knew Ronnie would whack him if he got the chance, so he decided to get rid of the ball in a hurry. He smashed a left-foot shot from forty yards and it screamed into the net. Nobody else would have dreamed of hitting it from there, but Tosh didn't want to get kicked!

We went on a pre-season tour of Italy in the summer of 1959. In one of the games, Johnny Haynes told Tosh to chip a free kick to the far post. Instead, Tosh smashed it straight at the defensive wall. He hit it so hard all their players jumped out of the way and the ball flew into the net.

'I thought I said chip it,' said Johnny.

'That was a chip,' said Tosh, keeping a straight face.

Johnny walked away, shaking his head in disbelief.

Tosh's antics drove Johnny Haynes mad, but away from the game they were like brothers. They grew up together in Edmonton. Tosh was always joking around, making Johnny laugh. Tosh brought out the best in him.

Johnny was never arrogant about his success. He didn't seek attention, but when he walked into a room, all eyes were on him. He had that indefinable gift of star quality. He was charismatic. It all came very naturally to him; he never went out of his way to impress other people. He had a great sense of style; always wore a shirt and tie. On the golf course, he would have the latest sweater and shoes. He always looked immaculate. Johnny Haynes and Denis Compton were the Brylcreem Boys. Their faces were seen everywhere in huge advertising campaigns. Johnny was the David Beckham of his day.

In football terms, Haynes was a genius. You can put him in the same class as Best, Law, Charlton and Maradona. It was 'the beautiful game' when he played it. Johnny was the best passer of a ball I ever saw. His ball control was superb, even on the worst pitches. They still call him 'The Maestro' at Fulham and that's what he was: a master of the game.

Johnny Haynes joined Fulham in May 1952 at the age of seventeen and stayed with the club throughout his League career. He made 657 appearances and scored 157 goals.

Johnny Haynes was the reason I joined Fulham. He was suave, a real man of the world. I looked up to him and tried to learn as much as I could from him as I settled into life in the First Division. He'd broken into the first team at seventeen, so he knew what I was going through.

One of our first big games in the 1959–60 season was away to Manchester City. We were staying in a very traditional hotel in the city centre. The team had dinner together on the Friday night before the game. I walked into the dining room and saw a long table laid out for us, glittering with glasses and cutlery. I'd never seen so many knives, forks and spoons in my life. At home we just had one of each.

The other players were used to this kind of living, but it was all new to me. I'd never been in such a posh hotel. In fact, I'd hardly ever eaten in a restaurant, apart from local cafés and fish and chip shops. I didn't want to make a fool of myself, so I made sure I sat next to Johnny Haynes. I decided to do exactly what he did. That way, I couldn't go wrong.

The head waiter was a short Italian, with greased-back hair and a big smile. He came over bowing and scraping and gave Johnny the real star treatment. Johnny looked through the menu and ordered half a dozen king prawns served on ice and a fillet steak, medium-rare, with French fries and a side salad. He discussed the various salad dressings available and decided on the blue cheese. The waiter looked at me.

'I'll have the same as him,' I said.

I was glad Johnny had ordered things I liked, because even if he'd ordered haggis and custard I would have gone for the same! When the prawns came, they looked delicious. At first, I didn't know how to eat them. Then I saw Johnny pick one up and start to peel it, so I did the same. Now I knew what to do, I got stuck in and really enjoyed the food. I'd finished my six prawns in no time.

I felt thirsty and saw a small bowl of water on the table. It had a slice of lemon in it and looked very refreshing, so I picked it up and drank it down in one. When I put it down, I realised everyone was looking at me. The whole team were in fits of laughter, but I had no idea why.

'What are they laughing at?' I asked Johnny.

Johnny didn't say a word. He just dipped his fingers in his bowl of water and dried them on his napkin. The penny dropped and I felt like sliding under the table. Players love things like that. I still get my leg pulled about it to this day when the old Fulham players get together.

I had another embarrassing incident at London's Savoy Hotel. Johnny had been invited to a party at the famous River Room and took me along. He probably thought it would be exciting for a young kid to go there and he was right. Johnny was in his MG sports car and I followed in my two-tone Triumph Herald. When we got to the Savoy, Johnny drove up to the main entrance and a doorman in a top hat ran out to greet him.

'Good evening, Mr Haynes,' he said. 'If you'd like to give me the keys, I'll park the car for you.'

I got out of my car and gave the doorman my keys, too.

'What are these for?' he asked.

'I'm with him,' I said, pointing to Johnny, who was disappearing into the hotel.

'Bugger off and park your own car,' said the doorman.

When I finally got back to the Savoy, Johnny was waiting for me in the foyer. He knew what had happened, but he didn't say a word. I was a kid with a lot to learn.

Luckily, I was doing better in games than in hotels.

I felt at home in the First Division. It was a big jump in standard, but I adapted easily. It felt very natural. Roy Bentley was still my mentor, talking me through every game.

Playing alongside George Cohen was a bonus, too. George was the fittest athlete at the club. He always looked confident and comfortable in matches. He had excellent levels of concentration and was totally focused in every game. George played right back and I was right half. We developed a kind of telepathy between us. If George pushed forward, I'd cover for him and vice-versa. We had a very good understanding.

Apart from the à la carte fiasco in Cardiff, George and I were no trouble to the manager. We were never tempted to go out drinking or chasing women on the night before a game. We had to be back in the hotel by 10.30 p.m. and we never broke the curfew. We'd get back from the pictures, have a hot drink, then be off to bed by 11 p.m. We lived for our football; a case of old heads on young shoulders.

We listened to the senior players and that stood us in good stead, until an away game at Leeds in December '59. Then things went horribly wrong, thanks to Jimmy Langley.

George and I were always the first to get up on the morning of a match. I'm still the same now; I hate lying in bed once I'm awake. Luckily, George was the same as me. We were both young and full of energy. We didn't want to laze around in our room, so we'd be first down for breakfast then out for a stroll around the town. I always bought a present for my mum, a box of chocolates or something like that.

A walk before the game was a good idea, but Jimmy Langley took it too far in Leeds. We'd just had our pre-match meal at the hotel. Jimmy had been at Leeds United as a player and he fancied seeing some of his old haunts.

'I'd like to walk to the ground today, gaffer,' he told Bedford Jezzard. 'I'll take the two boys with me if you like.'

Can you imagine three stars from a Premier League team walking to a match today? It would never happen, would it? But in those days it was nothing special.

'Are you sure you know the way?' Bedford asked.

'Of course,' said Jimmy. 'I know Leeds like the back of my hand.'

Ten minutes later George, me and Jimmy were on our way to the ground. I don't know which hand Jimmy kept his map on, but an hour later we were still walking. George and I were glancing at each other, both thinking the same. It was obvious Jimmy was lost. You could see by the look on his face he didn't have a clue where we were.

'Where's the ground, Jim?' asked George. 'The boss wants us there an hour before the game.'

'It's not far now,' said Jimmy, sounding vague.

We turned a corner and, to Jim's relief, saw a crowd of supporters heading for the game.

'There you are,' he said, pointing to the stadium in the distance. 'I told you I knew the way.'

We got to the ground and found the players' entrance. There was a big bruiser on the gate.

'Y'all right, lads?' he said.

'Yes,' said Jimmy confidently. 'We're players.'

'Oh, are ya? Who d'you play for then?'

'Fulham,' said Jimmy.

'Well, you're not playing 'ere,' said the bruiser. 'This is the rugby ground!'

Now Jimmy looked really nervous. It was gone 2 p.m. and Elland Road was on the other side of Leeds. Panic stations! A little Ford Anglia came slowly weaving through the crowd. Jimmy ran out in front of it. The driver had to stop. He looked quite nervous. He probably thought we were going to mug him.

Jimmy banged on the driver's window and he rolled it down.

'Look, we need a favour,' said Jimmy. 'We're playing for Fulham this afternoon, but we've come to the wrong place.'

'That were careless, weren't it?' said the man.

'Yeah, but we need a lift to the football ground,' said Jimmy. 'I'll give you a fiver.'

That was a quarter of Jim's wages.

'Oh, all right,' said the man, 'jump in.'

We eventually got to the ground at 2.30 p.m. We ran into the dressing room and there was Bedford Jezzard getting changed. He'd been a great goal scorer for Fulham in his day, but he hadn't played for years. He was furious with Jimmy and he gave him the dressing-down of all time. The way Beddy managed to string so many swearwords together was quite poetic. Jim was nearly in tears.

The manager wasn't angry with me and George. In his eyes, we were just kids. We got changed and kept our heads down. You could have cut the atmosphere in that dressing room with a knife. It was a dreadful way to prepare for a game.

Then we went out on the pitch and . . . beat Leeds 4–1.

Jimmy, George and I all had good games. What motivated us? A single word: fear!

A month later we started the 1960s with another classic Chamberlain cameo. We were playing Luton Town on a cold January afternoon at Kenilworth Road. Tosh started the game like a world-beater. He picked up the ball on the left wing, sped past their full-back Seamus Dunne and clipped in a perfect cross for Jimmy Hill to score with a header.

I ran over to Tosh to congratulate him and heard Seamus Dunne have a few quiet words with him.

'If you do that again,' he said, 'I'll kick you into the fucking stand.'

'No, you won't,' said Tosh.

'I will,' said Seamus.

'No, you won't,' smiled Tosh. 'I'm going to play on the right wing now!'

And that's what he did, switched wings for the rest of the game. Seamus never saw him, nor did anybody else. Tosh never had another kick.

It got so bad Roy Bentley had a word with the referee in the second half.

'Send Chamberlain off, ref.'

'Why? He hasn't done anything.'

'Exactly!' said Roy.

We lost the game 4–1, but Tosh stayed in one piece!

You never really knew what would happen from one week to the next. It was as funny as a Carry On film at times. But we finished tenth in the First Division that season, which was quite respectable. In fact, it proved to be our best-ever finish during my time with the club.

Fulham's First Division record for the period is as follows:

1959–60, tenth; 1960–61, seventeenth; 1961–62, twentieth; 1962–63, sixteenth; 1963–64, fifteenth.

My early years at Fulham were wonderful. I couldn't have wished to have been among a better group of players. They were fun to work with and immensely professional. Those friendships have lasted to this day.

My own game was improving rapidly and I was rewarded with the first of my three England Under-23 caps in November 1960, when I was picked to play against Italy at St James' Park. We drew 1–1 and playing in the same side as Bobby Charlton and Bobby Moore did wonders for my confidence.

Another big thrill came when I was asked to captain Fulham at the age of nineteen. Johnny Haynes was injured and he suggested I'd be a good replacement. That meant a lot to me. Pity the match turned into a personal nightmare.

I felt good leading the team out at the Cottage, but the afternoon went downhill from there.

We were playing Sheffield Wednesday. Our usual routine was for the ball to be played back to me from the kick-off. I'd hit a long ball out to Tosh on the left wing and we'd go straight on the attack. Wednesday forwards John Fantham and 'Bronco' Layne obviously knew the move and closed me down quickly.

Without looking, I kicked the ball back to Tony Macedo, which would have been fine except he was kicking the mud off his boots on the goalpost at the time. I screamed at him, but too late. The ball rolled over the line and I'd scored an own goal in the first few seconds of my big game as captain. That set the tone for the afternoon – we lost 6–1.

Luckily, Johnny Haynes was back as captain for the next game.

★　★　★

It was 1961 and a Fulham player was about to make historic head-lines; his name was Jimmy Hill, Chairman of the PFA. I admire what Jimmy has achieved in life, but I only ever saw him as an average player. No more than that. Jimmy had a high opinion of himself, but he was never as good as he thought he was.

He was an attacking inside forward and one of the club's leading goal scorers. He'd get around twenty goals a season, but missed many more. There was no doubting his love for the game. He had fantastic energy, he never stopped running, but his ball control left a lot to be desired. He'd be through on numerous occasions with only the keeper to beat and not score. Five minutes later he might smash the ball in the net from twenty-five yards. You never knew with Jim.

I never thought of him as a friend. Some players went out of their way to make me feel at home when I first got in the team, but Jimmy wasn't one of them. He wasn't unpleasant in any way, he just didn't take much interest in me, which was fair enough. He lived a very busy life, even then.

As Chairman of the PFA, he had a dream. He was determined to be the man who broke the £20-per-week maximum wage for professional footballers. He said it was outdated and unfair and he led the fight brilliantly. I'm not sure anyone else could have achieved what Jimmy did. He has to take all the credit for that. He didn't impress me as a player, but as a public speaker he was magnificent, very articulate and confident.

I remember seeing him speak onstage at a big PFA meeting in London in 1961 and all the top London players were there. Jimmy gave a passionate speech saying we should all go on strike if the clubs didn't abandon the wage-capping system we were working under. When he called for a vote backing the strike, a forest of hands soared in the air. The players were with Jimmy all the way and I went along with the vote. The PFA got the same level of backing all over the country.

In the end, as history shows, Jimmy Hill won the day and players enjoyed a new-found freedom. The most publicised pay rise came at Fulham. Our chairman, Tommy Trinder, supported the players' action and said that if we won, he'd pay Johnny Haynes £100 a week. When the time came, Tommy kept his word and said Johnny was worth every penny, which he was. Johnny never spoke to me about his big pay rise, but I hope he bought Jimmy Hill a drink. He owed him a huge debt of gratitude. We all did.

Jimmy Hill played nearly three hundred games for Fulham between 1952 and 1961. He left Fulham to become manager of Coventry City, where he proved to be an excellent coach, taking them from the Third to the First Division in five ground-breaking years. Hill was full of new ideas. Coventry City got a stylish continental strip to wear and a new nickname, the Sky Blues. An electronic scoreboard was built at Highfield Road and match-day radio, playing the latest pop hits, was introduced for home games.

Jimmy Hill is an important member of Fulham's Hall of Fame. He has filled every major role at the club: player, coach, manager, director and chairman. He has always shown great energy and enthusiasm, qualities that have contributed to his continued success in the highly competitive world of television.

Our best FA Cup run came in 1962. We got four home draws on the spin and prepared for each one with a five-day trip to Worthing. We stayed at the luxurious Warnes Hotel on the seafront. There were no hard training sessions; all we did was play golf, eat and drink. We had big fried breakfasts, English cream teas, a lovely meal in the evening, then a couple of pints down the pub.

It wasn't exactly a fitness regime, but we went into games relaxed and our team spirit was excellent. We beat Hartlepools, Walsall and Port Vale in the early rounds, but we knew our sixth-round tie, against Blackburn Rovers at the Cottage, would be tougher. We went to Worthing again and it looked like the good life had backfired on us the following Saturday when we went 2–0 down, but we fought back to draw 2–2. Maurice Cook got the winner in the replay at Ewood Park.

We drew Burnley in the semi-final. I could still taste the disappointment of seeing Fulham lose to United at Highbury four years before and I was determined we'd go one better this time. Burnley were an excellent side, pushing hard to regain the First Division title they had won in 1960. We started as underdogs, but Graham Leggat put us 1–0 up on a snowy day at Villa Park. We were brilliant in the first half, but Burnley came back after the break to draw level. Then we were denied a blatant penalty fifteen minutes from time, when Maurice Cook was pulled down in the box. That proved to be a major turning point. We were the better side on the day, but Burnley got away with it and won the replay 2–1 under the lights at Leicester.

Burnley had outstanding players including Irish international Jimmy McIlroy, England centre-forward Ray Pointer, England winger John Connelly, a very brave keeper in Adam Blacklaw and two excellent full-backs John Angus and Alex Elder. Captain Jimmy Adamson linked everything together in midfield. He was a really good wing-half and very unlucky never to win an England cap.

Despite all those stars, Burnley suffered an anticlimactic end to the season. They were chasing the Double, but finished as runners-up to Ipswich Town in the First Division and lost 3–1 to Spurs in the FA Cup final at Wembley. Danny Blanchflower, Bobby Smith and Jimmy Greaves got the goals for Tottenham.

I was very disappointed not to reach the final with Fulham, but I did have one major event to look forward to. My marriage to June. We'd been going out together for over two years. June was very pretty and that was the initial attraction. As we grew closer, I was sure I'd met the girl I wanted to spend the rest of my life with.

I decided to propose in style. We drove to Hyde Park and I rowed us out into the middle of the Serpentine and popped the question. June was surprised and delighted; I was very happy to hear her say, 'Yes'. Now we were keen to find our first home together. The search turned into a bit of a mystery story starring the Maltese Falcon . . .

Tony Macedo was born in Malta. He joined Fulham in 1957 and stayed for eleven years. Tony was a wheeler-dealer. Smart, good-looking and full of self-confidence. He'd go round local garages and tell them he played for Fulham. He'd talk them into giving him a car to test drive for them. He'd have them for a week here, a month there. Tony loved to barter.

His flamboyant character came through in his goalkeeping. He had a very continental style. He'd throw himself around and make flashy saves. That didn't go down well with everyone. He played for England Under-23s, but never won a senior cap. I think he got a raw deal.

To me, he was as good as any goalkeeper in the country. He was up there with Gordon Banks, Ron Springett and Alan Hodgkinson. Tony was a big man, but extremely agile. He dealt well with crosses, he was brave if he had to dive at a forward's feet and he was a great shot-stopper, too. Tony had the lot; he was a class act.

I trusted him as a keeper but, away from the game, I was never really sure where I stood with Tony. That came to light after a conversation with Frank Osborne at the Cottage. I told him June and I were looking for our first home. Frank had contacts everywhere. I thought he might be able to help us. Like all clubs, Fulham were keen to see their young players married, so Frank was happy to help. He suggested seeing Tony Macedo's flat in Raynes Park.

'Have a look and let me know what you think,' he said.

I asked Tony Macedo if we could come over.

'Of course,' he said, 'come for dinner.'

Tony's wife Margaret cooked us a very nice meal, then he showed us round. The flat was on the fourth floor of a block, overlooking the railway lines. It may not sound much, but June and I were impressed. She was sharing a flat with her mum in Ladbroke Grove. It was so small, she had to sleep in the kitchen. I was still at home in the terraced house in Notting Hill. Tony's flat was modern and spacious; we liked it a lot.

After the tour, Tony poured us all another glass of wine.

'What do you think of this place?' he asked.

'Very nice,' said June. I nodded.

'I might be interested in selling it,' he smiled. He said we could have it for £2,500. It sounded like a bargain to us. We were really excited and talked about it all the way home.

First thing next morning I went straight in to see Frank Osborne at the club.

'Thanks for telling me about Tony's flat,' I said. 'It's really nice. In fact, we're thinking of buying it, if we can get a mortgage.'

'What?'

'I'm thinking of buying Tony's flat. What's wrong with that?'

'I'll tell you what's wrong with it . . . he doesn't own it. It's a club flat!' shouted Frank, going red in the face. 'That scheming bastard, I'll skin him alive.'

Frank called Macedo in and gave him a terrible rollicking.

'How could you do something like that to a team-mate?' Frank screamed. 'You must have known you'd get found out, you bloody idiot!'

Tony wasn't fazed.

'It's all just a misunderstanding,' he said, lightly. Tony apologised and we left it at that, but to be honest I wasn't happy at all with his behaviour.

June and I were married on 23 June 1962. (We have now been happily married for forty-four years.) Our first home was in Worcester Park and we found it without any help from Tony Macedo.

Bobby Robson moved back to Fulham from West Brom that summer. He'd already had six successful years at Craven Cottage (1950–56) and it was good to know we had another England international in our side for the new season. We really needed Bobby's experience when a serious car crash put Johnny Haynes out of the game for a year.

We went up to Blackpool for a First Division game in October. I'd been out for a walk on the seafront with a few of the other players. On the way back to the hotel we saw the remains of a smashed-up sports car. Later we heard it was Johnny's car.

The crash left him with cruciate ligament damage in his knee. Sadly, he never played for England again. But for that crash, he would surely have been in England's World Cup-winning team in 1966. It was tragic.

(Johnny Haynes played for England at schoolboy, youth, Under-23 and B international levels. He made his senior debut in October 1954 and scored in England's 2–0 away win over Northern Ireland in Belfast. He became England captain in 1960 and led the team twenty-two times in a total of fifty-six international appearances. He died in a road accident in 2005.)

I took over as Fulham captain in Johnny's absence. Once again, I was surprised to be asked, especially as Bobby Robson was now in the team. But Bobby took it well and supported me, which I appreciated. He moved in near us and I got to know him very well. June and I spent a lot of time with him and his family and I thought of him as a friend.

Bobby was an intelligent player, a very good reader of the game. He had a good character, too, which he needed when he moved into coaching. He suffered a real baptism of fire, which I tried to warn him about.

In May 1967, I went on a long end-of-season tour with Spurs. We played Vancouver Royals, out on the west coast of Canada. I knew Bobby Robson was scheduled to join them as player/coach, but when I got to Vancouver all the talk was about the arrival of another coach, Real Madrid legend Ferenc Puskás. Bobby hardly got a mention. It didn't feel right to me.

As soon as I got back to England, I went round to Bobby's to tell him what was going on. I was shocked to see that his family were crating up their possessions and getting ready to emigrate to Canada. I had a quiet word with Bobby and he admitted he didn't know anything about Puskás joining the Royals. I tried my best to warn him that things didn't look good over there, but Bobby was already committed to the move and he went.

By the end of the year, he was back in England. Bobby and Puskás were doing the coaching together in Vancouver and that was never going to work. They were both strong personalities with their own ideas. As I feared, Puskás was the one the club backed and Bobby was out in the cold.

It seemed he had fallen on his feet when he was given the chance to manage Fulham in January 1968, but it was a difficult time for the club. Fulham were relegated, finishing bottom of the First Division. Nobody could blame Bobby for that; he'd inherited a poisoned chalice. But, when the team made a lacklustre start to the new season, he came under increasing pressure and was sacked in November. Johnny Haynes took over as manager for a brief spell.

Bobby had suffered two hammer blows in less than two years, but he was not beaten. He rebuilt his management career at Ipswich Town, with the same quiet determination he'd shown as a player. Later, of course, he went on to achieve great things at the highest level, especially with England and Barcelona.

To be honest, I felt a little let down by Bobby in later years.

I asked him about the manager's job at Ipswich Town in 1982, when he was leaving the club. It wasn't just a case of the old pals act. My management CV was strong at that time. I'd recently completed five successful years at Brighton, where we'd won promotion from the Third to the First Division in three years.

I saw Ipswich as a very similar, homely club and I was confident I could do a good job at Portman Road. I really fancied the challenge. Bobby had tremendous influence with the Cobbold family who owned the club. He said he'd see what he could do, but I thought his attitude was very cold. He never came back to me.

(Bobby Robson left Ipswich Town in 1982 after thirteen successful years there. He succeeded Ron Greenwood as England manager.

Bobby Ferguson, Robson's right-hand man at Ipswich, was promoted to manager at Portman Road, but was never able to emulate the success of the Robson years.)

There are no hard feelings now. I don't bear any grudges. Bobby is highly respected in the game and he deserves it. In his new role for the Football Association of Ireland, his experience and knowledge will prove invaluable to Steve Staunton and I'm sure the Republic of Ireland's team will benefit.

The 1962–63 season was full of contrasts. It was good to have Robson back, but terrible to lose Haynes. Then came the emergence of a precocious teenager called Rodney Marsh.

I first noticed Marshy in one of our weekly 'first team against reserves' practice games. He was a cocky little sod. He nutmegged me a couple of times in the first few minutes. I didn't like him making a fool of me, so I gave him a kick. He gave me a disdainful look, then got on with the game. He was always brave and always in trouble. He had his share of fights around the Cottage in those early days.

A lot of the Fulham players thought Marshy was arrogant, but I grew to like him. He loved to show his skills. He could do things with a football lesser players could only dream of. He was never blessed with pace, but he could shield the ball well and had brilliant ball control. He would dribble past players time and time again.

Rodney made a dream debut in March '63 when he scored our winner against Aston Villa with a spectacular volley. Then an awful head injury the following September nearly ended his career. He was badly hurt as he headed the winning goal at Leicester City. He suffered a fractured jaw and skull; he also permanently lost the hearing in his left ear.

Marshy was out of the game for almost six months and went through some hard times, but his self-belief remained intact and he went on to enjoy great success at QPR and Manchester City, before moving to America.

His best spell for Fulham came in the seventies when he teamed up at the Cottage with his mate George Best and the great Bobby Moore. Some of the football they played was wonderful. Pure showbiz! Of course, I'd left Fulham by then.

Rodney is an intelligent man. He is also a talented artist, which proves he has a sensitive side, but he was a rebel. As a kid at Fulham, he was always up to mischief. He liked to push things to see how far he could go. That characteristic has stayed with him, with serious results.

Rodney was making his way in the England team in 1973, when an off-the-cuff joke cost him his international career. Sir Alf Ramsey was giving a team talk before a game against Wales. He told Marshy he expected him to work hard in the first half.

'If you don't,' said Sir Alf, 'I will pull you off at half-time.'

'Blimey,' said Marshy. 'At Manchester City, all we get is a cup of tea and an orange.'

Sir Alf was not amused. Goodbye, England.

In January 2005, another unfortunate joke ended the Rodney Marsh era at Sky Sports. I don't think his bosses had any choice, but I was sorry to hear the news because we had shared some very good times at Sky Sports.

Rodney Marsh has always been a maverick character, but he was one of the most naturally gifted players I ever saw. I wish we'd had more games together for Fulham, but by the time he had recovered from that horrific injury, I was playing for Spurs.

The transfer came as a complete surprise to me. I had no thoughts of leaving, but my destiny was shaped by events elsewhere.

First, Dave Mackay broke his leg in a tackle with Noel Cantwell. It was a European game at Old Trafford in December 1963 and I saw it on TV. It was sickening to see Dave suffer such a serious injury. I felt sorry for him, but I didn't think the incident would affect my career in any way. Then I read an article in the *Evening Standard*. It said Spurs had also lost Danny Blanchflower, who needed a cartilage operation. Bill Nicholson needed to strengthen his squad and he was interested in signing Bobby Moore or me.

I went to see Frank Osborne at the club and asked what was happening.

'It's just newspaper talk, son,' he told me. 'Tottenham aren't interested in you. Bobby Moore's the player they want. You'll see in a couple of weeks, they'll sign Mooro. It's nothing to do with you, don't worry about it.'

I accepted what Frank said. Everything went quiet for a few weeks and I heard no more about it. I was expecting to hear that Bobby Moore had signed for Spurs, but nothing happened. Then, just before the transfer deadline in March, I got an urgent call from Frank one Friday night. He told me to come straight to his house.

When I arrived, his wife opened the door and she was crying. I knew her very well and asked what was wrong and she just shook her head and left me in the lounge with Frank.

'What's going on?' I asked him.

'She's a bit upset,' he said.

He asked me to sit down, then started talking nostalgically

about the scrapes I'd been in since joining Fulham as a kid: washing in the Thames, killing rats, arguing over my signing-on fee when I turned pro. I kept waiting for him to get to the point. I didn't want to be rude, but it was getting late and we were playing Liverpool the next day. I needed to go home and get some sleep.

'Fancy a sherry?' Frank asked.

'No, I don't want a drink, Frank,' I said. 'Look, what's this all about?'

'Spurs want to sign you.'

'You told me they wanted Bobby Moore.'

'I don't know what happened there,' said Frank, 'but Spurs came in for you two weeks ago. At first I told them no.'

'So what's changed your mind?'

'The money, Alan. They're now offering £72,500.'

Fulham was a fun club; a very close-knit community. June and I had settled well in Worcester Park. George Cohen, Bobby Robson, Eddie Lowe, Graham Leggat and Johnny Haynes all lived nearby. After games we'd go out for a meal, or back to someone's house for a few drinks. It was a good life and I felt settled.

'I don't want to go anywhere,' I said.

'You've got to go,' said Frank. He rang Tommy Trinder and put me on the line.

'We want to put a cover over the Hammersmith end of the ground,' said the Chairman. 'The only way we can do it is by selling you. They're offering a record fee, son. We're sorry to lose you, but we need the money.'

Now I knew why Frank's wife had been crying. Frank looked upset, too; he didn't know what to say. We sat in silence. My mind was in overdrive. Fulham had been my home for almost seven years. I'd played over two hundred games for the club and I was happy there.

Now one of the best clubs in the world wanted me. Tottenham

7

COME ON, YOU SPURS!

16 March 1964

The traffic was heavy on Tottenham High Road.

I'd been to White Hart Lane many times, but now I was arriving as a Spurs player. In the years ahead I would love playing for Tottenham, but on that first morning I was nervous.

I had left the safe and sleepy world of Fulham behind. Now I was joining the football élite. A famous club filled with world-class players. How would they react to me? What about the fans? Would they accept or reject me? I'd been thrown into the unknown and had no idea what lay ahead.

Suddenly, I was a stranger. I felt like John Wayne riding into town in some western movie, knowing I had to prove myself all over again.

An emotional weekend had turned my world upside down . . .

'Frank's told you we want to sign you?'

Bill Nicholson sat in Frank Osborne's house, looking calm and business-like. Eddie Baily, his assistant manager, sat beside him saying nothing.

'Yes, he's told me,' I said, 'but I'm happy at Fulham.'

When Bill Nicholson wanted something, he didn't take no for an answer. As I've said he asked if I could play right back so that he could sign Mike Bailey as his new right half.

'If we get you both, we'll have two very good players,' said Bill.

I told him if I came to Spurs it would be in midfield or not at all. He would have to choose between me and Bailey. He didn't hesitate.

'OK, you're the first choice. We'll take you. You'll be replacing Danny Blanchflower, because we don't think he's going to play again.'

'What about Dave Mackay?' I asked.

'He'll be back,' said Bill Nick.

Bill Nicholson was the best manager in Britain, if not the world. In the last three seasons he'd guided Spurs to the Double, a second FA Cup win, plus the European Cup Winners' Cup. Now he saw me as the replacement for one of his greatest players. I was impressed by his faith in me.

Bill sensed my change of heart. 'I don't want you to sign now,' he said, as if it had never been in doubt. 'I want you to play for Fulham tomorrow. Beat Liverpool if you can because that will give us a very good chance of winning the championship. Eddie and I will come and see you tomorrow night and get the forms signed. You'll get twice the money you're on at Fulham, plus a signing-on fee. Don't tell anyone except your wife. OK?'

My signing-on fee was only £20, but my weekly wage went up to £70, plus bonuses. That was very good money at twenty-two. Other pay rises were built into the contract. Bill also told Frank Osborne that Fulham owed me a £750 loyalty bonus for being with the club for seven years. Frank agreed to pay that out of the fee they were getting from Tottenham. Spurs were offering me a good deal, but I still felt let down by Fulham. I was surprised they were prepared to let one of their bright young players go. I drove home with mixed emotions.

Of course, I couldn't sleep that night.

The next day I tried to act normally, but once I got to the Cottage it was hard to hide my emotions. It was a relief to get out on the pitch and play. The first half was goalless; I sat next to Johnny Haynes during the break. The mood in the dressing room was relaxed.

'What are you doing after the game?' Johnny asked.

I couldn't hold the news in any more.

'I'm going to Tottenham,' I said.

'Is there a party over there?' said Johnny.

'No, I mean Tottenham Hotspur. I'm signing for Spurs tonight.'

'You're joking.'

'No, I'm leaving the club. This is my last game.'

Johnny looked shocked. He called the manager over.

'Do you know about this, Beddy?' Johnny asked.

'What's that?'

'Spurs are buying Mullers.'

'Is this true, Alan?' Bedford Jezzard looked angry.

'Yes, boss,' I said. 'I only heard about it last night. I met Bill Nicholson and Eddie Baily at Frank Osborne's house. I spoke to the chairman on the phone and he said I've got to go.'

'Did he?' snapped Beddy and stormed out.

He went to the boardroom and hammered on the door. Frank Osborne answered. Beddy asked him if what I'd said was true. Tommy Trinder and all the directors could hear every word. Frank was embarrassed, but had to admit my transfer had been negotiated in secret. Beddy was so angry he couldn't speak. He turned his back on Frank, walked out of the club and drove straight home.

(Bedford Jezzard was a man of integrity. The underhand way the sale of Alan Mullery to Spurs was handled left him feeling disillusioned with the club he had served as player and manager. He stayed on for nine months, but resigned in December 1964 to run the family's pub. He was thirty-seven years old and never worked in football again. Fulham went downhill after his departure and were relegated in 1968.)

Emotions were running high in the dressing room. The players all wanted to know why the manager had walked out. I had to tell them I was going to Spurs. I'd been part of that team for over five years, so naturally the news came as a shock. The club's cloak-and-dagger tactics had put me in a very awkward situation and I resented it. As we trooped out for the second half, the last thing I felt like doing was playing football.

No manager. A traumatic half-time break. Then Liverpool put five goals past our dispirited defence in the second half. That scenario would have made perfect sense, but this was Fulham, so we won 1–0!

After the game I said a quick goodbye to all the players. They wished me well, but it was all very rushed. A terrible way to say goodbye. I threw my boots in a bag and hurried out of Craven Cottage. There was no time to look back.

Bill Nicholson and Eddie Baily were waiting outside my house when I got home. They came in and I signed the forms. Bill told me to be at the ground by 9.30 Monday morning and that was it.

June and I went to a party that night. A friend of ours was talking about the Liverpool game. I told him I'd left Fulham.

'I'm a Spurs player now.'

'I don't believe it.'

'Neither do I,' I admitted.

A lot had happened in twenty-four hours . . .

I was so deep in thought, I nearly missed the turning into White Hart Lane. Bill Nicholson was standing in the car park, talking to one of the directors. He came over to greet me.

'Morning, boss,' I said.

'Don't call me boss, call me Bill,' he said, shaking me by the hand.

Everything at Tottenham was on a larger scale. The car park was massive, as big as a football pitch. The walls of the ground towered high above me. I felt a bit overawed. This was my chance to prove myself at the highest level. The question was, could I rise to the challenge?

I looked at Bill Nicholson. There was no doubt or uncertainty in his eyes. He was glad I was at the club, I could see it. He had bought me to do a job for Tottenham. His interest in me began and ended there. The ground rules had changed.

Fulham was fun, Tottenham was business.

At Spurs you were expected to win things. Failure would not be tolerated. I was playing for high stakes now, sink or swim. Bill directed me to the dressing rooms and I walked into the club that would be my home for the next eight years.

The first person I saw was Dave Mackay. He was running up and down a staircase, in the early stages of his long, lonely recovery from a broken leg. Then I walked into the dressing room and was instantly surrounded by a sea of famous faces. John White, Bobby Smith, Jimmy Greaves, Maurice Norman, Cliff Jones, Peter Baker, Ron Henry and Bill Brown. Double winners, European winners, the Kings of White Hart Lane.

My new training kit was hanging on a peg. White shirt and socks, blue shorts and a white tracksuit top with blue bottoms. I don't know how the club knew my size, but everything fitted perfectly. My initials had already been stamped on the shirt and tracksuit top. I was impressed by that. The dressing room was much bigger than the one I knew so well at Fulham. The baths were massive. At the Cottage we had one bath and one shower. At Fulham we had one table in the treatment room and at Tottenham there were four. I liked the quality of everything I saw that morning.

My transfer to Spurs had been pushed through in a hurry and it left me in a daze. But, as soon as I arrived at White Hart Lane, reality kicked in. All my competitive instincts rose to the surface. I was joining an outstanding Spurs team and I had a hell of a lot to live up to. It wouldn't be easy, but I was determined to succeed.

When you join a new club, it's a bit like being the new kid in school. If players make you feel welcome, it settles you down. That's what happened at Spurs, with one important exception. And that was Danny Blanchflower.

I always admired Danny. He was a truly great player. He was thirty-six years old when I arrived at the club. He'd enjoyed a magnificent career and he found it hard to accept it was over. Many of his strengths were still intact: his intelligence, his ability to read a game, his brilliant passing skills. Danny still had them all, but his body had let him down. There was no way back from his cartilage operation.

Taking over from a legend like Danny was a daunting prospect. He was a hero to every Spurs fan and rightly so.

(Danny Blanchflower joined Spurs from Aston Villa in 1954 for £30,000 and made 337 League appearances during his ten-year stay at the club.

He captained the Double-winning side in 1960–61. Spurs won their first eleven League games that season and went on to clinch the First Division by eight points. They then beat Leicester City 2–0 in the FA Cup final with goals by Bobby Smith and Terry Dyson. They were the first English team to win the Double since 1897.

Blanchflower also captained Tottenham to victory in the 1962 FA Cup final and the 1963 European Cup Winners' Cup final.

Blanchflower won fifty-six caps for Northern Ireland and reached the quarter-finals of the 1958 World Cup. Asked about the team's unexpected success, Danny explained with a smile: 'Well, we try to equalise before the other team have scored!'

Blanchflower was voted Footballer of the Year in 1958 and 1961.)

How do you follow a record like that? It was a huge task for a young player. Danny must have realised that. He could have done so much to ease the pressure, but I'm afraid he didn't help at all. In fact, he was quite aloof when I first arrived.

To be honest, Danny Blanchflower didn't rate me.

If he had been manager of Tottenham, he would never have bought me. I wasn't Danny's type of player. He loved people who showed finesse and silky skills. I'd come to the club to take his place and I'm sure he didn't see me as a worthy successor. I didn't have Danny's elegant style and I never would. My game was more direct and aggressive. Nobody could question my commitment and will to win, but he ignored those strengths.

Danny Blanchflower looked down on me.

A few words of encouragement in those early days would have meant a lot, but he kept his distance. This was probably partly due to the inner struggle he was going through. He was coming to the end of his days at Spurs and mine were just beginnning. It was a difficult time for both of us.

Danny was one of the best players of his generation. In the modern game, he would have been a multi-millionaire. Today's stars can retire knowing they never need to work again. I doubt if Danny had any real financial security when his career ended, although Spurs did give him a testimonial to reward ten years of loyal service.

Danny Blanchflower retired in April 1964, a month after I arrived at Spurs.

Danny was a very private man. When Eamonn Andrews appeared with his red book saying 'This Is Your Life', Danny said, 'No, it's not' and walked out on the live TV show.

He could be distant and elusive, but I'm happy to say we got on very well in later life. He often came to Brighton when I was manager there. He loved to reminisce about his days at Spurs. Those were the happiest times of his life. I always enjoyed hearing his stories and it was good to know I did finally win his respect as a player.

Danny had a very good sense of humour, when you got to know him. He told me that when he became Northern Ireland manager, there was a major panic because George Best had given his number 7 shirt to a fan before the game.

'So what's the problem?' asked Danny.

'Well, we only had the one shirt for Georgie,' said the kit man.

After ten years at Tottenham, where everything was so perfectly organised, Danny could not believe it!

Replacing Danny Blanchflower was hard enough, but I felt I was expected to replace Dave Mackay, too. Bill Nicholson was looking for me to supply the power and competitive spirit Spurs had lacked since Dave's injury. I could see the size of the task ahead and it worried me. Bill wasn't just looking for a new player. He wanted someone who would take the club into the future.

A new hero, if you like.

Spurs already had good midfield players in John Smith and Tony Marchi when I arrived, but Bill put me straight in the side. Spurs were an iconic team, not only for their success, but also for the wonderful way they played the game. No side had ever shown more class and style. From Jimmy Greaves and Bobby Smith up front to Maurice Norman and Bill Brown at the back, the team was full of top-class internationals. I'd never won a full cap.

I didn't talk to anyone about how I was feeling. I was much less open than I'd been at Fulham. If I felt apprehensive, I didn't want to show it. I thought things through, tried to get it all in perspective. I wasn't Danny Blanchflower. I wasn't Dave Mackay. I was Alan Mullery. I had to do things my way and play to my own strengths. That's why the manager had bought me. I wasn't frightened of failure, but I knew I faced a fight to win acceptance. At the end of the week, the team sheet went up and I was in the team to play Manchester United.

I made my Spurs debut at White Hart Lane on 21 March 1964.

Running out in front of 56,000 fans felt wonderful, but my worst fears were soon realised. I hit a poor pass in the first few minutes and a groan went round the ground. All eyes were on me. The crowd wanted Blanchflower and Mackay rolled into one. I couldn't live up to their expectations. To make things worse, United beat us 3–2. My Spurs career was off to a poor start.

The rest of the season was just as difficult. The comparisons between Danny, Dave and me continued and I found it hard to deal with the pressure. I was in an impossible situation and my form suffered. I was keeping international players out of the team and I felt awkward about that.

I managed to score a goal at Liverpool but overall I was disappointed with the way I played. We lost 7–2 to Burnley just before the end of the season and finished fourth in the League. Bill had hoped to boost his championship chances by signing me. Seen in those terms, my arrival had been a failure.

I took a break from football that summer and came back determined to do better in the 1964–65 season. I was looking forward to Dave Mackay's return. I knew that would give everybody a lift and take some of the pressure off me.

On 12 September, we were away to West Ham United. Dave was playing a comeback game in the reserves at Tottenham. The word was he'd be back in the first team in a couple of weeks. I'd often seen Dave running up and down the terraces at White Hart Lane to regain his strength. I admired his grit and determination. Now it seemed his long wait was almost over.

We lost 3–2 at Upton Park, despite two goals from Jimmy Greaves. We were all on the team coach waiting for Bill, who had gone to take a phone call after the match. I was in the front seat when Bill got on. He sat next to me and to my surprise I saw tears in his eyes.

They say tough men don't cry, but believe me they do.

'Are you OK?' I asked.

'I've just had some bad news,' said Bill. 'Dave Mackay has broken his leg again.'

The bond between Mackay and Nicholson was very strong. They saw the world through the same eyes. Even in his darkest hour, Dave's first thoughts were for the manager. 'Don't tell Bill Nick until the West Ham game's over!' he shouted at the Spurs staff, as he was carried to the ambulance.

Now Bill had heard the news and he looked shattered. Dave had worked like a demon to get back to full fitness, but he'd broken his left leg again and Bill really felt for him. You had to dig very deep to see the compassionate side of Bill Nicholson's character, but it was there. I saw it that day.

The news spread round the bus and all the players were genuinely upset. They thought the world of Dave. He was their leader, Bill's manager on the field. The mood was very subdued on the journey back to White Hart Lane. When a player breaks his leg for the second time, you can't help wondering if he'll ever come back. Bill didn't say a word.

Dave Mackay's new injury came hard on the heels of John White's death the previous July. John was struck by lightning while sheltering under a tree on a golf course during a thunderstorm. It was a tragic way to lose such a shining talent. These were difficult times for the club and I was desperate to repay the tremendous belief Bill Nicholson had shown in me. It was time to deliver on the field.

I was starting to feel more at home at Tottenham. I could sense my best form coming back, but I needed to win over the fans. Once they were on my side, I could start to enjoy my football again. That's what had been missing – the sheer joy of playing. Too many other pressures had got in the way.

Now what I longed for, more than anything else, was a stroke of luck. And it came in late October in a home game against Chelsea. They had a useful young winger called Albert Murray.

'I want you to get stuck into this lad,' Bill Nicholson told me before the game. 'Let him know you're there in the first five minutes.'

That was always the way in those days. You tried to get heavy tackles in early. The referees nearly always let them go. So, when Murray got the ball on the wing, I slid in on my backside and took the ball and man. I hit him so hard he flew through the air and landed in the crowd with the Spurs fans.

A lone voice rang out from the terraces.

'Come on, The Tank!'

I don't know who that man was, but I'd like to buy him a drink. That was the turning point. From that moment on, my life changed for the better. Spurs fans picked up on my new nickname. Suddenly I had my own identity. I wasn't Blanchflower and I wasn't Mackay. I was Alan Mullery. Strong and brave in battle, a fighter who never gave up.

The Tank had arrived.

Dave Mackay was the best all-round footballer I have ever seen. He was also the most inspirational captain I ever played under. You could be losing 5–0 and he still thought you could win 6–5. When he came back from his second broken leg, he was as hard as ever.

We played Leeds shortly after his return. Billy Bremner hit him with a late tackle and Dave was incensed. He leapt to his feet, grabbed the Leeds skipper by the shirt and virtually lifted him off the ground. Dave was steaming, but he kept his emotions in check and didn't throw a punch. Even so, Bremner looked terrified. The photograph of the incident is a classic. They've still got it up on the wall at Spurs. It was a fiery moment, but Dave Mackay's proud record of never getting sent off remained intact . . . just.

It was better to play with Dave than against him, but we were never on the same team in five-a-sides at the club. Our trainer,

Cecil Poynton, used to organise those games and he knew if Dave and I were up against each other, the sparks would fly. I think Cecil enjoyed it. I always sat next to Dave in the dressing room and when Cecil was giving out the shirts, Dave and I would never get the same colour. If I got red, he'd get blue.

The five-a-sides were played in an indoor training area at White Hart Lane called the ball court. There were goals painted on the walls and just one door in the corner. As soon as that door was shut, it was strictly no holds barred. Cecil Poynton never blew for a foul. Players were tripped, or barged into the wall.

Dave and I tackled the way we did in a match. The only difference was that we were wearing trainers not boots. We never hurt each other. The tackling was explosive but we never went over the top. Having said that, those sessions were not for the weak-hearted. It was like a volcano erupting at times, but they helped Dave and I build a mutual respect, which lasts to this day.

Things were not so harmonious when Terry Venables joined Spurs in 1966. On his first day at White Hart Lane, Terry and Dave clashed in a big way.

As usual, we finished training with a five-a-side game. Terry was always a confident person, but that morning he looked like a very lonely boy. I remembered feeling that way on my first day, so I talked to him as we walked over to the ball court.

'These five-a-sides can get a bit lively,' I warned him. 'You'll need to look after yourself in there.'

Terry thanked me for letting him know.

Cecil had put him on the opposite team to Dave Mackay. The game started and Terry had this annoying habit of sticking his backside out to keep other players away from the ball. He stood in the corner of the gym doing this, like he was killing time by the corner flag at the end of a game. Dave Mackay was behind him, tugging at his shirt and trying to win the ball, but there was no way past Venners.

We all knew Dave wouldn't put up with this for long. He stepped back a yard and booted Venners straight up the arse. Terry swung round and threw a punch. Dave hit him back. Cecil Poynton did nothing to stop the fight. In fact, he was egging them on. Then the door opened and in walked Bill Nicholson. He'd just paid Chelsea over £80,000 for Venners and there he was on his first day fighting the club captain.

'What's going on here?' shouted Bill.

Cecil immediately jumped between Dave and Terry, holding them apart and pretending to be shocked. 'Break it up, lads!' he shouted. 'What d'you think you're doing? We can't have this, it's disgraceful.'

'I don't want any more of that,' snapped Bill.

'Don't worry, it won't happen again,' said Cecil.

Bill walked out, slamming the door behind him.

Two minutes later, Terry and Dave were knocking each other silly again and Cecil was enjoying the fight.

'Go on, boys, get stuck in!'

I think Dave probably thought Terry was a flash East End lad from Dagenham. There was always an edge between them. But these days Terry always praises Dave Mackay, which is very fair considering the welcome he got on his first day at the club.

When I see Dave now I always give him a kiss on the cheek. Not many people can get away with that, but Dave knows how much I respect him.

Dave could play anywhere. He'd go in goal for training sessions at Spurs and make amazing saves. He even played in goal for Scotland once, when their keeper was hurt.

Naturally, he kept a clean sheet!

Those five-a-sides at White Hart Lane were X-rated. The other players told me that, before I arrived, Mackay's team always won. It evened out a bit when I got there; I hated losing as much as Dave did. I think Bill Nicholson recognised that quality in me.

He saw me as a potential leader, but I was happy to wait for my time to come.

If I had been offered the club captaincy while Dave Mackay was still at Tottenham, I would have turned it down flat. I always admired the way Dave led by example and I learnt a lot from playing with him. He was in his element when we won the FA Cup in 1967. I'll never forget the smile on his craggy face when he lifted the Cup.

It capped his courageous comeback.

Dave seemed to fall out of favour with Bill Nick during the following season and finally left Tottenham in July 1968. Bill cried when he heard Mackay had broken his leg for a second time, but he was ruthless when he felt it was time for Dave to go.

We were all having lunch at our training ground in Cheshunt. It was a warm sunny day and we were taking a break before going out to do another session in the afternoon.

A big chauffeur-driven car pulled up outside the canteen and out stepped Brian Clough, in that famous green jumper. Bill Nick introduced him to Dave Mackay. The rest of us sat there gobsmacked, as Cloughie successfully persuaded our captain to join Derby County. We were all whispering to each other, 'Dave's not going, is he?'

But that's exactly what was happening, all in public view. I was stunned. Maybe Dave was ready for a move and a new challenge, but he should never have been asked to discuss his transfer in public like that. I thought it was handled very badly. If Dave Mackay was playing today, he would be represented by a top football agency. Can you imagine an agent allowing Dave to sit there discussing his future over a bowl of salad in the staff canteen? It's ludicrous when you think of it.

Some things should happen behind closed doors, but the deal went through. Cloughie was delighted with his signing and Spurs lost a legend. There were no big speeches when Dave left. Bill

Nick never mentioned it. Mackay had gone and life went on. Now the manager had another big decision to make. Who was going to be his new captain?

A couple of days later, Bill called Terry Venables and me into his office. He was sitting at his desk and we both stood in front of him. He looked at us both and there was a moment's silence. It seemed like an age to me and I'm sure Terry felt the same.

'Alan, you're captain now,' said Nick.

'Thanks very much.'

'Terry, you can be vice-captain.'

Terry's face fell.

He was obviously very disappointed, but he knew there was no point in arguing. 'OK, Bill,' he said.

'Right, that's all.'

As ever, Bill Nick didn't waste words.

Terry and I walked out.

Venners was gracious enough to shake my hand and wish me well, but I could see how hurt he was. If the roles had been reversed, I would have felt just the same. Bill's decision that day had major repercussions on both our careers.

Terry left Tottenham for QPR the following year. I captained Spurs to two major Cup wins over the next four years. Taking over from Dave Mackay didn't weigh me down. I was ready for the responsibility and I loved being at the heart of things. I was Bill's new leader on the pitch. The promise he saw in me as a kid at Fulham had come to fruition.

From that point on, I played better than ever.

The game was tougher in those days.

I was known for my hard tackling. I didn't set out to hurt other players but, if somebody whacked me, I'd get my own back. Willie Carr of Coventry City went over-the-top on me once. Within five minutes, I saw my chance and did the same to him. It was a bad tackle and I nearly broke his leg. It happened in the heat of the moment and I wasn't proud of what I'd done.

That's the only time I can remember deliberately going over-the-top, other than when we played Leeds United. Those games were wars. Norman Hunter and Jack Charlton were hard, but I didn't think of them as dirty players. I was more wary of Allan Clarke, who would rarely back off in the tackle. I didn't trust Billy Bremner, but the Leeds player who was arguably the worst offender often got away with many of the things he did.

Johnny Giles was the most feared player in the game. He was a terrific footballer, but he had a fierce streak in him. He was also clever at hiding what he did. All the players knew it.

Bill Nicholson's team talks, before those Leeds games, were unique.

'If you get a 50–50 ball, look up to see who you're facing,' he'd say.

It was unheard-of for Bill Nick to talk like that, but such was the ferocity of our matches against Leeds that he feared losing one of us with a serious injury. Bill would rather lose a few tackles and keep all his players in one piece.

Tommy Smith and Ron 'Chopper' Harris are often described as the hard men of that era. They both were brutes at times. I remember Chopper hitting George Best up around the waist in one game. But I never minded tackling either of them, because in a 50–50 situation I knew they'd go for the ball.

Generally though, players didn't get the protection they do today. Some teams took advantage of that, but Bill Nick was not a cynical manager. He wanted his teams to play attacking, entertaining football. That philosophy was reflected in the way we trained. We had a very good training ground. The playing surfaces were excellent there. On the first day of pre-season training we'd be given a football each and all our work was done with a ball at our feet. Even in sprint sessions we'd run with the ball. The emphasis was on skill and control.

We all enjoyed training in the morning, but the afternoons were tougher. After lunch, we'd do a five-mile walk, with Bill striding out in the lead. He was following the training routines used by Arthur Rowe and his 'push-and-run' Spurs. Bill Nick and Eddie Baily were both part of that team and believed in Rowe's methods.

Twice a week, we'd be driven out on the team bus and dropped about ten miles from Cheshunt. Bill left those runs to Eddie Baily. He always had a bike with him and he'd happily cycle along as we ran back to the training ground. Jimmy Greaves loved playing in games and five-a-sides, but a ten-mile road run was not his idea of fun. So one day he nicked Eddie's bike and cycled to Cheshunt. Jim was waiting for us when we got back. He left Eddie's bike outside and jogged in with the rest of us. Bill Nick was impressed to see Jimmy finish with the front-runners. Greavsie wasn't even sweating!

When Eddie Baily finally got back he gave Greavsie a mouthful, but didn't tell Bill. It reminded me of Tosh Chamberlain and his milk-float rides at Fulham. Jimmy was a similar type of character, everyone loved him. He was fun to be with, always up for a laugh and joke. Nobody could really coach Jimmy. What he did came naturally. He was a born striker who made scoring goals look easy.

(Jimmy Greaves made his League debut for Chelsea in 1957, at the age of seventeen. He scored that day and went on to score in ever major debut of his career. In 1960, he became the youngest player to score a hundred League goals.

Greaves went to AC Milan in 1961, scoring nine goals in twelve games, during his brief stay.

Jimmy then signed for Spurs in the December of that year. Bill Nicholson paid £99,999 for him, holding back a single pound to save Jimmy from the pressure of being the first ever £100,000 player.

Jimmy stayed with Tottenham for nine years and scored a club record of 266 goals in 379 matches.)

People often ask me about Greavsie's drinking, but I can honestly say I never saw Jimmy Greaves in a drunken state when we were at Spurs – not even when we were celebrating winning the FA Cup in 1967. The news that Jimmy had a serious drink problem came as a real surprise to me.

Of course, that's not to say that a lot of the players didn't enjoy a drink. Alan Gilzean and Dave Mackay often went out on a Saturday night after a game. Bill Nick and Eddie Baily heard about these sessions and wanted to know what effect they were having. So they instigated a ten-lap race round the cinder track at White Hart Lane, first thing every Monday morning.

If the management were trying to catch Dave and Gilly out, they failed. The two Scotsmen came in first every time. They enjoyed a drink when the pressure was off, but they could handle it. They were both magnificent athletes, as those Monday morning races proved.

If a Spurs player had turned up for training or a match smelling of alcohol during my time as captain, I would have felt it was my job to confront them. I wouldn't have shied away from that, but it never happened with Greavsie or anyone else. I never heard of anyone going out to pubs or clubs the night before a game.

Standards were high at Tottenham. Bill Nick expected us to be professional and we expected it of each other, too. I was very hard on anyone who didn't pull their weight in games. I might have ruffled a few feathers, but I was there to win. I would have hammered anyone who turned up drunk, but it never arose.

Smoking wasn't seen as a problem. There's a famous picture of Jimmy Greaves smoking a cigarette in the dressing room after a game. I've also seen him puffing away on a pipe in a team meeting and Bill didn't say a word. Plenty of Spurs players smoked. I used to enjoy a cigar after a game. Smoking was part of everyday life then and we didn't give it a second thought.

Players never had health checks either. We got weighed at the start of the season and that was it. At Spurs, our club doctor was Brian Curtin. I can't remember him ever giving me a blood test, but he once jokingly offered me a glass of whisky and said it would make me feel better. Naturally, I declined.

Clubs didn't advise players on diet. My favourite pre-match meal was steak. Ask any nutritionist now and they'll tell you eating steak before exercise saps your strength. It never worked that way for me. Maybe it was psychological, but having a big steak always made me feel good and ready to play.

One of my first away games for Spurs was against Liverpool. Most of us had steaks for lunch at the hotel, before driving to Anfield. After the main course, a waiter came out with a huge dish of rice pudding. We all thought the same. How are we supposed to play if we eat that? Nobody touched it but, of course, rice pudding is high in carbohydrates and perfect energy food. Pity we didn't know it then because we lost the game 3–1.

Alec Stock always fancied himself as a bit of a visionary. He tried to bring in special diets during my last season at Fulham. We always had our pre-match meal before home games in the riverside stand. I arrived one day to find the team table covered with jugs of milk and boxes of cornflakes. I asked the chef what was going on.

'The manager wants you to eat cereals today,' he explained.

'I'll have a steak, thanks,' I told him. There must have been something in my tone of voice, because he didn't argue. I'd been a professional player for seventeen years. It seemed a bit late to change the habits of a lifetime.

Maybe I would have been a better player if I'd been given the perfect diet to follow all through my career. Who knows?

The modern game is so different with its health checks, psychologists and dieticians. Players are faster, fitter and stronger than they have ever been. But has that made the game more skilful and entertaining?

I'm not so sure . . .

Bill Nick often asked me to move closer to Cheshunt, while I was at Spurs. It used to take me nearly two hours to drive to the training ground every day, but I was happy living in Surrey. I didn't want to be part of any clique. A group of Spurs players regularly went out clubbing together, but it didn't interest me.

Was I an outsider at Spurs?

No, I don't think so. I got on well with all the team, but I always had a life away from the club and that's the way I liked it. I had plenty of friends outside the game, too. Denny Mancini the boxer was a good mate and so was Micky Stewart, the Surrey and England cricketer.

I spent a lot of time teaching Micky's son Alex how to bat and bowl, although he may say his dad was his best coach. It was a thrill to see A.J. Stewart grow up to achieve so much in his own career, as captain of Surrey and England.

I rarely socialised with my team-mates at Spurs, but I had great respect for them as players.

When I first arrived, Bill Brown was in goal. Dave Mackay was a big fan of his fellow Scot. He always said the bigger the game, the better Bill played. Peter Baker and Ron Henry were the full-backs from the Double team, both excellent players. Maurice Norman was the England centre-half, strong in the tackle and excellent in the air.

Sadly, I played with John White for a couple of months only, before his untimely death. He was a wonderful player. They called him 'The Ghost' because of his ability to drift into space unmarked and unnoticed. A man with immense style and grace.

Cliff Jones was one of the bravest little men I ever saw. A Welsh international winger with fantastic pace and ability, Cliff was totally fearless. He'd dive in where the boots were flying; two seconds later the ball would be in the net and Cliff would be on the ground with a cut eye. He got so many knocks, but it never changed him. What a player – he would be worth millions today.

Over the years, the faces changed.

For me, Pat Jennings was a better keeper than Bill Brown. Big Pat was a reassuring sight in goal, so reliable and consistent. He made unbelievable saves at times and I loved the way he'd come out and take crosses with those huge hands of his. Sometimes he needed only one hand to catch the ball. Pat was a giant in every sense of the word, one of the world's greatest goalkeepers.

Cyril Knowles came from Middlesbrough. He was as hard as nails, with a terrific left foot. Joe Kinnear was another first-class full-back. Phil Beal was very underrated. He had the tough task of taking over from Mackay when Dave went to Derby and I never thought Phil got the credit he deserved. John Pratt was another good club man who would play anywhere to help the team.

Mike England was a great player for Spurs, a centre-half in the Maurice Norman tradition. Big and strong in the heart of our defence and a wonderful header of the ball. Mike won most of his challenges, but he met his match one day at Everton.

Spurs had won a corner and a little winger called Johnny Morrissey decided to mark Mike England in the box. Johnny was quite a hard nut, but he was only about five foot five and Mike was six foot three. Seeing them standing together waiting for the corner was comical.

Not surprisingly, Mike really fancied his chances.

'Far post,' he kept shouting. 'Far post, I'm free!'

I took the corner and hit it to the far post as requested. I thought I'd put it straight on Mike's head, but the ball sailed harmlessly out of play for a goal kick. I couldn't work it out. Where was Mike? No sign of him. Then, as the box cleared, I saw our huge centre-half lying flat on his back in the mud. Johnny Morrissey had somehow knocked him out when the pair jumped as the ball came over, and then run away. When Mike England came round, he refused to go off. He spent the rest of the afternoon chasing Morrissey all over the pitch!

Frank Saul was involved in another off-the-ball incident in a game at Turf Moor. Frank was a hard centre-forward and Burnley's centre-half had been kicking him all afternoon. The referee was offering no protection, so Frank decided to take the law into his own hands. When the play was up the far end of the field, he got his revenge on the centre-half. They carried him off on a stretcher, with blood streaming from his nose. Frank wasn't a big man, but he could take care of himself. He'll always be remembered for scoring in the semi-final and final when Spurs won the FA Cup in 1967.

Jimmy Robertson scored that day at Wembley, too. He was the quickest player at the club: nobody could stay with him. Jimmy was a right winger with real ability. He was excellent at darting past the full-back and whipping in good crosses. In today's game I'd compare him to Shaun Wright-Phillips. Bill Nick liked to play two wingers and he expected them to tackle back when we lost the ball. Jimmy was always happy to do that. He was a very genuine player and I think Bill Nick made a mistake when he let him go to Arsenal.

For several seasons I had the pleasure of playing in the same side as the wonderful strike force of Greaves and Gilzean. Jimmy Greaves, one of England's best ever goal scorers and Alan Gilzean, a Scottish international with sublime skills. What a partnership!

They were prolific scorers. Jimmy could be out of the game for eighty minutes, then score two in the last ten. He was clinical. Jim had a powerful shot when he needed it, but he often preferred to pass the ball into the net. He had the knack of being in the right place at the right time. He did it better than anyone else I've ever seen.

Gilly had superb control. He could hold the ball up, or lay it off with subtle flicks, which Jimmy read perfectly. Alan scored some beautiful headers. He could hang in the air and place the ball with incredible accuracy.

Greaves and Gilzean. The 'G-Force'. If I hadn't been in the same team as them, I would have payed to watch them play.

Terry Venables had a much more difficult time at Tottenham. He was very much an individual player. Instead of hitting an early pass, he would often hold on to the ball too long. Bill Nick had played in a push-and-run side and that was the kind of football he wanted his teams to play. So Terry drove him mad.

'Don't fanny and fart arse about,' he'd shout at Venners. 'Move the ball early.'

But, to be fair to Terry, that was never his style. Bill must have thought he would fit into our side, but it wasn't a good signing. Maybe Bill thought Venners could be the new John White. Terry had tremendous skill and ability, but nobody could replace John. That was an impossible task.

Terry had his moments at Spurs, but there must have been times when he wondered why he'd ever left Chelsea. The Spurs fans never really took to him and the way Bill wanted him to play went against the grain. I think Venners had a rough deal at the Lane. Nobody really accepted him as a Tottenham player during his three years at the club.

It was a different story when a seventeen-year-old called Steve Perryman broke into the side in 1969, the year Terry left. Steve had come through the club's youth system and he was Tottenham through and through. The supporters recognised that from the start. Steve started his career in midfield, winning the ball with strong, crisp tackles. His distribution was good and he covered well in defence, too. I was impressed by his ability and attitude and he proved to be a very good Spurs captain, when the time came.

Probably my favourite player, during the later years of my stay at Spurs, was Martin Chivers. He signed from Southampton in

January 1968 for £125,000, a record fee at that time. Chivers was an inspired signing. He repayed all the faith the manager had shown in him, but Bill still moaned at him a lot. I don't know why.

I remember defending Martin after one game. He'd played very well and scored two good goals. We had won, but Bill was still moaning about a couple of chances that had got away. In the end I got sick of it.

'Hey, Bill,' I said, 'Chiv's just won us the game!'

A murmur of agreement went round the dressing room. Martin was a popular member of the team. He was big and brave. He scored fine goals, often when we needed them most. That's the sign of a truly great striker. A horrible knee injury kept him out of the game for a year, but Martin came back to replace Jimmy Greaves and forge a wonderful new striking partnership with Alan Gilzean.

Greavsie's move to The Hammers came as a bolt out of the blue. Once again, Bill Nicholson showed no sentiment when the time came to sell a star player. Jimmy was at home on transfer deadline day, 16 March 1970. The phone rang. Bill Nicholson said he had Martin Peters at the club. He was going to sign him from West Ham United and he wanted Jim to go to Upton Park as part of the £200,000 deal.

Jimmy had been at Tottenham for nine years. Now it was all over in one short phone call. Naturally, Jimmy was angry and upset.

'If you don't want me, I'll go,' he told Bill.

It was a sad end to a great career at Spurs. I missed Jimmy around the place. He had a lovely dry sense of humour, which proved to be an important part of the success he later enjoyed on TV with the *Saint and Greavsie* show. I count myself lucky to have played with one of the best natural goal scorers the world has ever seen.

Martin Peters was a very different character from Jimmy Greaves, but I liked him, too. We'd already played together for England when he joined Spurs and we got to know each other even better during that summer's World Cup finals in Mexico. Martin was a studious person, who only spoke when he had something worth saying. He'd listen to a conversation, then come in at the end with a really meaningful comment. He had a very good temperament; very placid, no nerves at all.

It was difficult for Martin to establish a strong identity as a Spurs player. Fans linked him closely with West Ham United. He was one of that club's three 1966 World Cup heroes, along with Bobby Moore and Geoff Hurst. But Martin was definitely an asset to our team. He could ghost into space and score goals from deep positions. He had his own very special way of playing the game.

I was at an England get-together before the 1966 World Cup finals. Alf was talking to all the players about the competition ahead. It was serious stuff and the players were hanging on his every word. Alf finished and asked if there were any questions.

Greavsie put his hand up.

'Yes, Jimmy.'

'Is it true you said Martin Peters is ten years ahead of his time?'

'Yes, I did say that.'

'Well,' smiled Greavsie, 'why are you playing him now?'

Everyone cracked up, including Martin. A gentle man and a pleasure to play alongside during my last two years at Spurs. He took over as Spurs captain when I left in 1972.

White Hart Lane is full of memories for me.

Earlier in this book, I told you about winning the UEFA Cup on a night of high emotion. Our FA Cup and League Cup wins at Wembley were wonderful occasions, too. I'll cover those in the next chapter. But, overall, what pleases me most is the way I managed to win the respect of the fans during my eight years at Tottenham.

I arrived as a nervous, naïve kid with so much to prove. I left with the cheers of 50,000 fans ringing in my ears as they carried me shoulder-high, before I walked off the pitch for the final time. I was sad to leave Spurs, but I couldn't have wished for a better farewell.

I still work for the club on match days. I'm part of a team of former players who do hospitality work in the various sponsorship lounges. It's good to see the familiar faces of Martin Chivers, Pat Jennings, Phil Beal, John Pratt, Martin Peters, Paul Allen, Ralph Coates and Cliff Jones. We talk to people about the game and answer questions about our own careers. I enjoy it.

That wasn't always the case.

Some of the previous regimes at the club were not particularly receptive to former players, but that's all changed now. The present chairman, Daniel Levy, goes out of his way to make us feel welcome. We get the same respect from all the other directors, the staff and the management. It's a treat to go back to Spurs these days.

I always like meeting current players. I was having lunch in the Gary Mabbutt lounge recently. Michael Dawson wasn't playing that day. He came in for a bite to eat and made a point of walking across the room to meet me. He was a very nice lad and I enjoyed talking football with him. I represent the past of the club, but talented young players like Michael are the future.

The best thing about going back to White Hart Lane is meeting the fans on match days. The club give me a car park pass, but sometimes I leave my car in the street. I park near the little terraced house that was home to Bill Nicholson through all his greatest years.

I'm surrounded by smiling Spurs fans as I take the five-minute walk to the ground.

'All right, Mullers?'

'Got your boots, Alan?'

'Come on, The Tank!'

It's jokes and banter all the way.

More than anything, I value that, the lasting bond I've built with the supporters of one of the greatest clubs in the world. I remember one-time chairman and lifelong fan Irving Scholar speaking to a group of former Spurs players at a testimonial dinner.

'You may think you're forgotten, but you're not,' he told us. 'Every time Tottenham plays, someone somewhere will think of you and the pleasure you gave them.'

Who could ask for more?

8

GLORY DAYS

I was running round Wembley with the FA Cup and 100,000 fans had seen a brilliant game of football. Now the roar of our supporters filled the best stadium in the world. The famous turf felt like carpet beneath my feet. Above me, the twin towers rose up towards the English sky. The thrill of the moment took my breath away.

Stanley Matthews ran up beside me.

'Well played, son.'

'You, too, Stan,' I smiled back.

Reporters were already calling the game, 'The Matthews and Mullery Final'. I didn't mind sharing the glory with the great man.

'Time you went home, Alan.'

I knew the voice. It was my Aunt Rose. What was she doing at Wembley?

'Come on, love, time for your tea.'

I drifted back into the real world. I was sitting in my aunt's flat in Notting Hill and I'd just seen my first Cup final, Saturday 2 May 1953. Blackpool had been 3–1 down but, thanks to a thrilling spell of wizardry from Matthews on the wing, the Seasiders had fought back to a 4–3 victory, with a Stan Mortensen hat-trick and a ninetieth-minute winner from Bill Perry.

I was eleven years old and my head was full of dreams.

Just six months later, after watching England play Hungary on that same old TV, I set my heart on becoming a professional footballer. That decision never changed or wavered. I wanted to play at Wembley in Cup finals and internationals.

It all came true at Tottenham . . .

1967 FA Cup Winners

Bill Nicholson went into every season believing his team could win everything.

'If you don't believe it,' he'd tell us, 'you're never going to do it.' Bill had the right idea. There is no point entering a competition unless you think you can win it. But I'd been at Spurs for three years and we hadn't won a thing.

In that time, the club had been through a major transformation.

Tottenham already had the reputation of being big spenders. Bill Nicholson bought every member of his Double team – Bill Brown, Peter Baker, Ron Henry, Danny Blanchflower, Maurice Norman, Dave Mackay, Cliff Jones, John White, Bobby Smith, Les Allen, Terry Dyson and Terry Medwin.

Now Bill had been busy again. Dave Mackay and Cliff Jones were still at the club, but all the other former heroes had gone. Bill had bought a whole new team. Joe Kinnear and Frank Saul were the only home-grown players. It was a new era, but we lived in the shadow of the Double side. The Press called us the 'Million Pound Spurs' and the pressure was on us to deliver. We needed to win a major trophy to establish our own identity.

I longed to see the glory days return to White Hart Lane.

We were playing well in the League and our confidence was high for the third round of the FA Cup. We were drawn away to Millwall from Division Two, on 28 January 1967. We were strong favourites, but The Den was a tough place to go. Journalists made a mental note: Possible Cup Shock!

We arrived at the cramped ground in Cold Blow Lane on a damp and dismal winter's afternoon. The South London fans decided to give us a hot reception. They surrounded our coach and started rocking it. Luckily, the police moved in before they could turn it over.

When we got to our dressing room, Jimmy Greaves suggested going out to have a look at the pitch. It was an hour before kick-off, but there were already 40,000 in the ground. The gates were locked and the atmosphere was hostile. The players' tunnel was surrounded by Millwall fans. There was a red shingle track all round the pitch, but it was only about a yard wide. The crowd were so close they could touch you.

We walked out to a storm of abuse.

The pitch was very muddy. We walked up to the centre circle, trying to look calm and unruffled, then two Millwall supporters jumped on to the field and ran towards us. One had a live cockerel under his arm and the other was carrying a miniature gallows. When they got to us, they rung the cockerel's neck, stuck the gallows in the mud and hung the bird from a noose.

'Right,' said Jimmy Greaves, 'I think we'll go back then, lads.'

We headed back to the dressing room, with the Spurs cockerel still swinging in the breeze. The Millwall supporters loved it, of course, but those two fans had made a big mistake. The Spurs team was full of strong characters and we didn't like playing the stooge for anyone. Bill Nick and Eddie Baily didn't need to motivate us. We were ready to go.

We held Millwall to a 0–0 draw at The Den, then beat them

1–0 in the replay, with a goal by Alan Gilzean. There were over 58,000 at White Hart Lane that night and once again it was very close. Millwall came out of those games with a lot of credit, especially their barrel-chested full-back, Harry Cripps, a cult figure with their fans. But we kept battling and deserved to go through.

We were on our way.

We were drawn at home against two Second Division sides in the next two rounds. We beat Portsmouth 3–1 in the fourth round with two goals by Alan Gilzean, including a spectacular diving header, and one by Jimmy Greaves. Greavsie got two more in our 2–0 win over Bristol City in the fifth round. We were going well and the 'G-Force' had scored all our goals. I can't think of a striking partnership today that can match the understanding those two enjoyed. They were deadly when they played together.

We trained on the Monday morning after beating City, then gathered round the radio to hear our draw for the sixth round. Away to Birmingham City. We'd now faced four Division Two sides in a row. It was 13 March. Were the fates smiling on us?

I always enjoyed playing at St Andrews. It was a big pitch and, if you played with wingers, as we did, there was always room to hit them with good long passes. The playing surface was excellent, too. I knew it would suit us.

I got up at 6.30 on the morning of the game and drove to White Hart Lane. The team bus left the ground at nine for the drive to Birmingham. Spurs fans were shouting to us from their cars on the M1 and waving their blue-and-white scarves. It was Cup fever all the way and it helped set the mood for the day.

We were going to St Andrews for a result. If we could win, fine, but we were determined not to lose. We kept things tight. Frank Saul missed our best chance in the first half, and the game ended 0–0. It had been a dour, dull affair. The replay at White Hart Lane was totally different. Over 52,000 saw us hammer

Birmingham City 6–0 with goals from Jimmy Greaves (2), Terry Venables (2), Alan Gilzean and Frank Saul. It was a powerful, confident display.

I was particularly pleased for Venners. He was often criticised, as I was, for not scoring enough goals, but Terry was really on song that night. Both his goals came from powerful twenty-yard shots. It was also good to see Frank Saul make up for that miss at St Andrews. The Tottenham fans were ecstatic; we sent them home dancing.

Wembley was just one game away.

Once again, we all crowded round the radio on Monday to hear whom we would play in the semi-final. Would it be Chelsea, Nottingham Forest or Leeds United? Chelsea had talent and potential; Leeds were fierce competitors; Forest were riding high in the League. There was very little to choose between them, they were all good sides. We were drawn to play Forest at Hillsborough on 29 April. We knew we'd have to be at our best to beat them.

Spurs and Nottingham Forest were closely matched in the 1966–67 season. Forest finished second in Division One, beating Spurs into third place only on goal average. Both teams were four points behind the champions, Manchester United.

We travelled to Sheffield on the eve of the game. I shared a hotel room with Terry Venables. He was working on his *Hazell* books at the time. Terry's stories about an East End private eye were very popular and were eventually turned into a successful TV series. I went to the cinema that night, but Terry was happy to stay in the room, tapping away at his typewriter. His one luxury was a glass of sherry from room service. He always said that helped him sleep well before a game.

It was only a short drive to Hillsborough the next day. The streets were packed with Spurs and Forest fans, singing and chanting. The atmosphere hit us long before we reached the ground. I wasn't nervous, I just wanted to get out there and play. Over 300,000 fans had watched our seven Cup ties so far. Now, could we clear the final hurdle?

Spurs had every reason to feel confident going into that semi-final. A wonderful solo goal from Jimmy Greaves crowned a 4–0 win over Newcastle United on 31 December 1966. Since the turn of the year, Spurs had lost just one League game in four months and were, of course, unbeaten in the Cup.

Nottingham Forest were in excellent form, too. Forest came to Hillsborough full of confidence. We were equally positive. FA Cup semi-finals are often tense and defensive, but our game with Forest was attacking and open. We treated 55,000 fans to a stunner. Jimmy Greaves opened the scoring for us with a fine shot from outside the area. Greavsie often placed the ball into the net, but this time he hit it hard and low into the corner.

Forest drew level and had chances before Frank Saul got the crucial goal. Forest battled all the way, but we held on for a 2–1 win. Even in our moment of victory, as we hugged each other and waved to our fans, I couldn't help feeling sorry for the Forest players. Losing in the semi-final was the ultimate kick in the teeth for them, especially when the game had been so close. They trudged off with heads bowed; we started to celebrate.

The singing and champagne started as soon as we got to our dressing room and lasted all the way back to London. All the players, directors, wives and girlfriends were on the train. The constant pop of champagne corks is all I remember about our victory ride home. The Spurs supporters were waiting for us at Euston station and they gave us a fantastic welcome, with horns blowing and scarves waving. We were totally engulfed by smiling, cheering fans.

June and I were staying with Terry Venables and his wife that night. We made our way through the crowds of well-wishers and caught a taxi to the Colony Club, which was owned by the American film star, George Raft. There were posters from his movies all over the walls. George had made a fortune from playing gangsters; one of his best friends in real life was Bugsy Siegel. George's gimmick was flicking a coin, while he told people what to do. Come to think of it, he would have made a good referee.

The Colony was the perfect place to relax. They had good food and music and we stayed until the early hours really enjoying ourselves. I didn't often drink much, but I was truly gone that night.

Morris Keston and his wife were with us at the Colony. Morris is a devoted Tottenham fan. He had always been a good friend to Spurs players and has helped to organise many testimonial games in the past. He has been a supporter for over fifty years and has travelled all over the world following his team. It was a great night for Spurs fans and it was good to celebrate reaching Wembley with Morris. The man's a legend!

The next morning June and I got a cab to White Hart Lane to pick up our car. The ground was surrounded by fans, with flags waving up and down Tottenham High Road. It was lovely to see them so happy, but the noise was hard on my hangover. All I wanted to do was get home!

The spirit at the club and among the players was excellent in the build-up to the final. There's nothing better than being in a winning team. Bill Nick and Eddie Baily made sure we didn't get ahead of ourselves, but we knew we had a good chance of lifting the Cup at Wembley. Chelsea had beaten Leeds 1–0 in the other semi-final. They were a young side, full of promise, but we were confident of winning the first-ever Cockney Cup final.

One enjoyable diversion from the pre-match pressures was recording an EP for EMI called 'The Spurs Go Marching On', which sold thousands of copies. The whole team went to Abbey Road for the recording session. This was, of course, the world-famous studio where The Beatles were currently recording all their classic songs. If John Lennon and Paul McCartney had turned up at Wembley to play in the final, they might have felt the way we did that day. We were like fish out of water.

We started singing to a backing track and it sounded bloody awful. The producer realised we were nervous and had the very sensible idea of sending out for some booze. The beer and wine were soon flowing and we started to have some fun. Venners sang 'Bye Bye Blackbird'; Joe Kinnear and Pat Jennings teamed up for 'When Irish Eyes Are Smiling'; Greavsie did a nice old song called 'Strollin''; and I chipped in with 'Maybe It's Because I'm a Londoner'. The rest of the lads all sang in the background. We recorded quite a few songs; in fact, they had a job to shut us up in the end. Funny what a few beers will do to a football team.

I was really enjoying life, but an injury during our last League game of the season wiped the smile off my face. Suddenly there was every chance I could miss the final. I'd damaged a muscle in my right thigh during the second half of our 2–0 home win over Sheffield United. Maybe I should have come off as a precaution, but that went against the grain. I played the whole game. As soon as it was over, my leg started to tighten up.

Bill Nick was annoyed.

'Don't tell anyone about this,' he told me. 'You might make the final, we'll have to see how it goes.' I only had seven days to recover. I was a quick healer, but I knew it was touch and go. One word summed up how I felt that night: gutted.

I had treatment twice a day, but the leg was slow to respond. We had a Press open day at Cheshunt in the middle of the week. I sat smiling for the photographers, while the rest of the team trained. Of course, the journalists soon read the situation and the story was all over the papers the following morning.

'Mullery Heartbreak'.

'Spurs Star to Miss Final?'

I always try to stay optimistic, but I was worried sick that week.

It seemed so ironic. I was hardly ever injured. Now, with the biggest match of my Spurs career at stake, I was forced to play the waiting game. It was the last thing I thought about at night and the first when I woke up in the morning. I'd slowly get out of bed and take a few tentative steps. Did the leg feel better or was the muscle still tight? Talk about walking a tightrope.

Of course, I played it all down when I was with the rest of the players. They were in high spirits, looking forward to the game. I didn't want to spoil things for them, but dark thoughts of sitting at Wembley watching them play filled my head. I was so close to seeing my childhood dream come true, I could almost touch it. Almost, but not quite. Maybe the dream would become a nightmare and there was nothing I could do about it.

After six days that felt like six years, the waiting was finally over. I had the crucial fitness test on the day before the game. When I got up that morning, the leg felt much better, but I still felt very nervous. I drove to White Hart Lane not knowing if I would play in the final.

Bill Nicholson, Eddie Baily and Cecil Poynton all came out on to the pitch for the test. There was no question of hiding anything from them. I would have to tell them the truth, even if it meant missing out. I had to put the good of the team ahead of my own feelings. That was never in question.

Cecil asked me to jog, sprint, twist and turn. Then I had to hit long and short passes. I held back on kicking the ball with maximum power, because I was frightened the muscle might go again, but everything else was fine.

'OK, you're playing,' said Bill.

What a relief. Now I could actually start thinking about the game . . .

The Cup final was important to all of us, but it had an extra edge for Terry Venables, who had left Stamford Bridge just one year before. He would be facing his old team-mates, which is never easy. The Chelsea fans were sure to give him a hard time, too, and like me, he'd been under more than his fair share of pressure.

We shared a room on the night before the game. All we wanted was a relaxing stay at the team hotel and a good night's sleep. What we got was noise, hassle and steamy sound effects from our sexy next-door neighbours,

Bill Nicholson's arrangements were usually impeccable, but he got things badly wrong for the final. The Spurs players were all expecting to stay at a country hotel before going to Wembley, somewhere quiet and private, where we could focus our minds on the game ahead. Instead of trees and grass, we got concrete and glass.

Bill booked us into the Mayfair Hotel in the heart of London. It was the worst possible choice, crowded and busy. Word had got out of where we were staying, so every time we stepped out of our rooms we were surrounded by supporters wishing us well and asking for autographs. They didn't mean any harm, but the timing was all wrong. We needed some space.

On the Friday night, we all walked up to a cinema at Marble Arch. I was glad to get out of the hotel; it was starting to feel very oppressive in there. We saw a western called *The Professionals*, starring Burt Lancaster, Claudia Cardinale and Robert Ryan. I really enjoyed the film and felt relaxed for the first time that day. Then the lights went up and we were surrounded by autograph hunters again. There was no escape.

When we got back to the hotel, there must have been over two hundred people milling around in reception. Terry and I took one look and decided to go straight to our room. I rang room service and ordered a hot drink for myself and a glass of sherry for Terry. We both agreed the only way to get some peace and quiet was to have an early night. We had our drinks, then turned out the light and settled down for a good sleep.

I was just drifting off, when I started to hear voices in the next room. It was a man and a woman fooling around together. The woman had the dirtiest laugh I'd ever heard. The noise quietened down and I was almost asleep, when I heard a soft tapping noise on the wall. As I listened in the darkness, the sounds of passion grew louder. The man started to grunt and the woman started to moan. The banging got faster and faster. Their headboard was knocking against our wall and they were obviously enjoying themselves thoroughly!

Terry woke up and turned on the light. Half an hour later the sexual athletes were still at it. We started shouting through the wall.

'Shut up in there!'

'Haven't you had enough yet?'

The answer was no. Our sexy neighbours didn't take any notice of us. An hour later the wall was still shaking and the screams of pleasure were louder than ever. I phoned down to reception and complained about the noise.

'Can't you do something?' I asked. 'We're playing in the Cup final tomorrow.'

'Well, sir, it's a bit awkward, isn't it?' said an embarrassed voice.

He was right. There was nothing we could do but turn up the TV and wait for the kinky couple to complete their steamy session. It was two hours of non-stop action. Of course, Terry and I ended up laughing about it. We both agreed the man next door should play for us in midfield at Wembley. Nobody could match him for stamina.

The following morning, we were dying to see what the couple next door looked like. We dared each other to knock on their door, but we both chickened out. We never did meet them, but Terry and I both thought their performance was worthy of a gold medal in the Bedroom Bonking Olympics.

It wasn't the best preparation for the final, but it gave the rest of the team a laugh when we told them the story over breakfast. Venners and I had missed out on some sleep, but we were soon caught up in the excitement of Cup final morning. TV cameras were at the hotel to provide live coverage of the build-up to the game. I'd seen every final since 1953 and now I was part of the greatest football event of the year. Having come so close to missing out, I was determined to make the most of the day.

We had our pre-match meal in a private room, before leaving the hotel. Bill Nicholson gave us a short team talk. He said we all knew we were good enough to win the Cup, now it was up to us to go out and prove it. I had no doubts we'd do just that. I felt we would be far too experienced for Chelsea. Spurs had never lost at Wembley. The club had already won four FA Cups; I knew we could make it five.

I'd heard on the grapevine that the Chelsea players were unhappy with their win bonus and ticket allocation. We didn't have any niggles like that. Manager Tommy Docherty was sure to get the most from his young team, but he had lost Peter Osgood with a broken leg and that would hurt their chances.

I enjoyed the coach journey to Wembley. I'd never played there before so the atmosphere was all new to me. At first we saw mainly Chelsea flags and supporters, but as we got closer to the ground the Spurs fans came into view, thousands of them, waving, smiling and thoroughly enjoying their day. Finally, we turned into Empire Way and there in front of us was the magnificent stadium with its famous twin towers. My mind raced back to my Aunt Rose's flat where I saw The Matthews Final. Notting Hill was only ten miles away, but it had taken a very special journey to get me here . . .

We went out for a walk on the pitch before the game. The playing surface was immaculate, like a billiard table. I looked all around, trying to lock the scene in my memory. Being there was spectacular. It lived up to all my expectations and more. I was enjoying the thrill of the moment, then Bill Nicholson walked into my line of vision. He didn't speak but the look on his face spoke volumes.

We were here to win; it was time to focus.

I was careful to warm up properly in the dressing room. My leg felt fine, but I didn't want to take any chances. I felt up for the game. I wasn't anxious, I wasn't nervous, I was ready. We lined up next to Chelsea, waiting to walk up the tunnel. Dave Mackay started to throw a football at the wall behind them and head the rebounds. The ball was flying just above their heads. Dave was fired up and determined to intimidate Chelsea if he could. They looked edgy.

'Look at this lot,' he shouted to us. 'They're shitting themselves!'

Dave had grabbed the psychological high ground before we'd even got on the pitch. We went into the game full of confidence.

Our team was: Pat Jennings, Joe Kinnear, Cyril Knowles, Alan Mullery, Mike England, Dave Mackay, Terry Venables, Jimmy Robertson, Alan Gilzean, Jimmy Greaves and Frank Saul. Our substitute, not used, was Cliff Jones.

Chelsea had some very talented players. Peter Bonetti was a top keeper; Ron Harris, Eddie McCreadie, John Hollins and Marvin Hinton were all strong at the back; Charlie Cooke could scare defences with his close control and mazy runs; Tony Hateley was a big, brave centre-forward and excellent in the air. They could all play on their day, but 20 May 1967 belonged to Tottenham Hotspur.

We dominated from the start and went into the lead when I hit a shot that rebounded off Ron Harris to Robertson. It fell just right for Jimmy and he smacked it into the net. We went in 1–0 up at half-time. Bill Nick warned us not to get complacent and we kept the pressure on in the second half. Chelsea's main tactic seemed to be hitting high balls towards Tony Hateley, but Mike England stayed close to him and Pat Jennings had no problem dealing with their crosses.

We doubled our lead when Dave Mackay took a long throw into the box and Jimmy Robertson headed it on to Frank Saul who spun and hit a hard, low shot past Bonetti. We should have cruised it from there, but Chelsea came back well in the last fifteen minutes and Bobby Tambling scored with a header five minutes from time. Chelsea tried to put us under pressure, but we held on to win 2–1.

My first feeling when the referee blew for full-time was elation. The second, just a few seconds later, was complete and utter exhaustion. I'd never run more in a game and the Wembley turf really took it out of you. The thigh injury that had caused so much worry was fine, but my feet were killing me. We'd been paid to wear new boots for the game. At least we knew of the deal, unlike the Fulham fiasco eight years later but I was left with terrible blisters on my heels. They were very sore.

I forgot the pain as we climbed the famous steps to the royal box, led by our captain, Dave Mackay. This win meant so much to him. At the final whistle, his eyes had shone with tears. Now he was all smiles, as he raised the Cup in triumph to the Tottenham fans. He'd come back from two broken legs – nobody deserved the glory more.

As soon as we got back down to the pitch, I took my boots and socks off and gave them to Cecil Poynton with my winners' medal, for safe keeping. The turf felt fresh and cool on my feet, which were covered in blood. I did the lap of honour, even put the Cup on my head, but I couldn't shake the tiredness that filled my body.

I'm sure a lot of that was due to the hard work I'd put in, but some of it was mental, too. I'd concentrated so hard in the game that, when it was all over and the adrenalin dropped, I felt completely drained. Very happy, but 'out' to the world. I'd always dreamt of walking around Wembley as a winner, but when it happened for real, I was almost too tired to enjoy it.

Television viewers had voted me Man of the Match, so I had to pull myself together to do some live TV interviews. I think that did me good. When I finally got back to our dressing room, the celebrations were already in full swing. There were cases of champagne everywhere. Players were drinking it and throwing it all over each other. Bill got covered, but he was happy to take it. Spurs were winners again.

Terry Venables had played well against his old club and he celebrated by taking a bottle of champers into the bath and starting a big sing-song. We all joined in at the tops of our voices. I felt much better when I'd freshened up and Cecil had dressed the wounds on my feet. We all piled into the team bus and headed off for a night at the Savoy.

A team of police outriders guided us through the busy London streets to the hotel that had refused to park my car when I was a kid at Fulham. There was no danger of being turned away now. We got VIP treatment all the way and we were in the mood for a party.

As soon as we got into the big banqueting room, Dave Mackay ordered six bottles of champagne for the guests on his table. I did the same and the room was soon shaking with noise and laughter. Bill Nick was sitting at the top table with his wife, Darkie, and the directors. Suddenly, he jumped to his feet and banged the table.

'Oi, you lot down there!' he yelled. 'Don't think you're a good team yet, just because you've won the bloody Cup final. Shut your noise . . . now!'

The room went deathly quiet.

OK, I admit we were being a bit loud, but Bill's reaction was totally over the top. We were just letting off steam, having some fun after the tensions of the day. Maybe we shouldn't have ordered all that champagne before the meal was served, but we meant no harm. We were there for a celebration, after all. But Bill's reaction was to tell us to shut up. He made it clear to everyone in the room that we weren't as good as we thought we were.

Of course, we all felt embarrassed and it took a while for the mood to pick up again. The meal was delicious, as you would expect at the Savoy, but now we felt we had to be on our best behaviour. Should we order another bottle of wine? It was pretty subdued, to be fair.

After the meal, Bill gave a speech and we all applauded. He had the FA Cup beside him on the table and he was delighted we'd won. The earlier flare-up was forgotten, but the party was fading fast. An old-fashioned band started to play. It was ideal if you wanted a quiet evening with a few waltzes, but that's not what we had in mind. The players knew Morris Keston was having a party across town. We were all invited and it was sure to be a lot more fun than what was happening at the Savoy.

A crowd of us jumped into a line of taxis outside the hotel and ten minutes later we were at the Hilton. Morris welcomed us with open arms. There were about a hundred people at the private party and they were all Spurs fans. They gave us a tremendous cheer when we walked in. People were talking, laughing, smiling, joking, giving us drinks, offering us food, telling us how well we'd played at Wembley and how happy they were we'd won the Cup.

The centrepiece of the room was a huge cockerel carved in ice. Sixties music pumped out of speakers around the room, then a great live band kicked into action. They had more rhythm than the steamy stars of the Bedroom Bonking Olympics. Soon we were all dancing and having the time of our lives. At last we could relax and have some fun.

I don't remember leaving the Hilton. I woke up in the back of a cab heading for Worcester Park. June didn't think it was a good idea for me to go back to the Savoy in the state I was in. She was probably worried we'd bump into Bill Nick. When we got home, I stumbled out of the taxi, fell in through the front door and that's the last thing I remember until waking up with someone hitting me over the head with a hammer. Well, that's what it felt like!

I would have loved to have stayed in bed that Sunday morning, but I had to get to White Hart Lane to meet the other players. The club had arranged an open-topped bus tour and this time the organisation was perfect. Thousands of supporters lined the streets and seeing how much our win meant to them made me feel very emotional. It meant a lot to all the players, too, I could see it in their faces.

The FA Cup was back in N17 and that felt good, very good indeed.

Tottenham Hotspur didn't win another major trophy for four years. That statistic looks cold and clinical in print, but it hides the reality of many high-quality matches against stylish opponents. I played some of the best football of my career during that time.

Our first match of the 1967–68 season was a classic. We played Manchester United for the Charity Shield at Old Trafford. We went into the lead after eight minutes. Nothing surprising about that, until you hear the name of the goal scorer: Pat Jennings. Pat launched a long kick upfield. Alex Stepney was out of his goal and the ball bounced over his head and into the empty net.

United were the reigning champions and their pride was hurt. They stormed back at us and Brian Kidd passed to Bobby Charlton, who crashed it into the net from fully thirty yards. The TV commentator, Kenneth 'they think it's all over . . . it is now' Wolstenholme, was drooling into his microphone.

'That was a goal good enough to win the League, the Cup, the World Cup and even the Grand National!' raved Ken.

The game ended 3–3. Spurs and United were declared joint winners of the Charity Shield and were cheered off the field by 54,000 totally satisfied supporters. Two weeks later we beat West Ham United 5–1 in the League. I scored and felt ecstatic. One week later we lost 5–1 to Burnley and I felt deflated. Our defence of the FA Cup ended in the fifth round, when Liverpool beat us

2–1 at Anfield, having held us 1–1 at the Lane. Our best Cup performances came in the third round when we held Manchester United to a 2–2 away draw, with two goals from Chivers, and then beat them 1–0 in the replay, with an extra-time winner from Jimmy Robertson. The Lane was rocking with suspense, tension and finally exhilaration. What a night!

So, although we didn't win another trophy until 1971, there were still some good times at the Lane. We never stopped believing or competing and Bill Nicholson made sure we never got complacent.

He marked my card in the summer of 1969. I'd just got back from England's tour of South America. The phone rang at home one afternoon. It was Bill.

'How did it go over there?' he asked.

'Quite well, thanks. I played in all the games and Alf seemed happy.'

'Well, we've got a young lad coming through at the club,' said Bill. 'His name's Perryman and he might take your place.'

'He might take someone's place, Bill, but he won't take my place.'

I put the phone down and smiled. I knew what Bill was up to. It was his way of telling me not to get too carried away with my good form for England. At Spurs I still had to fight for my place. I didn't mind that. I was now playing at the highest level of world football with the best players and I knew I had to work hard to stay there.

Bobby Moore, Bobby Charlton, Geoff Hurst and Gordon Banks were my England team-mates. Jimmy Greaves, Alan Gilzean, Dave Mackay and Pat Jennings had all shared my life at Tottenham. I'd played against Pelé in Rio and won the FA Cup at Wembley. These were golden days and I wanted to ride the wave of success for as long as I could.

A couple of weeks after Bill's call, I was honoured to be selected for a Rest of the United Kingdom side to play against

Wales at Ninian Park, Cardiff, in a game to celebrate the investiture of Prince Charles as Prince of Wales and to raise money for the Aberfan Disaster Fund. 'I was honoured' may sound a glib phrase, but in this case it was true. I was honoured to be picked in that side. Just look at the team and you'll know why.

Rest of the United Kingdom: Pat Jennings, Tottenham Hotspur and Northern Ireland; Tommy Gemmell, Celtic and Scotland; Terry Cooper, Leeds United and England; Billy Bremner, Leeds United and Scotland; Jack Charlton, Leeds United and England; Alan Mullery, Tottenham Hotspur and England; George Best, Manchester United and Northern Ireland; Francis Lee, Manchester City and England; Derek Dougan, Wolverhampton Wanderers and Northern Ireland; Bobby Charlton, Manchester United and England; John Hughes, Celtic and Scotland.

It was a wonderful group of British players and the best of them all was Georgie.

Sir Alf Ramsey had selected the side and he was waiting for me in reception when I arrived at the team hotel in Cardiff.

'I've put you in a room with George Best,' he said.

'Blimey, Alf, do me a favour.'

Everyone knew Besty's reputation.

'You know him pretty well,' Alf told me. 'I thought you could keep an eye on him.' The truth was nobody could keep an eye on Georgie. He was a free spirit who sometimes walked on the wild side.

He didn't look very wild when I walked into our room. He was asleep in bed with the curtains pulled. He said something that sounded like 'whasserrrmarrerrr?'

'See you later, George,' I said and went down to get some lunch.

He'd had a heavy night and slept for most of the day. He got up for some tea and toast before the game, then went out and played a blinder. We won the game and it was quite late by the time we'd all had a meal together. I was getting ready to go back to the hotel when George came over.

'What you doing tonight, Mullers?' he asked.

'I'm going to bed. I've got to drive back to London in the morning.'

'Come and have a drink first.' George smiled. 'I know a place.'

I liked George. He was at the peak of his fame then. United had won the European Cup a year before and the world was at his feet. That night I saw what it was like to be a true superstar.

We called a taxi and talked about the game as we drove through the late-night streets. It was around midnight when we arrived at the club. The moment we walked through the door, I started to feel like an extra in an old Hollywood movie.

The place was packed, but the manager lifted a table from the back of the room and carried it right to the front of the stage. I was amazed by the big-star treatment, but George took it all in his stride. We sat down. Nobody was interested in me, they were all staring at Georgie.

The waiter came over. George ordered beer for me and champagne on ice for himself. Then he asked for a bottle of gin, a bottle of vodka, a bottle of brandy, plus ice, mixers and some extra glasses. I was bemused.

'Planning a big night, George?' I asked.

'It's not all for me.' He smiled.

'Who's it for, then?'

'The girls who'll be sitting here in five minutes.'

I found all this amazing, but George was right. Five minutes later he was surrounded by beautiful women he'd never met before. And it was easy to see what they all had in mind.

I left the hotel at eight the next morning. George still wasn't back . . .

On a personal level, life was good and full of achievements. But pressures were mounting at Tottenham, especially when another trophy-less season slipped by. It felt like a journey through the mountains. High one moment, low the next.

The World Cup finals in Mexico in 1970 fired my ambitions. I hated coming home a loser from that tournament. I had one message for the lads back at Tottenham.

This season we win something . . .

1971 League Cup Winners

1970–71 was a much better season.

Jimmy Greaves had gone to West Ham United, but I never worried that our goals would dry up. I'd spent the summer playing with Martin Peters for England and knew he would score for Spurs from midfield. Martin Chivers was also back from a serious knee injury and raring to go. Even without Greavsie, our goal threat was enough to scare most teams.

We finished third in Division One and got through to the sixth round of the FA Cup, only losing to Liverpool after a replay. But the crowning glory was wining the League Cup at Wembley. Right from the start, the omens felt good. We had home draws all the way to the semi-final.

We beat Third Division Swansea City on 9 September, with goals from Perryman, Peters and Morgan. The names of the scorers tell you how the team had changed since 1967. Steve, Martin and Roger were all new faces. Martin Chivers was now a major force in our side and he scored in our win over Sheffield United on 7 October. United were a good Second Division side who won promotion that year but Jimmy Pearce, another new face, added a second in our 2–1 win.

We got our first Division One side in the fourth round and it proved to be our easiest tie to date, as we thrashed West Bromwich Albion 5–0 at the Lane. Martin Peters got a hat-trick and Gilly, who was still playing very well, got the other two. We enjoyed another big win over First Division opposition, Coventry City, in round five. This time our hat-trick hero was Chivers. Gilly added another, as we won 4–1.

Bristol City were struggling in Division Two that season, but they gave us two good games, home and away, in the semi-finals. Gerry Gow was a tiger in the middle of the park and inspired the underdogs to play well above themselves. Martin Chivers and Jimmy Pearce gave us a 2–0 win away. For the second leg on 23 December 30,000 fans packed into Ashton Gate. A goal from Alan Gilzean earned us a hard-fought 1–1 draw. Spurs were on their way to Wembley again . . . the perfect Christmas present!

We were expecting to play Manchester United in the final but Aston Villa beat them 3–2 on aggregate in the semi-finals. It was a real shock because Villa were a Third Division side. We knew we could beat them, but the danger signs were there: take this team lightly at your peril. Villa had some fine players including Ron Wylie, Andy Lochhead, Brian Little and Bruce Rioch.

Our team for the League Cup final, on Saturday 27 February 1971, was Pat Jennings, Joe Kinnear, Cyril Knowles, Alan Mullery, Peter Collins, Phil Beal, Alan Gilzean, Steve Perryman, Martin Chivers, Martin Peters, Jimmy Neighbour. Our sub was Jimmy Pearce, but he stayed on the bench.

There was a sell-out crowd of 100,000 at Wembley to see the game.

We started as overwhelming favourites, but Villa were inspired. Andy Lochhead put himself about and upset a few people. Villa definitely came to compete and they were unlucky. They played better than us, but we had Martin Chivers and he scored twice in the second half to give us our 2–0 win. We had to wait until the seventy-eighth minute for our first goal. There was a scramble in the goalmouth, the ball broke to Martin and he smashed it in from short range. I played Chiv in for his second three minutes later. He took my pass, went past the centre-half and hammered the ball home. Martin showed true ability that day. He was good leader of the line and hungry for goals.

For the second time in my career, I climbed the steps to the royal box. It was a totally different feeling, going up as captain. This time I was the leader of a team who had come through a Cup run together and were now getting the prize. It's amazing how many thoughts flashed through my mind, as I made my way through cheering supporters on either side.

I thought of Dave Mackay who'd been such a marvellous captain for Tottenham. I thought of my friend Bobby Moore who had lifted the World Cup for England just five years before. I was proud to walk in their footsteps. I held the League Cup high in the air and the cheers of the Spurs supporters rang out in the cold afternoon air. It was a beautiful noise.

We threw Bill in the bath after our lap of honour. I don't think he was too amused, but somebody found him a spare suit and he soon recovered. I had a picture taken on the team coach with the Cup and all the wives and girlfriends. When I first arrived at Spurs, I thought it was just a business, but I was wrong. It felt like family now.

A couple of days later, the club let me take the trophy home. My little girl Samantha had been ill and I wanted to surprise her. We ended up eating Smarties out of the League Cup together. Well, she was a bit young for champagne.

The old Wembley has gone now.

The new stadium will write its own stories of great games and heroes, winners and losers. But I'll never forget the two finals I played there for Tottenham. I'm grateful I had my share of glory beneath the twin towers.

9

THREE LIONS ON MY SHIRT

I won all of my thirty-five full England caps while I was at Tottenham Hotspur.

My debut against Holland in December 1964 came as a complete surprise. A reporter phoned me at home to break the news, but I didn't believe him. I was still struggling to establish myself at Spurs. Things were slowly improving (I'd just been given my nickname, The Tank) but I was far from happy with my game and my confidence was low.

It made no sense for Alf Ramsey to pick me. That's why I dismissed the journalist's call, but the next morning I got a letter from the FA confirming I'd been included in the England squad. The timing could not have been worse, as far as I was concerned.

From the minute I met up with Alf and the players in London, everything felt wrong. We flew out to Holland and stayed at the Amsterdam Hilton. When Alf told me I was in the team, I pretended to be pleased, but I had a sinking feeling inside. I'd waited all my life to win a full cap, why did it have to come now?

England drew 1–1, with a goal from Jimmy Greaves, but I took my poor form into the game and trudged off at the end knowing my debut had been a complete disaster. I thought I'd never play for England again. Luckily, I was wrong about that, but I did have to wait another two and a half years for my next cap.

By early 1966, I was playing much better for Spurs and I was included in Alf's World Cup 'get-togethers'. These gave him the chance to assess the top forty players in the country. I always felt on the fringe of these events and didn't play in any of the friendly games Alf organised, but I was still bitterly disappointed when I was left out of the final World Cup squad. Nobby Stiles and Gordon Milne were chosen ahead of me. I thought I was a better player than both of them.

Once the World Cup started, I could see Alf had made the right decision. Nobby was outstanding throughout the tournament. His job was to sit in front of the back four; if there was a specific opposing player to mark, such as Eusebio, he'd take care of that. It was exactly the same job Alf asked me to do when I got into the team a year later.

Nobby was as blind as a bat. A little man, no more than five feet seven, nine and a half stone dripping wet, but as hard as nails. Nobby would run through walls for his team. The public loved him. He symbolised the spirit of '66 with his tenacity and strength. He was a superb motivator and the World Cup win was his finest hour.

Alf also made the right decision when he picked Geoff Hurst to play in the final, ahead of Jimmy Greaves. Greavsie must have felt terrible, but the wisdom of Alf's decision is there for all to see in the record books. I watched the game at home on TV, like millions of others. I was delighted with the win, but disappointed not to be part of it all. It sharpened my England ambitions. When my next chance came, I'd be ready.

24 May 1967

I walked out at Wembley to play for England against Spain just four days after winning the FA Cup there with Spurs. I'd been voted Man of the Match in the final and my confidence was sky high. Amsterdam was a distant memory. My England career started here and now, as far as I was concerned. I wore the shirt with pride that night and we won 2–0 with goals from Jimmy Greaves and Roger Hunt.

Alf only picked me for the game because Manchester United had gone on a close-season tour of Australia, taking with them all their big stars, including Nobby Stiles. Once I was in the England team, I had to try and keep Nobby out. It was a straight fight between the two of us. I expected Alf to pick Nobby again as soon as he was available, but he didn't, he stuck with me. That gave me all the incentive I needed and between May 1967 and April 1971, I missed just five of England's thirty-eight inter-nationals. If Nobby had not gone on tour with United, I might have spent a lot more time waiting around in his shadow.

England's next game was against Austria in Vienna, three days later. When we arrived, we were invited to a Strauss evening at a huge banqueting hall in the heart of the city. It was a beautiful building, with long tables laid out for dinner and an orchestra playing the music of the local hero. The England players were all in suits, but we still felt underdressed. Everyone else was in evening dress.

As we were being shown to our table, the orchestra started to play one of my favourite Strauss melodies. I grabbed Geoff Hurst and we waltzed off across the dance floor, much to the amuse-ment of the rest of the team. I don't know what Vienna is like now, but the Austrians didn't have much of a sense of humour then. They looked shocked. Alf wasn't too impressed either. He had that certain look Victor Meldrew made famous years later: 'I don't believe it!'

We won the game 1–0. Alan Ball hit our winner. When we got back to the hotel, I was hungry and ready for a good meal. I was sharing a room with Bobby Moore, but he didn't have dinner with the rest of us.

'I can't eat after a game,' Bobby told me. 'I never feel hungry.'

He stood quietly at the bar, drinking the local chilled lager and looking as cool as ever. Every time I glanced at him his glass was full. He seemed to be on the same pint for ages. The truth was, every time he finished a beer, the barman had the next one waiting.

Bobby loved a few drinks after a game, it was his way of relaxing. But he overdid it that night. The combination of playing the game, having no food and drinking strong lager on an empty stomach caught up with him. I'd finished my meal and was chatting to a few of the other lads at the table, when I saw Bobby slowly sliding down the bar in the corner. Nobody else had noticed, so I went over and gently guided him out of the room.

When we got to the lift I could see he was really out of it. I had a quick look round to make sure nobody was watching us, then slung Mooro over my shoulder in a fireman's lift. I carried him back to our room and laid him out on his bed, where he slept until the morning. Bobby and I shared a room on every England trip after that. I think he was impressed by the way I looked after him.

Rooming with Mooro was never boring.

We got back to Hendon Hall one night, after a game at Wembley. It was quiet hotel in a leafy London suburb. I can't remember whom we'd played, but Alf wanted us to get up early the next morning, so we all went straight to our rooms. As usual after a match, Bobby wasn't remotely tired. I went into the bathroom and changed into my pyjamas. When I came out, Bobby had changed too . . . into a suit.

'Going to bed?' he asked.

'That's the general idea, Mooro. What are you doing, then?'

'I'm going to a club in town, sure you don't fancy it?'

'No, thanks.'

'OK, see you later.' He smiled.

Bobby opened the window and climbed out into the night. We were on the first floor, so he slid down the drainpipe to the hotel garden. I went to the window to make sure he was OK. He gave me a wave and ran off across the lawn, through the shrubbery and away.

About five o'clock the next morning, I heard Mooro tapping on the window. I opened it and he climbed back in.

'Good night?' I asked.

'Yeah, fine.' Bobby grinned.

He grabbed a couple of hours' sleep, had a shower, then joined the rest of the team downstairs for breakfast. You would never have guessed he'd been up all night. In fact, he looked better than I did!

Certain rules apply to every football team, whether you're playing for England or a Sunday morning pub team. It's always good to get on well with the captain. It's even better to get on with the manager. Alf had very definite views on how he wanted his players to play. We each had a specific role in the team and he expected us to stick to that. He made this clear to me when we beat Northern Ireland 2–0 at Wembley in November 1967.

I won the ball in the first half with a good tackle, then dropped my shoulder and beat another man. A third player came in quickly to close me down. I pushed the ball past him and hit a perfect twenty-five-yard pass to set up an attack from which Geoff Hurst scored. I felt pretty pleased with myself when we walked in at half-time. Alf Ramsey came straight up to me in the dressing room. I was expecting some praise, but I was wrong.

'What were you doing out there?' Alf asked, in that crisp voice of his.

'When?'

'When you beat three players and hit that long pass . . .'

I smiled. 'I enjoyed that.'

'You may have enjoyed it, Alan, but that's not your job.'

I looked at Alf. He wasn't joking.

'Your job,' he continued, 'is to win the ball and give it to Bobby Charlton.'

'OK, Alf,' I said.

And that's exactly what I did for the next four years in the England team, win tackles and try to give the ball to Bobby. Of course, it wasn't always possible to pass to him, but Alf was a good tactician and his message to me was clear: keep it simple. He knew exactly how he wanted me to play and I was happy to go along with that.

All I wanted to do was play for England . . .

In 1968, I was selected for our quarter-final against Spain in the European Nations Cup. Bobby Charlton scored in front of a full house at Wembley to give us a slender 1–0 lead in the tie. We went to Madrid for the away leg knowing we needed to produce a great performance.

I was thrilled to be playing at the Bernabeu. It was another ambition achieved. I had been a huge fan of Real Madrid since their classic 1960 European Cup final at Hampden Park, where they beat Eintracht Frankfurt 7–3, in front of 130,000 fans.

What a wonderful game! Di Stefano got a hat-trick; Puskás went one better. Seven goals between them – was there ever a better striking partnership? I'd seen it all on Aunt Rose's TV, now I was going to play at Real's home ground. To me, it was magical. But, as usual, I left sentiment behind when it was time for the game.

The Spanish fans were loud and confident as we drove through Madrid to the stadium on a warm evening in early May. A vast crowd of 120,000 filled the Bernabeu and the packed terraces seemed to stretch up into the night sky. Spain had just won the Eurovision Song Contest and their fans were all singing this bloody silly song. Somehow, it didn't quite match the drama of the moment.

George Cohen was right back and had to mark Gento, who was a hero at Real Madrid. Gento was known for his extreme pace, but George matched him and kept him quiet all night. That battle summed up the match. We silenced the stadium with a 2–1 win. Martin Peters and Norman Hunter scored.

Winning in the Bernabeu was an excellent result and we were feeling optimistic about our chances in the finals. We played a warm-up game at Wembley against Sweden, just before flying out for the competition. Martin Peters, Bobby Charlton and Roger Hunt all scored in a comfortable 3–1 victory. It was England's last win over Sweden for many years.

I was involved in a horrible clash with Sweden's goalkeeper, Larsson. As I ran into the box and slid in for the ball, he dived at my feet and my knee crashed into his head. My knee was really sore, but I was more worried about the keeper. He was out cold and they had to carry him off on a stretcher.

After the game, I heard he had been taken to hospital for X-rays, which revealed a fractured skull. It was a pure accident, but naturally I felt very sorry for him. I talked to Alf and he arranged for me to visit Larsson at the hospital in London a couple of days later. His family had flown over from Sweden and were obviously worried. His head was swathed in bandages and he looked very shaken up, but he spoke English and made it clear he didn't blame me for what had happened. Thankfully, he made a full recovery.

I always played the game hard, but that accidental clash was the worst incident I ever had of hurting another player. I'm grateful it didn't crop up too often in my career.

In early June 1968, England flew to Italy for the European Nations Cup finals. We stayed in an elegant hotel in the hills above Florence. Mooro had just bought a state-of-the-art portable record player. It was the about size of today's laptops; I'd never seen one before. The sound quality was very good, but I can't say the same for Mooro's choice of music. He played an Engelbert Humperdinck LP day and night.

The game against Yugoslavia was a nightmare for me and the team. I became the first English player to be sent off. I was ashamed and expected Alf to banish me for ever, but he stood by me. Earlier in this book I wrote in detail about the South American tour of 1969 and the 1970 World Cup finals in Mexico. Looking back now, those were the greatest years of my England career and I have Alf to thank for that. If he had reacted differently to my sending off, I would have missed out on all those wonderful memories.

When I got back from Mexico in the summer of 1970, friends told me Malcolm Allison had been slagging me off on ITV's World Cup panel, while I'd been away. He and Joe Mercer were a successful management team at Manchester City. Of course, Malcolm was heavily biased in favour of Colin Bell and he kept saying I should be dropped in favour of 'Nijinsky'. I liked and respected Colin and I had no interest in what Allison had been saying behind my back. I knew I'd done well in Mexico. If I needed any reassurance on that score, the London *Evening Standard* had voted me England's 'Player of the Tournament'.

Jimmy Hill and Brian Moore both phoned me several times, asking me to go on ITV's top football show, *The Big Match*, for a face-to-face confrontation with Malcolm Allison. They obviously knew it would make great TV, but I told them to forget it. I didn't want to know.

My mum and dad hadn't said anything to me about all this, but when I went to see them one day, my brother Teddy was there and he was seething. 'Allison was really out of order,' he told me. 'He was sniping at you every chance he got. It really upset Mum.'

That changed things. I've always been able to take criticism, it's part of being a footballer. But when people upset your family, that's a different matter. When Brian Moore rang again, I told him I'd meet Allison, but I wanted to lay down the ground rules. No rehearsals. Just one take. Brian agreed.

When I arrived at the television studios in London, Malcolm was already waiting in the Green Room. He turned his back and totally ignored me. I was carrying a plastic carrier bag. Nobody knew what was in it. When the head-to-head started, I asked Allison how many England caps he'd won. He tried to avoid the question, but I forced him to admit he hadn't won any. I took an England cap out of the bag and offered it to him.

'You can have this one,' I told him. 'Go on, take it. I've got another thirty at home.'

My argument was simple, but effective. Allison had never won a cap. I'd played for England thirty-one times at that stage. So why did I need advice from him? Who cared what he thought? In the end, he was speechless. I knew I'd won the day and friends who saw *The Big Match* confirmed that. I went round to see my mum a couple of days later. I asked her if she'd seen the show.

'Yes,' she said. 'I'm glad you put him in his place, Alan.'

That was all I needed to hear.

Malcolm Allison bore a grudge for a long time. He didn't talk to me again for ten years.

We finally broke the deadlock when Malcolm brought Manchester City to Brighton for a First Division game. We beat them and Michael Robinson, whom I'd signed from City, was outstanding. At the final whistle, Malcolm walked over and shook me by the hand.

'I don't know what you've done with Robinson,' he grinned, 'but it's working. I could never get him to play for me like that!'

We shared a bottle of champagne before he left that night. I'm glad we resolved our differences. Malcolm was a great character and a very talented coach, especially when he combined his fire and passion with the experience of the great Joe Mercer.

I played only four more times for England after our shattering 3–2 World Cup defeat by West Germany in León, Mexico. We beat East Germany, Malta, Greece and Switzerland. For me, the most memorable of these games was our 1–0 win in Malta in February 1971. Bobby Moore was unavailable and Alf made me captain for the day, an honour I still treasure, but my time was running out. Our 3–0 home win over Greece, the following April, was an enjoyable night. I had no idea I had just played my last international at Wembley.

I won my thirty-fifth and final cap against Switzerland in Basle on 13 October 1971. We had to fight hard for our 3–2 win and I played well, despite being troubled by a painful pelvic condition which was threatening to wreck my season. I missed the next two England games through injury, but I was back in late April 1972 for a vital European Championship qualifier against West Germany at Wembley.

I'd made a successful comeback for Spurs earlier that month and had helped the club to beat AC Milan over two legs and win a place in the UEFA Cup final. After a long lay-off, I was back to my best form and eager to play against the Germans. I was disappointed when Alf told me I was on the bench. It was frustrating, especially when Gunter Netzer started to rip England apart in midfield. I'd marked Pelé in the World Cup and I knew I could do a similar job on Netzer. I was longing to get out on the pitch.

Midway through the second half, Alf turned towards me.

'Get changed,' he said.

My spirits soared. At last I had a chance to show what I could do. I stood up and started to take off my tracksuit.

'No,' said Alf, 'I meant Rodney.'

I turned to Rodney Marsh who was beside me.

'Go on, mate, on you go,' I said to him.

Outwardly, I showed no emotion, but I was crushed inside. In that brief moment, I knew my England career was over. I had the experience to deal with Gunter Netzer. I'd recently hit the national headlines with my performances against AC Milan. Alf knew I was match fit and sharp. I could have done the job for him that night, but he left me on the bench. That told me all I needed to know. Netzer continued to run riot and West Germany ran out easy 3–1 winners.

I had a lot of thinking to do after the game. I was thirty years old. I'd be thirty-three by the time the next World Cup came around and I couldn't see myself being picked for that. I'd thoroughly enjoyed playing for England and I didn't want it all to end in a trail of disappointment. It was clear now that in Alf's eyes my best years were over. I didn't want to slog around the world just to sit on the sub's bench. My mind was made up by the time I went to bed that night. I knew what I had to do.

I put all thoughts of my England career to one side for the next few days. Spurs played Wolves in the first leg of the UEFA Cup the following Wednesday. We won 2–1 at Molineux with two goals from Martin Chivers. I was totally caught up in the excitement of the game but, when my head cleared, I still felt the same way about England.

I rang Sir Alf Ramsey at the FA. I wasn't angry or emotional. Alf had always been very fair with me and I just wanted him to be the first to know my decision.

'Alf, I'm going to retire from international football,' I said. 'After the West Germany game, I think the time has come to say thank you very much, but it's time to go.'

Alf didn't try to change my mind, but he was very gracious.

'If that's the decision you want to make, Alan, all I can say is thank you very much for all you've done. You've been a credit to your country.'

It was the perfect way to end my days as an England player. No regrets and some genuine words of respect from a great manager. A few years later, Bobby Moore picked a team of the best England players he ever played alongside. Mooro selected me in the heart of midfield. Receiving a tribute like that from England's greatest-ever captain meant the world to me. It was always a joy and a privilege to play for my country, but I knew it was time to say goodbye.

Now I was free to concentrate on winning the UEFA Cup for Tottenham Hotspur. I was sure that would be just the start of many more good times at the club.

How wrong I was . . .

10

YESTERDAY'S GONE

I scored the goal that won the UEFA Cup for Spurs on 17 May 1972.

I should have been ecstatic that night, but instead I sat alone, brooding, until dawn.

The problem was Bill Nicholson. Let me make this clear, I had then, and I still have, great respect for Bill and for all he achieved at Tottenham. He had his own way of doing things and he was very successful. He lived and breathed for the football club. If the team played badly, he made sure we knew exactly how he felt. I didn't mind that; he wanted the best from his players and wouldn't accept anything less.

Bill Nick wasn't one to throw praise around. If he said 'well played' once in a season, that was the most you could expect. But when he did say it, it really meant something. I worked closely with Bill at Spurs for over eight years and I enjoyed nearly all of that time.

If he'd given me a pat on the back the night we won the UEFA Cup, it would have meant the world to me. All he had to say was, 'Well done, Alan. Good to have you back.' But he never said a word and I couldn't help wondering why. I was starting to sense that, despite the UEFA win, Bill felt it was time for me to leave the club. I knew he could be ruthless in that situation, even when it came to his biggest stars. He'd got rid of Greaves and Mackay. Was I next?

A rollercoaster season was over, but I sensed trouble ahead.

I spent the summer with June and our little girl, Samantha, who was four. Being at home was a great leveller. I was treated as a celebrity by the outside world, but with my family I was an everyday husband and father. I enjoyed the break from football, but I often found myself thinking about Bill Nicholson. I still bore a grudge for the way I'd been treated.

I returned to pre-season training with Spurs in July 1972. I waited for a week to see if Bill would give me some kind of pep talk to make me feel part of the season ahead, but he hardly spoke to me.

I've always been a proud person. I didn't want to wait around to be told to go. If I was going to leave Spurs, I would be the one to make the first move.

I knew the UEFA Cup final would be hard to top. Scoring the winner. Lifting the trophy. Being carried shoulder-high round White Hart Lane by thousands of happy, cheering fans. What a lovely memory to go out on, if that proved to be my last ever game for Spurs.

So, a week into pre-season, I went to Bill's office at the training ground, feeling anxious as I knocked on the door. The truth was, I didn't want to leave Tottenham, but did Bill Nick still want me at the club?

Bill asked me in and I told him I thought it was maybe time

for me to move on. What I wanted to hear was, 'Don't be silly. What do you want to leave for? We're back in Europe and I want you here.' If I'd heard that, I would have been very happy to stay. I was still only thirty and I knew I had at least two more good years in me. I wouldn't let him or the club down.

But Bill just said, 'I can't let you go immediately. I'll have to find a replacement.'

He spoke without any emotion. It was cold and business-like, that's what hurt.

'I don't want to hang around, Bill,' I said. 'I want to go now.'

He reached across to a sheet of paper on his desk and pushed it towards me.

'OK,' he said. 'Six clubs have been on the phone for you. Here's a list of the numbers.'

I looked at the names. Stoke, Leicester, Nottingham Forest, West Ham, Crystal Palace and Fulham. They all wanted me to play for them, but Bill was quite happy to see me go.

'Speak to the managers if you like, but I will need to find someone to take your place.'

I'd been trying to keep my emotions under control, but I felt a sudden stab of anger. 'You don't need to buy anyone, Bill,' I snapped. 'You've already played three players in front of me. Phil Holder, John Pratt and Phil Beal.'

Bill looked at me in silence, then stood up.

'You can use this phone,' he said.

Then he walked out and left me alone in his office.

I was disappointed, but not surprised. At least it was all out in the open now; I knew where I stood. I didn't have time to sit around feeling sorry for myself. If I was on the way out of Spurs, it was up to me to get the best deal for myself and my family.

Can you imagine one of today's top players ringing up a list of Premier League managers and saying, 'I believe you want to buy me'? Well, that's exactly what I had to do. Without an agent to help me, I was out there on my own.

I sat at Bill's desk and spoke to all the managers. The one who impressed me most was Bert Head at Crystal Palace who was very open and straightforward. I was on £150 a week at Tottenham. Bert said he would raise that to £250 a week, plus a £25,000 signing-on fee. I told him it was a good offer and I would see him the next day to talk about it.

The last manager on the list was Alec Stock at Fulham. When I rang him, he went straight into the world of cloak and dagger. 'Don't speak to anyone before you speak to me in person. I must see you first,' he said. I explained I'd already spoken to several other managers on the phone, but I agreed to see Alec the next day, before meeting Bert Head.

When I got to Fulham, Alec outlined his offer which was £150 a week, the same as Spurs were paying me, plus £5000 for signing a four-year contract.

'How does that grab you?'

'It doesn't,' I said. 'Crystal Palace have offered me a much better deal to join them.'

'Have they?' said Alec. 'Well, here's my *pièce de résistance*. I promise you the manager's job at Fulham, at the end of your four years. You can have my job and I'll move upstairs. You've got my word on that.'

That stopped me in my tracks. I asked if I could phone Bert Head, then and there. I told him about Alec Stock's offer and asked if he could match it. Would there be any chance of me becoming Palace manager when I packed up playing in four years' time? Bert said he couldn't promise anything like that. It was too far ahead and he couldn't guarantee what would happen in the future. But he stressed he wanted me as a player and the money they were offering was still very much on the table.

I told Alec I needed time to think things over, so I went home and talked it all through with my wife. We were a young family and the extra money from Palace would have come in very handy. But Alec Stock was offering me a future in the game beyond my playing days and, in the end, I decided to opt for that.

I saw Alec the next day. He repeated his promise to pass on his experience and train me for the manager's job. There was nothing in writing, but we shook hands on the deal and I was happy with that. Alec was known as a gentleman and I knew I was putting my trust in the right person. Fulham paid £65,000 for me, just £7,500 less than they'd received from Spurs eight years before.

It was a wrench to leave Spurs.

I left with a sad heart. Bill Nicholson had made a mistake by selling me too soon. I was very disappointed, but it was time to move on.

Fulham now had an impressive training ground and an excellent coach, Bill Taylor, who went on to work with the England team under Ron Greenwood. It was only two years since I'd played for England in the World Cup, so Bill and the players were delighted to have me in the team and made me feel welcome. Second Division football was relatively easy for me. I had a lot more time and space; I could savour my last few years as a player.

I didn't give the manager's job much thought. That was something for the future.

My resentment towards Bill Nick simmered on for another two years, until he came to Fulham for a pre-season friendly in 1974. I met him outside the Cottage and he looked troubled. I asked what was wrong and he opened up to me.

'I think I've lost the respect of the players,' he said.

Bill Nick and I had clashed, but I never lost my respect for him as a manager. He had always been strong, but now he looked a forlorn figure. He wasn't the man I'd known for eight exciting years. I could see he was sinking and I felt sorry for him. Any bitterness I felt towards Bill melted away that night. After that, I always wished him well.

Bill resigned as manager of Tottenham Hotspur in September 1974. It must have broken his heart. He advised the club to appoint Danny Blanchflower and Johnny Giles as his successors but they went for another Irishman instead, former Arsenal player and captain, Terry Neill. Bill was so angry, he severed all contact with the club.

When Terry Neill took over, he asked me to return to White Hart Lane. He said it would be great to have me at the club as a player and leader. I appreciated his belief in me, but I didn't want to leave Fulham because of the promise of the manager's job. Also, by then it was all too late. I made the right decision; Terry had two difficult seasons at Spurs.

When Terry Neill left Tottenham in 1976, he was succeeded by Yorkshireman Keith Burkinshaw, who had been Spurs' first-team coach and who was keen for Bill Nicholson to come back to the club he loved. Bill Nick returned as a consultant in 1976, having been awarded on OBE for services to football the previous year. He became club president in 1991.

Bill Nicholson died on 23 October 2004 at the age of eighty-five. A road near his beloved White Hart Lane has been named in his memory . . . Bill Nicholson Way.

As for me, instead of going back to Spurs in 1974, I started looking to the future at Fulham. I helped Alec Stock to sign Bobby Moore and that impressed him. From then on, I worked more closely with Alec as his apprentice. I spent a lot of time helping in the office and driving him around in the evenings. It was often inconvenient and I got no extra money, but it was all leading somewhere, because in a couple of years I would be manager of Fulham football club.

I was still playing well and won the 1973–74 *Match of the Day* 'goal of the season' award for one I scored in an FA Cup tie against Leicester City at the Cottage. We were attacking and as I ran into the 'D' on the edge of the box, Barry Lloyd played the ball in over my left shoulder and it fell perfectly into my stride. I hit it first time on the volley with my right foot and it flew into the top right-hand corner.

Peter Shilton was in goal. As we walked off at half-time, he tapped me on the shoulder.

'I got my fingers to it,' said Shilts.

'If you'd got your fingers to that one, Peter, your hand would have landed in Hammersmith.'

He didn't get anywhere near it!

The funny thing about that goal is that it gets better every year. I work at Fulham on match days and people often talk about it. 'You must have been forty yards out when you hit that one,' a Fulham fan said to me recently.

'Was it that far?' I asked.

'At least, Alan,' he said. 'Maybe forty-five yards.'

The myth surrounding that goal has grown with the years, but even then it received a lot of publicity. Martin Shaw, of the hit TV series *The Professionals*, spent a week with Fulham around that time. He was doing research for a film about football and I remember him asking me lots of questions about the game.

Some time later, Martin was a special guest on *The Big Match*, part of a series on 'famous fans'. I was sitting at home watching the show with June and our two children, Neal and Samantha. Brian Moore asked Martin to name the best goal he'd ever seen and he picked mine against Leicester. He said some fans may have thought it was lucky, but he'd often seen me practising volleys from the edge of the box after training sessions. (I used to put in some extra time, like Johnny Haynes had done years before.)

Martin said it was like an actor rehearsing his role, then delivering a great performance on stage. A lot of hard work had gone into that goal and he respected my dedication. They showed the goal a few times while Martin was talking and I was as pleased as Punch. It was nice to be praised by a famous actor, especially with all my family watching. My little girl Samantha was very impressed, but not by my goal.

'Dad, do you really know one of the Professionals?' she said.

The definite highlight of my last spell at Fulham was our Cup run to Wembley in 1975. It was a succession of amazing events that finally ended in disappointment on the big day. I was very down at the end of final, but it was typical of the Fulham players that our official dinner turned into a happy and hilarious night. It was the wake of all time.

I came back after the summer break feeling optimistic about the season ahead. It was a beautiful day in early July. After training, Alec Stock and I sat in the sun at the training ground drinking tea. I had just one more year to go as a player and would soon be Fulham's new manager so, with that in mind, I spoke to Alec about bringing in three or four new players to boost our squad. That's what we needed to help us really kick-start our new season. Promotion was not out of the question. I said I could use my contacts to help Alec sign the necessary players. I already had a few names in mind and was very enthusiastic.

Alec sat there listening and sipping his tea. When I'd finished, he told me there was no money for new players. Fulham must have made £100,000 from the Cup final, which was a fortune in those days, but it had all gone on paying off debts, including the new stand. There was no money left to invest in the future.

'Well, if that's the case,' I told him, 'this will be my last season as a player. I'll be looking to take over as manager after that.'

'If that's what you want to do, that's fine,' said Alec.

It was all agreed and discussed a year in advance. I continued to help Alec in the office and drive him around. Things were quite amicable between us, but there was a sense of anticlimax at the club. After the thrill of reaching Wembley, the new season proved to be a non-event. I was annoyed because, if we'd signed the players

I had in mind, we could have been pushing for promotion.

In the March of that final season, I had a brief break from my problems at the club. A TV crew came to the ground one afternoon to film a fun game between Fulham and a bunch of kids from All Saints School. I was told it was all for a future children's television programme.

I was enjoying the game and didn't realise I was being set up until I felt someone tapping on my shoulder, as I was about to take a throw-in. I turned round and there was Eamonn Andrews with his famous red book.

'Alan Mullery . . . This Is Your Life!'

I was amazed. How June and my family managed to keep it all from me, I'll never know. But it turned into a really enjoyable night of laughter and nostalgia. I received tributes from many great players including Pelé, Bobby Moore, Bobby Charlton, George Cohen, Tosh Chamberlain, Roy Bentley, Bill Nicholson, Dave Mackay, Jimmy Greaves, Martin Chivers, Gordon Banks, Nobby Stiles and Sir Alf Ramsey.

My mates Jimmy Tarbuck and England wicketkeeper John Murray were there too. But glamorous *Avengers* star Honor Blackman got the biggest laugh of the night when she told Eamonn, 'The best thing about supporting Fulham is seeing Alan Mullery's legs!'

It was a lovely evening for June and me. Neal and Samantha enjoyed being on TV too. My mum and dad were there, along with my brother Ted and sister Kathy. My father was seriously ill with lung cancer at the time and died later that summer. I'm just so glad he was well enough to share that very special night with us all.

Only one thing marred the show for me. That was when Alec Stock blurted out the news that I was going to retire at the end of the current season. I hadn't told anyone about my decision. Alec Stock was the only person who knew. He also knew I was expecting to succeed him as Fulham manager, but he didn't mention that. He had no right to tell the world my playing days were numbered. But that was Alec Stock.

Back at Fulham, things got steadily worse between us. We'd never been friends as such, but we'd always had a good working relationship. Suddenly, he seemed more distant. Things came to a head when Fulham played West Brom at the Hawthorns. I walked into the away dressing room and started to get changed.

Bill Taylor, Fulham's coach, came over, looking very embarrassed.

'What's up, Bill?' I said.

'I thought Stocky had told you.'

'Told me what?'

'You're not playing today, Alan. You're on the bench.'

'Where's Stock now?'

'In the boardroom upstairs.'

'Right.'

I got dressed and went straight up to the boardroom. I banged on the door and asked for Alec Stock.

'What's your game?' I asked him.

'What d'you mean?'

'I thought I was playing today.'

'Well, you're not, you're on the bench.'

'You didn't have the bottle to tell me that face-to-face, did you?'

He didn't know what to say.

I was furious. If it had been a home game I would have walked out and gone straight home, like Bedford Jezzard had done a few years before, but we were up in the Midlands so I had to stick around. When I'd cooled, I decided to get changed and sit on the bench. I eventually came on as sub and did my best to prove the manager wrong. I was near the end of my career and every match was important to me. I knew I deserved my place in the team on merit, but Stock was starting to mess me around.

When it came to the last game of the season, at home to

Blackburn Rovers, I was on the bench again. Stock finally put me on for the last ten minutes. Not the best way to end my career as a player. I didn't go out on a wave of glory, but I didn't dwell on it. My mind was already on the future and my new career as a manager.

June and I took the kids to Majorca for our summer holiday and I came back feeling fit, tanned and raring to go. On my first morning back, I drove to Craven Cottage to see Alec Stock. He was sitting behind the desk in his office. When I walked in, he gave me a big smile. 'I know why you're here. You've come back to play, haven't you?'

'No, I've come for my job as manager.'

Alec swivelled on his chair and looked out of the big window behind him. I was left staring at the back of his head.

'I don't want to give up yet,' he said.

The room went silent. I realised he was going back on all the promises he'd ever made to me. What made it worse was he didn't have the guts or decency to look me in the eye as he said it. We'd had our ups and downs, but I'd never questioned his word. Everyone said Alec Stock was a man of honour, yet here I was with my career plans in tatters. Four years of broken promises and he didn't even appear to feel guilty. I was bitterly disappointed at the way things had turned out and in him as a man.

'You gave me your word,' I said. 'I want the job you promised me.'

'You haven't got a job,' he said.

His back was still to me. I felt so angry, I wanted to spin him round on his chair and smash him in the face. If he had been a younger man, I would have done it, too. But he was in his sixties and he had a weak heart, so I couldn't hit him. I walked out without another word. I wanted nothing more to do with the man. And that's how I felt for the next ten years. There were various reunions and dinners involving him, but I wouldn't attend any of them. I still felt very bitter about the way I'd been treated. I never spoke to Alec Stock again.

When I left his office, all I wanted to do was get some fresh air, but I bumped into the first-team players on the stairs. They knew why I'd gone to see Stock that morning and I think they were looking forward to me taking over as manager. There was plenty of light-hearted banter. 'What do we call you now, then, boss or gaffer?'

When I told them what had just happened, they couldn't believe it. They all felt sorry for me and I appreciated that, but I just wanted to be alone. I can remember driving home and feeling like my head was bursting. I'd been through a few tough times in my playing career, but nothing like this. For four years I'd lived with the dream of becoming Fulham manager. Alec Stock had stolen that away from me and the chance never came again.

The strange thing is, I was warned this would happen. Shortly after rejoining Fulham in 1972, I received an anonymous letter, which said that I would never ever be manager of Fulham football club while Alec Stock was there. That turned out to be one hundred per cent correct. I could never find out who sent the letter, but that person knew exactly how things would turn out, four years beforehand. Creepy, isn't it?

When I got home, June could see I was upset but we didn't want to talk in front of Neal. He was such a gentle little lad. If we got upset, it upset him, too, so June told me to take him to playschool. I can remember walking up the road holding Neal by the hand and chatting to him as if everything was all right, while inside I felt totally confused and let down. I was in a terrible state, to be honest.

I'd started the day full of hope, but the optimism had been knocked out of me – and fate hadn't finished with its games. When I got back indoors, the phone was ringing. It was Ken Calver, the secretary at Brighton and Hove Albion football club. He said Mike Bamber, the chairman, would like to speak to me.

Mike came on the phone and asked me what I was doing at the moment.

I said, 'Not a lot, to be fair. I've just been sacked by Fulham.'

'Well, jump in your car and come and see me. Peter Taylor resigned last night. I want you to be our new manager at Brighton.'

After the day from hell, I was on a high again. I drove straight down to the Goldstone ground in Hove. On the way, I thought about an incident three years before, when I hit a Fulham player who I felt wasn't trying hard enough in a match. Our opponents that day? Brighton! Our centre-half, was hurt in a clash of heads and I asked an Irish player called Jimmy Dunne to mark Brighton's centre-forward, Ken Beamish. Two minutes later the ball broke to Beamish, who was totally unmarked and who scored.

'I told you to keep an eye on him,' I shouted at Jimmy Dunne.

'It's nothing to do with me,' he said.

As captain, I had every right to tell Jimmy what to do, but he didn't want to know.

'You worry about your own game,' he snarled and pushed me away.

The next thing I knew, I'd punched him in the face. He went down like a sack of spuds. I moved away, but when Dunne stumbled to his feet I could see he had a cut under his eye. The referee had no idea what had gone on and soon blew for half-time. My first reaction was to go over to Jimmy and apologise, but he ran off ahead of me. When I got near the dressing rooms, he jumped out and tried to hit me, so I thumped him again.

They had to carry Jimmy in and our physio spent most of the break bringing him round. Meanwhile, Alec Stock raged at me for hitting one of our own players. Everyone was shouting at the same time, but the aggravation seemed to do us good. We went out and beat Brighton 5–2. It was one of our best wins of the season. Jimmy Dunne and I shook hands afterwards. I was sorry I'd hit him, but my attitude was the same as it had always been: I expected every player to try his best in every game. As I drove into Brighton, I had to hope that incident wouldn't go against me now.

When I arrived at the Goldstone, Mike Bamber led me to the boardroom, where two other directors were waiting. Brighton were a Third Division team who had just missed promotion the previous season by one place. Their manager, Peter Taylor, had unexpectedly resigned to join Brian Clough at Nottingham Forest and Bamber was keen for me to take over as manager.

'Why me?' I asked.

'I saw you thump one of your own players once,' he said. 'Anyone who wants to win that much, I want as our next manager.'

He explained how he'd dreamt about the incident the night before. 'When I woke up, I knew you were the right man for the job.'

A dream and a punch-up are not the usual criteria for appointing a new manager. It all felt a bit strange and I suddenly felt very tired.

'I'll need to think it over,' I said.

'I understand that, Alan,' said Bamber, 'but the players have already started pre-season training. We can't wait long.'

'I'll give you my answer in the morning,' I told him.

I had a good feeling about Brighton the minute I walked into the stadium. Maybe being cheated by Alec Stock was fate. There was a new challenge waiting for me on the south coast and I decided to take it on.

At the end of the week, I stood in the Brighton boardroom again, this time surrounded by all the directors and players of the club. I knew some of them. I'd played with Joe Kinnear and Phil Beal at Tottenham, now I was their manager. It felt strange. I was entering a whole new world and all eyes were on me. The room was hot and crowded. I felt nervous, but I kept it well hidden. I wanted to project confidence and a strong belief in what we could achieve together.

'Anyone who doesn't believe we can get promotion this season can go now,' I told them. 'I don't want you at this football club if you feel like that. Come and see me in my office and we'll get you sorted out immediately. I look forward to working with the rest of you. See you at training on Monday.'

When everyone had left, Mike Bamber poured us both a glass of whisky. 'You handled that well, Alan,' he said. 'Here's to the future.'

When I left the Goldstone that afternoon, I went down to the seafront for a stroll. I wanted to clear my head before driving home. As I walked on to the pebble beach and gazed out to sea, memories flashed through my mind. Johnny Haynes, Jimmy Greaves, Bobby Moore, Pelé, Wembley stadium, the Maracana. I'd travelled the world as a player. Now I was starting a new chapter in my life: Alan Mullery, manager. If I could achieve a fraction of what Sir Alf and Bill Nick had done, I'd be a happy man.

I was thirty-four years old and the best five years of my football life were about to begin.

11

THE SEAGULLS

Sir Alf Ramsey, Bill Nicholson, Bedford Jezzard and Alec Stock were all with me on my first day as manager of Brighton and Hove Albion football club in July 1976. Not literally, of course, but they were all there in spirit. I had learnt something different from each of them.

Alf was very studious; when he spoke to you he gave you words of wisdom. He trusted his players to do the job he'd selected them to do for the team. Bill Nick was a fantastic coach with a photographic memory. He knew everything about the game and, tactically, he was superb. Bedford Jezzard knew how to boost the confidence of his players. He was very tactile; when you played well he'd give you a big hug and say, 'Well done.'

Alec Stock had a different skill. In my opinion he was the biggest bullshitter I'd ever met. I've seen him give the Fulham players a real rollicking after a game, then go out and tell the Press there were definite positives to take from the team's performance. He taught me how to deal with journalists. His PR skills were exceptional.

It's one thing to learn from other managers, but using that knowledge to make your own mark in management is something else again. I'd been a professional footballer for nearly twenty years, but there's a world of difference between being a player and a manager. What made me think I could succeed in this new role?

I'd passed my FA coaching badge under Don Howe and Steve Burkinshaw. Terry Venables and I did the course together. So I had some qualifications to go with the drive and optimism I brought to the Brighton job. More important than all of that, I set myself clear and definite targets. I wanted to create a team in the Bill Nicholson tradition, a team that played pure football, but that also had enough battlers to see you through in a fight.

Like Bill Nick, I wanted wide attacking players left and right supplying two good strikers who could get me goals. I also needed defenders who could tackle hard and win the ball, plus a good, reliable keeper. When you list the various pieces of the jigsaw, they all make perfect sense. But assembling your dream team can be a long, hard road. It's a delicate balancing act involving tough decisions, judgement and luck.

The big advantage I had at Brighton was inheriting a good squad from Peter Taylor. He had just missed promotion by three points. It was now my job to guide the club to the Second Division in the season ahead.

There were about thirty-six professionals at Brighton when I arrived. That was far too many. I think twenty-four is an ideal squad size. To get closer to that, I had to get rid of quite a few players. I watched them all closely in training and pre-season friendly games. Who would go? I had some tough decisions to make.

Joe Kinnear and Phil Beal were both clearly past their best and they topped my hit list. We'd been team-mates at Tottenham, but I was building for the future and I couldn't base my decisions on friendship or sentiment. I also knew my standing in the eyes of the rest of the players depended on how I approached my dealings with the two former Spurs stars. Any favouritism would be spotted right away. I had to stamp my authority on the situation and deal with the senior players first. It was me or them.

I phoned Bill Nicholson for advice. He told me to back my judgement. If I was sure it was time for Joe and Phil to go, I had to act on that decision. He warned it wouldn't be easy, especially if they were sitting on good contracts, but I had to stay strong. I'd been on the wrong end of some of Bill's decisions in the past, but now he was talking to me as a fellow manager and he was happy to share some of the secrets of the trade with me.

I often turned to Bill Nick for advice in those early days as a manager. I phoned him at least once a month during my first season at Brighton. He always took my call and offered me valuable words of wisdom. He was the master and I was a young manager who was keen to learn. As the season progressed, he said a few times, 'You're doing very well.' Coming from Bill, that meant a lot to me. He'd made the transition from player to manager himself and knew how tough it could be.

Phil took the news reasonably well, but Joe was angry. I said he was overweight, but he denied it. I told him he'd have to do extra training to get fit, but he refused. I said he was no good to me in his present condition and I felt it would be best for him to leave the club. He accused me of betraying our friendship. It all got very personal and unpleasant, and Derek Dougan of the PFA got involved, but I stood my ground.

The club came to financial agreements with Joe and Phil and they left, along with former Millwall star Dennis Burnett, another good player who was reaching the end of his career. Things ended amicably with Phil and Dennis, but Joe Kinnear remained bitter and bore a grudge for some time. He wouldn't talk to me for at least five years, but that's all in the past now. Joe became a fantastic manager at Wimbledon and I'm sure he discovered that tough decisions have to be made sometimes.

There were also plenty of positives to enjoy at Brighton.

I hadn't seen the team play during the previous season, so I arranged a 'first team against reserves' game to see what I had to work with. I soon realised I wouldn't need to buy any new players. It was good to have experienced people such as goalkeeper Peter Grummitt and Welsh winger Peter O'Sullivan, but it was a skinny kid called Peter Ward who really caught my eye.

He was playing for the reserves and scored three goals in the first half. Not only that, but he was gliding past first-team defenders with ease. I put Wardy in the first team for the second half and he scored three more. I juggled some other players around and the new formation worked immediately. Everything fell into place.

I'd never heard of Peter Ward before. The coaching staff told me he had scored six goals in the last eight games of the previous season. That only served to confirm a decision I had already made. From now on, Wardy was our star striker. I came off the training pitch feeling very happy with the day's work.

I got back to my office at the Goldstone ground around four. I was working at my desk when in walked Fred Binney, the club's leading goal scorer and a hero to the fans. He was probably only four years younger than me.

'Come in, Fred,' I said. 'What can I do for you?'

Having dropped him to the reserves that afternoon, I knew what was coming.

'You're very new,' he said. 'This is your first job as a manager. Can I give you some advice?'

'Please do.'

'The little, skinny fella, Wardy. He's not strong enough for the Third Division. You should play me. I got over twenty goals last season, you know.'

'Thanks for the advice, Fred,' I said.

I let Fred have his say, but nothing could shake my belief in Wardy. I played Binney and Ward as a twin strike force for the first ten games of 1976–77 season, but eventually dropped Fred and he was transferred to Exeter City. It was a controversial move at the time and it could have come back to haunt me, but I was confident I'd got it right.

Peter went on to score thirty-six League and Cup goals that season and become the country's top goal scorer in all four divisions. I pushed a midfield player called Ian Mellor up to partner Wardy and he scored fifteen goals. They both had electric pace. Fifty-one goals from my new strike force was enough to silence any potential critics.

Peter Ward was one of the main reasons my first season as a manager was so successful. The other was Brian 'Nobby' Horton. I was registered to play for Brighton if required, but the first time I saw Nobby play I knew I'd never be needed. Brian was me on the football pitch, the best captain I ever had. If the players had any problems, he would come and see me and we'd sort things out. We trusted and respected each other for five years.

You couldn't ask for a better leader than Brian Horton. He had real authority on the field and led by example. He won nearly every 50–50 ball and never stopped urging the team on. I've seen him flying into tackles in five-a-sides at the club, because he hated to lose. It reminded me of my clashes with Dave Mackay on the ball court at White Hart Lane. Dave had been Bill Nick's manager on the pitch at Spurs. I followed him into that role.

Now I was the manager and Brian Horton represented everything I believed in on the field. We had some talented players at Brighton, but Horton and Ward were outstanding. The only time the team stuttered in our push for promotion was when Brian missed a couple of games with injury. We missed his drive and will to win. He played a vital role in my transition from player to manager.

We made a good start to the season, but I was unhappy in my new life. For twenty years I'd been a player, one of the lads. I loved the banter and camaraderie that goes with being a professional footballer. Now I was on the outside of that group and it took me a while to make the adjustment.

The truth of my new situation came home clearly when we went to play an away game, early in the season. We were staying at a hotel on the Friday night and as I walked into the restaurant for dinner, I heard a buzz of conversation and laughter coming from the players' table. That's always a good sign at any club, it shows the team spirit is right.

Without thinking, I sat down with the players and the conversation stopped dead. Complete silence. At first, I didn't guess what was wrong. I looked round the table and the lads were all staring at their soup to avoid eye contact. I'd made a big mistake; I didn't belong with the players any more.

I cursed myself for making such a stupid error. I knew the rules. Players are always left to eat in their own company. They can talk about their wives, lovers, or even the manager. Their space is never invaded, but I'd done just that. There was no easy way out of the awkward position I'd put us all in. I got up and found another table. The other members of the coaching staff soon joined me and the atmosphere picked up again.

I'm sure the incident was soon forgotten by everyone but me. It's still in my mind thirty years later. Why? Because that was the moment my playing career finally ended. I hadn't faced up to it until then. The life I'd known for so long was over and it was never coming back.

The truth came rushing in that night and it shook me to the core.

It was a hard lesson, but one I had to learn quickly. As a player, I'd been used to having everything done for me. Now I was picking the team, planning the training sessions, organising hotel rooms and booking the travel. I was involved with every aspect of arrangements for the team. I didn't mind the responsibility, in fact, I found it rewarding. I was keen to build a family atmosphere at the club and I worked well with the rest of the staff. I always got in early and had a cup of tea with the cleaning ladies before starting work. I wanted everyone to feel part of the future we were building at Brighton. I learned to love my new life, but leaving a successful playing career behind proved far more difficult than I'd ever visualised.

Players don't really know what they have until it's gone . . .

We won promotion that first season. Mansfield Town deserved to be champions. We finished as runners-up, one place ahead of Crystal Palace, which delighted our supporters. The atmosphere at the club was excellent. Winning is everything in football. The players, fans and directors were all happy and I'd moved on.

The player had gone for ever. I was now a manager and I had my own way of doing things. As a player I always hated having to knock and wait outside Bill Nicholson's closed office door at Tottenham. So I decided my door would always be open, unless personal business was being discussed.

Coaching was the best part of the job. I had the ability to show players what I intended them to do. I could demonstrate how I wanted them to pass, move or shoot. That was very valuable, especially when I was working with individual players, explaining the role I wanted them to fill in the team.

I remember one session where I was talking about cutting in from the left and shooting from the edge of the box with your right foot. I went through the move to show what I meant and hammered the ball straight into the top corner. The players were impressed and asked me to do it again, but I followed the first rule of coaching: if you've done it perfectly first time, leave it!

I was pleased with how my players had performed and we were confident of winning promotion, but I knew we needed to strengthen the squad if we were to succeed in Division Two. Fortunately, the directors felt the same and they called me in for a meeting just before the end of the season. Keith Wickenden, the vice-chairman, was waiting with some leading questions.

'If we give you two hundred and fifty thousand pounds to spend on new players, will that make us a good Second Division side?' Keith asked.

I said I thought it would.

He came straight back at me. 'If we give you half a million, will you get us promotion?'

I was wary of promising too much.

'If I have half a million, we'll have a better chance,' I said.

'OK, you've got it. Now tell me who you want to buy.'

I didn't have to think twice. 'Mark Lawrenson,' I said.

'I've never heard of him,' said Keith.

'You will,' I told him. 'He's a young central defender at Preston; one of the most exciting prospects in the game. He's playing at Crystal Palace tonight. We can go and see him if you like.'

'Right,' said Keith, 'let's go.'

The board meeting ended there and then. I rang Nobby Stiles, who was assistant manager to Harry Catterick at Preston North End. He confirmed Mark was playing that night and fifteen minutes later several directors and I were on our way to south London. We had a club limousine driven by a great character called Ernie. I enjoyed the spirit and spontaneity we had at the club then. We were full of enthusiasm and all eyes were on the future.

Crystal Palace had just paid Charlton £750,000 for a powerful striker called Mike Flanagan. That was a huge fee in 1977, even for a proven goal scorer, but Lawrenson didn't give Flanagan an inch of space that night. He was absolutely brilliant.

After the game, I asked Keith Wickenden and Mike Bamber what they thought of Mark's performance.

'Go and buy him now,' said Keith.

'I agree,' said Mike.

I went straight down to the dressing rooms to find Nobby Stiles.

I asked if Lawrenson was for sale. Nobby told me Liverpool had just bid £75,000 for him. I went back to Keith and Mike and they told me to offer £100,000. By then Nobby Stiles and the team had left, so I phoned him the next morning and he called back with good news later in the day.

'Liverpool won't match your offer,' Nobby told me. 'Lawrenson is yours for £100,000, as long as he wants to make the move.'

Mark came down with his stepfather, Tom Gore, who was on the board at Preston. I did all I could to sell the club to the player and offered him a very good financial package. I knew he was worth it. Mark sat there listening, but not saying much. Finally, his dad said, 'If I were you, Mark, I'd sign for Alan. I've got a feeling he's going to do great things here.'

Mark agreed. Now all that was left was the formality of the medical. Mark was extremely fit, so I was amazed when the club doctor asked to speak to me in private.

'I think this player may be diabetic,' the doc said. 'My advice is not to sign him.'

This made no sense to me, so I went back to Mark for an explanation. It turned out that Preston had put him on a steak-and-Guinness diet to build him up. He hated Guinness, so the club said he could add a drop of blackcurrant cordial to make it taste nicer. Mark admitted he'd gone a bit over the top. His drinks were more blackcurrant than Guinness. That's why his blood-sugar levels were sky high. He wasn't diabetic after all.

With that last-minute scare out of the way, I was free to make the best signing of my entire managerial career. It took a few weeks to sort things out. In fact, I think Mark was on holiday in Spain when he decided to sign for the Albion. He joined us in June 1977 for a then club record fee of £112,000. Brighton made a profit of almost £800,000 when they sold him to Liverpool four years later.

Any manager would love to have a player of Mark's ability in their side. He had a calm, strong temperament, he never caused any problems and he always performed brilliantly on the field. His presence helped to lift the team to a whole new level of performance in the 1977–78 season.

A young left back called Gary Williams also joined Brighton as part of the Lawrenson deal. Paul Clark, a tough midfield player, was another excellent addition to the side. We adapted well to the Second Division and started playing good, attacking football. I enjoyed taking my team to White Hart Lane. Things had gone downhill since my glory days at Tottenham and the club had been relegated the previous season. Now they were our rivals for promotion. There was a lot riding on the game, but I was determined to enjoy my return.

I went out on the pitch before the game to knock a few balls around and the Spurs fans gave me a great welcome. They were not so happy at the end of the game. We held Spurs to a 0–0 draw and beat them 3–1 at our place. Three points out of four from my old club was a good indication of our League form.

By the end of the season, Brighton were at the heart of a tense and exciting battle for promotion to Division One. Only two points separated the top four clubs: Bolton, Spurs, Southampton and ourselves. We had to win our last home game and hope for the right result between Southampton and Spurs, farther along the south coast. We won 2–1 and our crowd swarmed on to the pitch and started to celebrate.

But I knew it could all be premature. I kept asking for a radio. I needed to know what was happening at The Dell. News came through it was 0–0 and the teams were still playing. Southampton had to win to give us promotion. Right at the death, the Saints attacked. Someone thought they'd scored; someone else said they'd hit the post. It was agonising not knowing what was going on. When I finally heard the result, it was shattering. Spurs had got a draw. That put them level on points with us, but ahead on goal average.

Our dreams came crashing down by the narrowest of margins. Football supporters are often ripped apart in the media, but I was proud of the Brighton fans that day. As the bad news spread among them, I would have understood if they had turned and quietly walked away. Instead they kicked their disappointment aside and started to stamp, cheer and roar as never before.

The team came out into the directors' box and waved at the sea of faces filling the pitch below. I was totally caught up in the emotion of it all. Tears were rolling down my face. Somebody handed me a microphone and I promised we'd definitely go up next time around. We walked back to the boardroom with the roar of over 30,000 loyal fans still ringing in our ears.

One of the Brighton directors came up to me. 'Do you realise what you said out there?'

'What's that?'

'You've just promised them promotion next year.'

'Well, I'd better make sure we deliver,' I replied.

I was convinced we could do just that.

The board shared my optimism going into the 1978–79 campaign and they backed me to sign the players I needed to improve our chances. I bought two internationals, Gerry Ryan of the Republic of Ireland and Peter Sayer of Wales. I also paid Fulham £200,000 for a talented young striker called Teddy Maybank to play alongside Peter Ward. Mark Lawrenson and Brian Horton were the spine of my team; I built everything around them.

Once again, we started well and were never far from the top of the table. We had a good group of players and they were hungry for success. I didn't have many disciplinary problems to deal with, so it came as a surprise when I got a letter from a fan saying Teddy Maybank and Peter Sayer had been seen in a Brighton nightclub two days before a bad four-goal defeat at Leicester.

The rules I set out for our players were clear. Nobody was allowed to go out for three days before a game. They weren't even allowed to play golf, so nightclubs were certainly out of the question. Now two players had broken the rules and I had to make an example of them.

I called all the players together before training.

'I can't believe the result we had at Leicester on Saturday,' I told them. 'I've been trying to work out why we were so poor. This morning I got a letter saying that all of you, the whole team, were seen drunk in a nightclub late on Thursday night. There may be nothing to this story, but I'll be writing back asking the man to name the players he saw. If he can't do that, I'll sue him for defamation of character. But if any of you were in that club, I'd advise you to come and see me this afternoon and tell the truth, if you are man enough to do that.

'If you don't come and talk to me and I discover you were there, I'll put you straight on the transfer list.'

Then I walked out and left them to ponder on what I'd said. I knew there would be some peer pressure on Maybank and Sayer to own up and was interested to see what they would do. Sure enough, they came in that afternoon at different times. They both claimed they'd been alone at the club and swore they were only drinking orange juice. At least they showed some character by trying to cover for each other.

In the end I fined each of them two weeks' wages. A very nice lady, who looked like Joyce Grenfell, came to the club on behalf of my favourite charity, Guide Dogs for the Blind. I made Peter and Teddy write out their cheques for £250 there and then.

The tweedy lady was delighted. 'Thank you so much for your generosity.'

'Knowing these two,' I smiled, 'they'll probably be making another donation soon . . .'

But they never did.

By early May 1979, we were in with a serious chance of bringing First Division football to Brighton. Once again, things were incredibly tight at the top of Division Two. (Only two points divided the top four teams at the end of the season.) It all came down to our last away game at Newcastle. It would be heartbreaking to fall at the final hurdle again. But if we won, we were up.

I arranged for the team to travel up on the Wednesday before the game. We stayed at the Post House hotel in Washington and went to St James' Park that night to see Newcastle play. They put five goals past Bristol Rovers and it was the best result we could have had, because now the players knew what to expect. Newcastle were a good side and, unless we were at our best on Saturday, they would rip our dreams to shreds.

Sunderland let us use their training ground on Thursday and Friday, which was very good of them considering they were also in the promotion race. Having some extra time to prepare for the game was a novelty for my players and it proved to be very successful. By the time the game came around, they were fully focused and ready to go.

Everyone from the club came up by train on The Seagulls Special. It was packed with directors, staff, wives, girlfriends, families and supporters. Other people travelled by coach, car and minibus to be there on our big day. All roads led to the North East that weekend; we had 10,000 fans in the stadium by the start of the game. It was like a Cup final.

We got off to a dream start and went 3–0 up. Brian Horton got the first with a header, then Peter Ward and Gerry Ryan added two more before half-time. In the break, I warned the players Newcastle's pride was hurt and they would come at us in the second half, but although they pulled one goal back, our dream result was never in doubt. Near the end of the game, the Magpie fans were listening to the day's other scores on their radios. It came down to a simple equation. If we went up, Sunderland would stay down. The Geordies liked the sound of that, so we were roared home by nearly 30,000 voices at the final whistle.

I ran out on to the pitch and hugged the players. We waved to our supporters and the Newcastle fans joined in the celebration. Once again, tears filled my eyes, but this time they were of happiness, not disappointment.

We travelled home by train and The Seagulls Special became The Paralytic Express. There was champagne everywhere. The journey back seemed to take a lifetime, but nobody cared. I walked the length of the train with the team, thanking the fans for their support. Everyone who was on that train will remember it for ever.

June and I got off in London and it took ages to find a minicab to take us home. We finally got to bed in the early hours, then we had to be up early the next morning to drive to the club for an open-topped bus tour. We got caught in a traffic jam going into Brighton. We couldn't work out why the roads were so busy on a Sunday morning. I saw a policeman controlling the traffic and asked him if he knew why there were so many cars about.

He smiled. 'It's your fault, Mr Mullery.'

'My fault?'

'Yes, they've all come to see you and the team.'

'The way things are going, I'll miss the bus.'

'Don't worry, I'll get you there.'

He disappeared for a minute, came back on his motorbike and gave us a police escort all the way to the Goldstone. I appreciated his help – we wouldn't have got there without him. The streets were packed with fans. I was anticipating a reasonable turnout, but nothing like this. There were 250,000 people lining the streets that day.

Ask me to name the high point of my career at Brighton and I would choose that open-topped bus tour. Brighton had never seen anything like it before. We'd given the whole town a sense of achievement. I'd been at similar celebrations as a player, but being there as manager was different again. I was proud of the players and what we'd achieved together.

An hour later, the bubble burst.

After the parade, we went for a celebratory lunch at a hotel in

Brighton. All the players and directors were there with their families. Everyone was in a good mood, laughing and joking. Then someone in Mike Bamber's party stood up and called for silence. She told us that when Mike took over as chairman he said Brighton would be a top club in five years.

'Now he's done it,' said the woman. 'He's given you promotion to the First Division!'

I could see the players looking at each other, as if to say, 'What have we done then?'

The woman nodded to the organist in the corner and started to sing her own version of the old Ritchie Valens hit 'La Bamba', only she called it 'Mike Bamber' and the words were all in praise of the chairman. It was so embarrassing, it killed the event dead. I was expecting Mike to stand up and say the players deserved the glory not him, but he loved it.

The good times were over, almost before they had begun . . .

A couple of days later I caught a cab across town. The driver was a Brighton supporter.

'Best three years ever,' he told me. 'Next stop Europe!' He believed it, too. Success was affecting everyone from the chairman to the fans. Suddenly we were Big Time.

'Now it gets tough,' I thought.

'Robert Redford's here, Alan. He wants to talk to you.'

I thought my secretary was joking, but I went out to investigate and found myself face-to-face with Redford.

'Hello, Robert,' I said, trying to look casual, 'nice to meet you.'

I asked him into my office. On closer inspection, I realised this wasn't the famous Hollywood star. But if Redford needed a double, this man would be first in line!

'I'm Robert Bell,' said the stranger, 'owner of San Diego Sockers in California.' He explained he wanted to live and work with an English team for a month, to see how things were run. In return, he'd fly everyone from the club out to the States the following summer. He'd arrange games in San Diego, Portland and Las Vegas and pay for everything out of his own pocket. I told him he had a deal.

This had all happened back in our promotion season and Robert Bell proved to be as good as his word. Just four days after beating Newcastle, sixty of us were on our way to the USA. What better way to celebrate our arrival in the First Division? It should have been a dream trip, but it turned into a three-week nightmare.

The omens were bad when the pilot came on the Tannoy, halfway across the Atlantic, and announced that Crystal Palace, under Terry Venables, had won their last game of the season to become Second Division champions by a single point. We were second. Losing out to Palace was annoying, but we still had the States to look forward to.

I can't remember who first realised that parts of our hotel in San Diego were effectively being used as an impromptu knocking shop. I'm sure Robert Bell didn't know what was going on, but that's what turned out to be happening on the nights when we were there. It was a pleasant hotel with nice grounds and a good golf course, but at night local prostitutes hung around in the bars and nightclub, waiting to pick up sailors from the local port. The first hint of trouble came when some of the players' wives were propositioned by a group of sailors who mistook them for local hookers. Things went rapidly downhill from there.

June and I were asleep in our room when we were woken by angry shouts and screams. My first thought was that one of the players was being robbed at gunpoint. I pulled on a pair of shorts and ran out to see what was going on. A bedroom door down the corridor burst open and one of my players ran towards me, closely followed by a beautiful naked blonde brandishing a pair of scissors.

She clearly intended to use them and, as I'd recently paid a decent amount of money for him, I thought I'd better save him. I grabbed the girl as she ran past me and managed to pull the scissors out of her hand. Apparently, another blonde had been eyeing him up earlier that evening and his girlfriend was the jealous type. I carried her back to their room, still screaming and struggling.

'She thinks I was flirting with a girl in the nightclub, but I wasn't,' said the player.

'You bloody liar!' screamed the blonde.

'Shut up, the pair of you. If I hear any more noise out of you tonight, you're both on the plane home in the morning.'

I left them alone, but took the scissors with me.

Another quiet night in California.

I'd been looking forward to a relaxing holiday in America, but I never had a minute's peace. In the main, the players were well behaved. My biggest problem was Mike Bamber.

My relationship with Bamber had never been easy, but there was always a buffer between us. His name was Harry Bloom. Harry was a lovely man in his seventies, one of the main directors of the club. Like Bamber, Harry was a self-made millionaire. Harry started out selling second-hand cars from home and built that into a big successful business. He was always honest and straightforward with me and I liked him very much.

When Bamber tried to interfere with transfers or players' wages, Harry would say, 'Leave that to Alan, he knows what he's doing.' By the same token, if I had too much to say on the financial side of things, Harry would tell me to leave the money to Mike. He nipped any arguments in the bud and kept things on an even keel.

Harry Bloom had chosen not to take the California trip and, without him there, Bamber's ego seemed to take control.

It started with Bamber being given a suite at the hotel. Everyone else was sharing double rooms, but Mike was upgraded. Then when he got to the pool on the first morning, the players had taken all the sunbeds. He told me I'd have to move a couple of them so he and his wife could lie down. I refused to order my players around like that and Mike was far from happy.

A few days later, Robert Bell invited everyone out for dinner at a really nice restaurant. All sixty of us went. June and I sat at the head table with the directors. The players were at long tables with their wives and girlfriends. Beer and wine were flowing and we all ordered crab claws and big steaks. The waitresses started to bring out the food and I actually started to relax for once. Then it started. Trouble.

Mike Bamber stood up.

'Hey! Excuse me! Where's mine?' he snapped at a young waitress who was serving food to the players. The poor girl looked embarrassed.

'Sorry, sir?'

'Where's mine?' said Bamber. 'I'm the chairman of this football club. I should be served first.'

The mood in the room dropped like a stone. It was like the Brighton dinner all over again.

When we got back to our room that night, June told me she was really upset by the way Bamber had behaved. She wasn't the only one to feel that way. That tour definitely had a lasting effect on team morale. The chairman made it clear he felt he was more important than the players and the staff. They resented it and I didn't blame them. Everyone was unhappy and couldn't wait to get back to England. Things were never the same at the club. The spirit of 'all for one' was lost forever.

During that trip, Robert Bell asked me if I'd like to manage San Diego Sockers. When the Brighton in-fighting was at its worst, I was almost tempted, but at that point I was fully committed to taking the club into the First Division. In spite of everything, that still excited me.

But first, I needed a rest. Looking after sixty people for three weeks and dealing with all the bickering had left me exhausted. Robert Bell offered me his condominium in California for two weeks.

Samantha and Neal were flown out to join us and we had a really enjoyable family holiday in the sun. Believe me, I was ready for it.

I walked straight back into more stress and turmoil when I returned to the club for the 1979–80 season. Moving up to the First Division was a quantum leap. I wanted to give the players who'd won promotion the chance to prove themselves at the highest level. My priority was to rekindle the team spirit we'd had before our dreadful Stateside tour, but that dream was soon shattered.

I found myself in a head-on confrontation with the players. They had all been offered pay rises to play in Division One, but they were insisting on doubling their wages. I thought that was unreasonable and I felt let down by them. Brian Horton was their spokesman and I didn't like arguing with him. We'd come a long way together in a short time. I thought the world of Brian, but we were trapped in an uncomfortable situation where we both had to fight for what we thought was right.

We played some pre-season games in Scotland. I had hoped we could sort everything out while we were all away together, but it didn't happen. A week before the season was due to start, the players threatened to go on strike. They said that, if they didn't get the wages and bonuses they were asking for, they wouldn't play against Arsenal on Saturday.

We were still deadlocked on Thursday morning, two days before the game. I got all the players and the coaching staff together on the pitch at the Goldstone and announced that, if the first team did strike, I would play apprentices and kids from the reserves against Arsenal. When we got stuffed, as we certainly would, I'd tell the media my first team had refused to play because they were too greedy. I would have done it, too. I wasn't prepared to cover for the players on this one.

I said they had until two o'clock that afternoon to sign their new contracts, or I would start to prepare the kids for the game. I felt I had to stand my ground on the issue and one by one the players came in and signed. I didn't see it as a victory. In my eyes, we were all losers. Going into the First Division was tough enough, without tearing each other to bits. The result of the Arsenal game was totally predictable. They whipped us 4–0 at home. We got what we deserved.

The following Monday morning, I set about building bridges between myself and the players. I didn't want any bad feelings about money lingering around for the rest of the season. I assured the players we would assess their performances during the year ahead and those who did well would be rewarded with improved contracts. In other words, they had to prove they were worth First Division money. I knew some of them would thrive at the top level, but others would fall by the wayside.

We'd had a shambolic start to the season and things got even worse when Mark Lawrenson was injured at White Hart Lane. I knew I'd lost my best defender for several weeks and I had to juggle the side. Cover was very thin on the ground, so I decided to take a chance on a young lad of seventeen called Gary Stevens.

Bobby Robson had let Gary go from Ipswich a year before and I'd signed him as an apprentice. He was a good central defender, but I played him at right back in the first team and he settled in surprisingly well. Gary had a good match temperament and played twenty-six League games for us that season. He showed real promise right from the start and went on to play for Spurs and England later in his career.

Steve Foster, John Gregory and Neil McNab were also import-ant additions to the squad. I bought Steve from Portsmouth and he proved to be a great player for Brighton. He was big and brave, strong in the tackle and good in the air. Fozzie led the defence well and gave us much-needed stability at the back.

John Gregory was a stylish right back. He came from Aston Villa for £164K and was worth every penny. (The club made £90K profit when they later sold John to QPR.)

Neil McNab was a Scottish whippet, a fierce competitor in midfield who never stopped running or competing. I bought him halfway through the season from Bolton Wanderers and he gave us the extra edge we needed. Brian Horton continued to drive the team on.

Mark Lawrenson was excellent when he came back from injury. Peter Ward was still scoring goals, but finding much less space in the top flight.

It wasn't an easy season for any of us, but Bill Shankly provided some welcome light relief when we travelled away to play Everton. I met him on the Friday night at Tranmere. I'd gone there to see a match, but Bill kept me talking all evening instead.

'They don't play football here, son,' he told me. 'They do that up the road at Anfield.'

We sat in the boardroom together for a couple of hours and it was wonderful. Bill talked non-stop about the game. He had a way with words. Nobody loved football more.

The following afternoon, I was giving my team talk in the dressing room at Goodison Park. A commissionaire knocked on the door and said Mr Shankly wanted to see me. Before I could reply, Bill burst in with a big smile on his face.

'Getting ready for the game, son?' he said. 'Well, you'll beat this lot, no problem.'

A minute later, he'd taken over the team talk and my players were hanging on every word. I let him get on with it. There was no stopping Bill Shankly when he was in full flow!

We finished sixteenth in our first season in the First Division, which was a reasonable achievement. When teams get promoted to the Premier League now, managers always say their priority is survival. We achieved that. Now we needed to improve.

Once again, I faced confrontation in the close season. Not with the players this time, but with the chairman. Mike Bamber was keen to cash in on our First Division status by developing the ground and building sponsors' lounges. I told him our first invest-ment should be in new players. We needed to add quality to the team. Mike started to shout me down, but Harry Bloom stepped in with his usual words of wisdom.

'Michael,' he said to Bamber, 'the boy knows what he's talking about. We'll get the players first and we'll have all the corporate business afterwards, when we've consolidated in the First Division.'

To be fair, Mike did listen. Harry Bloom was now vice-chairman and he was like a father figure to Bamber. All the time Harry was with us, life moved forward at the club and I received the go-ahead to make some major signings in the summer of 1980.

I bought Michael Robinson from Manchester City for £450,000. Malcolm Allison had paid £750,000 for him just a year before. Michael scored eight goals for City in thirty games. He played forty-two games for Brighton in his first season and scored nineteen goals. I could see he'd lost confidence at City and I made a point of praising him every chance I got. I asked him to lead the line like an old-fashioned centre-forward and he did the job very well.

Agents were rare at that time, but Michael Robinson had one and he nearly ruined the whole deal. He came to my house with Michael to discuss terms and started making what I considered to be ridiculous demands. I threw them both out. Michael phoned me later and I told him my original offer was still on the table. I said I'd be happy to sign him, but his agent could stay at home. Michael agreed and signed the next day. It's just as well I was a manager at a time when agents were still a novelty. I haven't got the patience to deal with all that . . .

Sadly, Gordon Smith is remembered at Brighton as the man who missed the last-minute chance to win the FA Cup in 1983. That's a shame because he was one of the best players I ever worked with. He reminded me of Trevor Brooking. A midfield player with silky skills who could read the game perfectly. I signed Gordon from Glasgow Rangers for £400,000. He played thirty-eight games in his first season for us and scored ten goals from midfield. I couldn't ask for more than that.

We were a far better team in 1980–81, but we continued to struggle in the First Division. Peter Ward had been a Roy of the Rovers figure at Brighton, but when Peter Taylor phoned to ask if he was available for transfer, I had to consider it. I talked it over with Mike Bamber and Harry Bloom and we agreed we would sell him for £400,000. I knew I had a good chance of signing Andy Ritchie from Manchester United for a similar fee and I felt the time was right for a change.

I then found myself in a drawn-out game of cat and mouse with Brian Clough and Peter Taylor. Peter would phone and say they definitely wanted Wardy and would pay £400,000. Ten minutes later I'd get a call from Brian saying he didn't want Ward at any price. This went on for far too long. I even met them at a hotel in Brighton, on the night before our home game with Nottingham Forest, and we still got nowhere.

The next day Wardy had his best game of the season. Forest wanted him more than ever, but the good guy/bad guy routine went on . . . and on . . . and on. Obviously, they were trying to wear us down to the point where we would sell Peter on the cheap.

Mike Bamber was abroad on business and Harry Bloom came in every morning to see how things were going. I asked him what he thought of Clough and Taylor, who had both worked at Brighton.

'They'll keep on to you every day,' he said. 'One will say the deal is on, the other will say it's off. That's the way the two of them work. They can be a pain in the arse to deal with.'

Harry was absolutely right. In the end, I'd had enough. Cloughie phoned me up yet again. 'The deal is off,' he said. 'Don't take any notice of what Peter Taylor says, I make the decisions here.'

He was about to ring off.

'Brian, before you go, let me give you a word of warning,' I said quietly. 'If you have not done this deal by twelve o'clock this lunchtime, it is off. I will then drive up to Nottingham, wait for you in the car park and I will run you over. How do you feel about that?'

Of course, I had no intention of doing any such thing, but I wanted to shock Cloughie into seeing the game was finally up. Either he paid the fee we were asking or he could stop wasting my time. Just before midday that day a fax arrived from Nottingham Forest football club saying they would pay £400,000 for Peter Ward. The whole ridiculous saga was finally over and I could sleep at night again.

Brian Clough was one of the great characters of British football, but I'm glad I didn't have to deal with him too often during my career.

Peter Ward left Brighton in October 1980 with thanks from me for all he had done for the club. Peter was happy to be one-third of an unusual transfer triangle, in which Forest striker Garry Birtles moved to Old Trafford and bought Andy Ritchie from Manchester United for £400,000. Andy was only nineteen but I saw great potential in him.

Inside two weeks, Harry Bloom was dead. He died beside me on the team coach in Stoke. He had won £700 playing cards on the way up and he was well pleased with that. I can still see him in his trilby hat and bright-red braces. He was a great character, always full of life. I was joking with Harry about winning all that money. I turned away to talk to somebody else and felt him slump forward. I immediately feared the worst. We laid Harry in the aisle of the coach and one of our medical staff tried to revive him but it was no good. Harry had died of a heart attack. I'd lost a good friend.

From that day, things went rapidly downhill between me and Mike Bamber. There was no buffer between us any more. Whatever Bamber wanted he got and I couldn't do anything about it. Results were going against us and I could feel his increasingly critical eye on me all the time. Those last six months at the club were very difficult. I had to watch my back, but I also had to appear relaxed and confident in front of the players.

I don't think they lost faith in me as their manager. At one point relegation looked a probability, but we stuck together and won the last four games at the end of the season to beat the drop by two points. The team showed good spirit under pressure and I admired them for that.

But pressures were building off the field. Our lack of success meant falling attendances. Money was tight and Mike Bamber started to go behind my back. I found he'd been talking to players about contracts, which he had never done before. He'd always left that to me.

At the end of the season, he called me in and told me to sack all my backroom staff, including Ken Craggs and George Aitken who had worked so hard for the club. He even wanted to get rid of the kit-man Glen Wilson, who had been at Brighton for years. The club meant the world to him. I couldn't have lived with myself if I'd fired these people. Bamber knew that; he was doing all he could to undermine me.

Next he said we needed to raise £400,000 to pay off the club's debts. I reluctantly suggested selling Mark Lawrenson. I hated to lose Mark, but the money from his transfer would cover what we owed and leave enough to invest in new players. I told Bamber I valued Mark at a million pounds and Liverpool, Arsenal and Spurs could all be interested. But I had another manager I wanted to approach first. Bamber agreed to leave it all to me.

I went straight to my office and phoned Ron Atkinson.

Rumours were rife that Ron was about to leave West Brom to become the new manager at Manchester United. He confirmed the rumours were true.

'How would you like Mark Lawrenson to be your first signing?' I asked him.

'Are you letting him go, then?' said Ron.

'I've got to,' I said. 'We need the money. I want four hundred grand clear plus my pick of two United players.'

'Well, I agree to the four hundred grand,' said Ron, 'but I'll have to look at the players when I get to United. If you choose the right two, I'll be quite willing to let them go.'

'OK, Ron,' I said. 'You've got a deal.'

He asked if I was going to a football dinner in London later that week and we agreed to meet there to finalise everything. I met Ron and we shook hands on the deal. I reported back to Mike Bamber at the Goldstone the following morning.

'I've done the Lawrenson deal,' I told him. 'He's going to Manchester United.'

'No, he's not,' said Bamber. 'I've done a deal with Liverpool.'

I couldn't believe what I was hearing.

'But I've spoken to Ron Atkinson,' I said. 'I've given him my word.'

'You'll have to tell him we've changed our mind. Liverpool are offering £900,000 and they're happy to pay that in full when the transfer goes through. I want the money.'

I was livid.

'First you start dealing with the players,' I said. 'Now you're doing the transfers. You'll be picking the team next.'

'I've been thinking about that,' he said facetiously.

'Look,' I snapped, 'if you make me break my word to Ron Atkinson, I'll resign.'

'I've told you what I'm going to do.' His voice was as cold as ice.

'Right, you can find yourself a new manager.'

It was all over.

I felt too angry and upset to drive home. I found myself taking a familiar route down to the seafront. Five years before I'd walked on that pebble beach. Then, the world was full of hope and promise. Now, I faced an uncertain future.

The truth was, my best years as a manager were already behind me.

12

ON THE ROAD AGAIN

Angry.

That's how I felt in the days after I left Brighton. I thought I'd achieved more than any previous manager at the club. I'd started with a decent Third Division team and developed it into a Division One side filled with top-level players – Mark Lawrenson, one of the best defenders of modern times; John Gregory, Steve Foster and Gary Stevens, all of whom went on to play for England; Michael Robinson of Eire; Neil McNab and Gordon Smith, both Scottish internationals.

Players of that calibre would never have dreamed of joining Brighton and Hove Albion before I took over. My credibility definitely helped me to sign them. I'm not saying I deserve all the praise for the rapid rise the club enjoyed during my five-year stay, but I sure as hell played my part. Our first two seasons in the top flight were tough, there's no denying that, but any club should expect a similar period of transition.

If I had continued to enjoy the backing I'd received while Harry Bloom was alive, I'm sure we could have consolidated our position as a First Division club. Instead, I was out in the cold and Brighton went on to be relegated just two seasons later.

Did I regret walking out after my confrontation with Mike Bamber? Was I too headstrong? The honest answer is yes. I was fiery and prone to rush into emotional decisions. I should have taken my time to think things through before resigning, but it wouldn't have changed anything in the long term. If I'd backed down over the Lawrenson transfer, I believe Bamber would have walked all over me from that moment on. And my pride was too strong to allow that. Our split was inevitable.

I went to see Brian Horton at his home, a few days after leaving the club. I told him I felt I had no alternative but to resign. Bamber wanted me out and he'd got his way. Brian was upset about how I'd been treated. We'd worked well together for five years and he was sorry to see me go. Maybe the club saw Brian's loyalty to me as a potential problem, because during that summer he was sold to Luton Town. Brian's transfer may have made life easier off the field, but I'm sure the team missed their leader on it.

It was a shame life had turned so sour at Brighton, but it was time to move on. Within a month, Mike Bailey had taken my job at the Goldstone and I'd replaced him at Charlton. It looked like a swap deal, but that wasn't the case. When Bailey left The Valley, Charlton's young chairman, Michael Gliksten, invited me to lunch and sold the job to me. His family owned the club, but The Addicks were going through hard times.

'We're not expecting promotion next year, so don't worry about it, Alan,' Michael told me, in his classic, public-school accent. 'We'd like you to do your best. That's all we ask.'

Michael was like a breath of fresh air, after the unpleasant turmoil at Brighton. He was open and honest and I liked him from the day we met. He offered to match the money I'd been earning at

A proud young international. Playing for the under-23s gave me my first chance to wear the three lions

Mexico 1970. England line up before a classic match with Brazil, the best team I ever played against

Teaching Pelé how to fly!

The *Mirror* spells out the horror story
of two goals that counted for nothing

The ice man cometh.
Johnny Giles closes in on me

The new England captain. For one day only, on the sand in Malta

Give me back the Cup! Celebrating the 1972 UEFA win with the Spurs' fans

Looking smart and feeling good. I've just been voted 1975 Footballer of the Year

The best player I ever bought. Mark Lawrenson in action for Brighton

A sweet strike. Scoring for Spurs against Coventry City

Welcome to The Valley. My first week at Charlton with (*l to r*) Martin Robinson, Terry Naylor and Don McAllister

Just before being sacked at QPR. The tension shows in my face

A new career dawns. Commentating on Spurs v Liverpool, December 1993

Celebration of 100 years of the Football League. I was honoured to be part of his elite group. Can you name them all? Answers at the back of the book

Family team picture (*l to r*) Neal and Tracy, me and June and Samantha

With my lovely wife June, summer 2006. Still so happy together after forty-four years

Brighton and I decided to join him. It was like working with a character from *Tom Brown's Schooldays*. A jolly decent chap! His warm personality threw a positive spin on life at The Valley but, in truth, the famous old ground was in a ramshackle state. I was surprised how bad things were when I looked around.

An enormous area of terracing on the far side of the pitch was literally crumbling away. It was too dangerous to be used by fans on match days; weeds sprouted from every crack in the concrete. The overall atmosphere was one of decay. When I asked to see my office, I was led to a battered Portakabin in the club car park. This was home to Benny Fenton, the general manager, plus the coaching staff, the scouting staff and me.

Deluxe it was not.

Walking into those cramped offices could have been depressing but, within seconds, I was involved in a comedy sketch worthy of Monty Python!

Benny Fenton was standing by his desk holding an open umbrella above his head.

'What's the brolly for?' I asked.

'It's gonna rain,' he said, as if stating the obvious. He looked annoyed.

'I've gotta tell you something, son,' he said. 'I was manager of Millwall when you went back to Fulham on loan from Spurs. You beat us 1–0 and you were the best player on the field. You cost us promotion and that ruined me for life.'

What a welcome!

My first day at the club and a man in a Portakabin, holding an open brolly, tells me he has hated me for years. I started to explain my playing days were all in the past. Then the heavens opened and rain poured in through the roof straight on to Benny's brolly. He stayed nice and dry, but the water splashed all over me.

'Told you it was gonna rain,' he said, with a grin.

Benny wasn't so crazy after all.

The Portakabin door banged open and a groundsman rushed in loaded down with buckets. He put them in various strategic places to catch the drips. This was obviously a regular routine. Nobody else seemed to take much notice, but I've never forgotten it.

'Do I need a brolly, too?' I asked Benny.

'No, your office is dry.'

'Where is it then?'

'Down there.'

Benny pointed to a thin partition at the end of the room. On the other side was a desk and a chair. I wouldn't have been surprised if I'd seen a Norwegian Blue parrot in there, too!

I'd found my new home.

Once I got past his early John Cleese impressions, I enjoyed working with Benny Fenton. He was a former manager and player and brother of Ted Fenton, who managed West Ham United. Like me, Benny had a genuine love of the game. Chief scout Les Gore came into that category, too. His discoveries included Paul Walsh, one of Charlton's rising stars.

Life in the Portakabin was never dull.

I was working in my office behind the partition one morning when I heard some loud claps of thunder. It always amused me when Benny put his umbrella up, so I went out to see him in action. To my surprise, he was sitting quietly at his desk.

'Where's your brolly then, Benny?' I asked.

'Don't need it.'

'Didn't you hear the thunder?'

'Thunder?' Benny looked confused, then he smiled. 'That's not thunder, it's just Derek Hales and his gun out on the pitch.'

'OK,' I thought. 'Monty Python time again!'

I walked out on to the pitch and, sure enough, there was Derek Hales holding a shotgun. Derek was a brave striker with a terrific left foot; a real tough nut with long curly hair and a big black beard. Maurice the groundsman was throwing stones up at the rafters in the main stand and, as the pigeons flew out, Derek was shooting them. He had a pile of dead birds at his feet.

'Derek, what are you doing?'

Ask a silly question . . .

'I'm shooting pigeons, boss,' he replied. 'I do it twice a week.'

'Why?'

'I like pigeon pie,' said Halesy.

'And,' added Maurice with feeling, 'it stops them shitting all over the seats!'

They had logic on their side. I laughed all the way back to the Portakabin.

Ken Craggs joined me as assistant manager from Brighton. It was good to have a trusted friend to work with and we soon got busy. There was no money to buy players, but we brought eight free transfers into the club, including Steve Harrison, who went on to coach England under Graham Taylor, and Welsh international Leighton Phillips. Now we had some real quality and, once the new players had settled in, we went on an unbeaten run of twelve games around the turn of the year. Paul Walsh was rapidly making a name for himself and I also gave a debut to a promising young defender called Paul Elliott, who later enjoyed a fine career with Chelsea and Celtic.

Suddenly, we were in with a chance of promotion. I asked Michael Gliksten if I could buy Archie Gemmill. Archie's drive and competitive edge were just what we needed. Michael asked how much it would cost. When I told him, he explained he couldn't afford to pay the extra money out of his own pocket. I believed him. His family had been subsidising the club for years. I understood Michael's situation, but missing out on Gemmill still came as a disappointment. Ken Craggs and I had used all our contacts and experience to create a useful side. A couple more good experienced players would have made all the difference.

Things got worse when Michael told me he was selling the club to Mark Hulyer. I'd first met Mark when he arrived un-announced at The Valley early in the season with a cheque for £50,000, which he offered to give the club in return for his company's name being over the main stand for five years. Mark was an ambitious young man and, within a year, he owned the club.

I joined Charlton Athletic because I liked Michael Gliksten. He was the best chairman I ever worked for. I didn't feel the same about Mark Hulyer. I saw the season through, but all my motiv-ation had gone. The team won just once in the last eleven games and I left in the close season. I still had two years on my contract. I was sorry to leave a good group of players, but I really had no choice.

It was June 1982 and I was on the road again.

I didn't have to wait long for the phone to ring.

The name of the caller was a major surprise. Ron Noades wanted me to take over at Crystal Palace. I knew the vast majority of Palace fans still hated me from my time as Brighton manager, where I'd been accused of fanning the flames of rivalry between the two clubs. Trouble flared with Palace when a contro-versial penalty incident knocked Brighton out of the FA Cup. I was furious and at the final whistle I remonstrated with the referee.

As I walked back down the tunnel, Palace fans spat all over me. I gave them two fingers, then did an awful interview bad-mouthing those supporters and saying I wouldn't give a fiver for any of the Palace players. I could have handled things better, but I just totally lost it. It didn't go down too well at Selhurst Park and I knew the fans there still held a grudge.

I reminded Ron Noades of all this, but he was still confident I was the man for the job. We met for lunch at a hotel in Richmond and I was extremely wary. I wanted some stability in my life and I was far from sure I'd find it at Palace.

'I don't know if we'll be able to work together,' I said to Ron. 'We're both volatile people.'

We agreed on a six-month trial period, to see how things went. Ron showed his good faith by making me a director of the club, which enabled me to attend board meeting and know exactly what was going on. I got through the trial period, but in time all my doubts proved well founded. The Palace supporters never accepted me.

The players were terrific. I got on as well with them as any team I ever managed, including Brighton. Jim Cannon, Jerry Murphy, Billy Gilbert, Peter Nicholas and Vince Hilaire all played their hearts out for me but, once again, there was no money to invest in building for the future. Ron Noades and the board were under tremendous pressure just to keep the club alive. So, for me, it was out of the frying pan into the fire.

I regularly received abusive phone calls and anonymous letters at Palace. OK, we had two disappointing seasons, finishing fifteenth and eighteenth in the Second Division, but nothing could justify some of the filth directed at me. I found the constant abuse very difficult to deal with.

Threats eventually turned to violence.

As I walked to my car after a humiliating home defeat, a gang of Palace supporters attacked me. A friend helped to keep them at bay until the police arrived, but it was a nasty incident. It really scared me. I always felt edgy on match days after that. In many ways, I shared the fans' frustration. I knew what I needed to do to improve the team. I also knew it was impossible without a budget.

After what I'd achieved at Brighton, every club I joined thought I was a miracle worker. They all wanted me to turn a poor team into a good team. Experience has taught me that is totally impossible. You can make the most of the players you have and get them better organised, but without real talent to work with you can never move up to the next level.

A poor player who tries his hardest is still a poor player. That's the reality of the game. We won promotion twice in three seasons at Brighton, but I could buy players there. Charlton and Palace had bugger all to spend. I was on a loser from the start.

In the end, inevitably, I fell out with Ron Noades. We'd got rid of so many players, I found myself playing outside right for the reserves one afternoon, just to make up the numbers. Then, as manager, I had to take the first team to West Ham for a League game in the evening. It was a farce and it couldn't go on.

Ron and I agreed to go our separate ways after two seasons. He knew I wanted to go and he wanted me out, so it suited both of us. I was relieved it was all over.

I was out of work yet again.

When you're hungry you hunt and I was soon on Jim Gregory's trail.

Terry Venables had left Queens Park Rangers in a blaze of glory, having led them to fifth place in the First Division. His reward was a glamorous new assignment as the boss of Barcelona. QPR needed a new manager and I wanted the job. I knew Terry well and I could have asked him to put in a word for me, but I didn't want any favours. I'd succeed Venners on my own initiative, or not at all.

Some high-quality coaches were being linked with QPR. David Pleat, Gordon Jago and John Lyall were all mentioned in the Press as possible candidates. I was keen to add my name to the list. I knew QPR chairman Jim Gregory from my early days at Fulham, where he'd been a director. Jim grew up in Notting Hill, so we came from the same streets.

I tried to phone him at QPR, but I was told he was away for

a few days. I knew Jim often went to a certain health farm in Surrey and I was pretty sure that's where he'd be. The next day I read David Pleat was out of the running for the job and I decided to act fast.

It was time for some detective work. I phoned the health farm and asked for Mr Gregory.

'We don't have anyone of that name here,' said a snooty voice on the other end of the line.

'Look,' I snapped. 'I know Mister Gregory is there and I've got a very important message. I must speak to him *now*.'

The line went dead for a moment, then the snooty voice came back. 'Hold on, sir, we'll put you through.'

I put the phone down.

Now I knew where Jim was staying. I got in my car and drove straight to the health farm. As I walked into the reception area, I saw Jim walking downstairs in a white towelling robe.

'So you're the clever bastard who's been playing games,' he smiled. 'Well, now you're here, you'd better come and have a glass of champagne.'

We went to his suite.

'I'll tell you what, Alan,' said Jim, 'I'm impressed by the way you tracked me down. It shows you're keen and I like that. I've got one more person to see about the job. If that doesn't work out, we'll have a chat.'

The following day I read Gordon Jago hadn't got the job. Then I got the call from Jim Gregory. Two hours later we were sitting face to face. Jim had his own offbeat way of doing things. He was a rough diamond; a powerful little man who didn't suffer fools gladly.

'I'm going to ask you one question,' he said. 'Get it right and I'll give you the manager's job. Get it wrong and . . .'

He left me to complete the sentence. Jim was like that. He liked to test people to see how they would react.

'What's the question?' I asked, keeping my voice relaxed.

'Before Terry knew he was going to Barcelona, he told me he wanted to sign a centre-forward for QPR. Who was it?'

I had no idea. Jim's eyes were on me, but I tried to look cool. My mind was racing. 'The job depends on this. Bloody hell!' I had no way of knowing what Terry had been thinking, so I had to guess. I pictured the QPR team. Who would improve it?

'Mick Harford,' I said.

'You've been talking to Terry Venables, haven't you?'

'No, Jim, but that's who I'd buy.'

That answer got me the job.

At last, after three years of hard times, I had the chance to work with a top-class First Division side and a chairman who could afford new players when we needed them. It felt too good to be true. And it was.

The first hint of trouble came when I arrived to start work at Loftus Road in June 1984. As I hung my jacket in a wardrobe in the office, I found a pair of shoes belonging to Terry Venables. I soon discovered they were impossible to fill.

Later that morning, I asked one of the secretaries to do some work for me. 'Terry wouldn't have done it like this,' she said.

'I don't care what Terry would have done,' I told her. 'Can you do it my way, please?'

That went down like a lead balloon. I soon realised Terry Venables was everywhere. The chairman still loved him. The players still loved him. The staff still loved him. Terry had done a brilliant job at QPR and won the total loyalty of everyone in the place. He cast a long shadow. Venners was impossible to replace.

My organisation of a pre-season tour of Ireland was all wrong. 'Terry wouldn't have done it like this.'

Some of the players were difficult, too. I'd kept Terry's coach, Frank Sibley, and we got on well together, but I ran into problems at an early training session with a full-back called Warren Neill. We were concentrating on how I wanted the team to work as a defensive unit. Terry Venables had regularly played the offside trap. I didn't want to do that. I thought it left us too square and a well-timed pass and run could cut us in two.

Frank and I were explaining some new ideas. Warren Neill was not impressed.

'Terry didn't do it like this,' he told me.

I could see other players were thinking the same. They were missing Venners. I was the new face nobody wanted to see. Anyone taking over that job would have faced the same problems. I didn't lose the dressing room at QPR. The truth is, the players never gave me a chance. The coach they wanted was starting a new life thousands of miles away in the sunshine of Catalonia.

Maybe I could have turned the situation around with the help of the chairman, but the support I needed was never there. I saw whose side Jim Gregory was on when I left Warren Neill out for a midweek game away at Southampton and decided to give a lad called Wayne Fereday a chance in his place. I told Warren my decision the day before the game. He wasn't very happy, but then players never are when they're dropped. I thought no more about it.

I was fast asleep at home that night when the phone rang at 2.00 a.m. It was Jim Gregory. I don't know where he was, but I could hear music in the background. He said he'd heard about me dropping Warren Neill.

'What's your team for tomorrow?' he asked.

'It's two o'clock in the morning,' I said.

Jim wouldn't be put off. He wanted the team there and then, so I told him.

'If I was you, I'd think about changing that and putting Warren back in.'

'What happens if I don't?' I asked.

'That's up to you,' he said. 'The consequences of that . . .'

I'd heard enough. I put the phone down on him.

Ironically, one of my first-team players was injured in a warm-up session the following day and Warren Neill played after all. Jim Gregory came down to Southampton in his Rolls-Royce the following night.

'I see you changed your mind, then.'

'No, not really, Jim. One of the lads had to pull out this morning. That's the only reason Warren's not on the bench.'

I have to admit that the team played badly and Jim made a point of seeing me before he left.

'You're not doing very well, are you?' he said.

He was a hard man and he certainly knew how to apply the pressure.

Terry Venables' success the previous season meant QPR were in the UEFA Cup. We beat Partizan Belgrade 6–2 in the second round and flew out to the away leg feeling confident. From the moment we arrived at the stadium, everything went wrong. The crowd pelted us with bottles and ball bearings and we were battered in every way. We ended up losing the game 4–0. We were out of Europe.

I got back on our private plane in a foul mood. No team should ever lose a four-goal lead. I was so angry I felt physically sick. I assumed all the players felt the same. One of my players who'd done nothing worthwhile in the game, started singing. I jumped to my feet.

'Haven't you got any pride?' I screamed. 'How can you sing when you've just lost 4–0?'

'That wasn't our fault.'

'Whose fault was it, then?'

'Yours,' he said cockily. 'I think this is possibly the finish of you.'

When a player talks to you like that in front of the rest of the team, either he goes or you do. I already knew the chairman would side with the player, not me. I had the player in my office first thing the next morning and told him exactly what I thought of him, but it was water off a duck's back. Players are shrewd. He knew I was living on borrowed time, the whole team did.

I went into the boardroom after our next home game, which we drew. Jim Gregory had his own suite at Loftus Road, so he could stay over at the club whenever he wanted to. He took me there for a quiet word. I knew what was coming.

He poured himself a glass of champagne and drank it down in one.

'I think it's arrivederci time,' he said.

'I don't know a lot of Italian, Jim,' I said, 'but arrivederci means goodbye, right?'

'Yeah,' said Jim, putting down his empty glass. 'Goodbye.'

There was no emotion. Jim went back to the boardroom. I found June and we drove straight home. We sat talking and drinking until about three in the morning. I'd just left my fourth club in three and a half years. That was a worry, but I had no regrets about leaving Loftus Road.

It was fitting my sacking should come at Christmas because I'd been haunted by the Ghost of Venables Past since my first day. The chairman acted like Scrooge to the very last. At 8.00 a.m. the next day, two men from the club were at my house to collect my company car. I threw the keys at them and slammed the door.

Managing QPR was the worst job I ever had in football.

I was out of the game for the next eighteen months. It was my longest spell away from football since signing for Fulham when I was fifteen. I was forty-three and I'd spent the last twenty-eight years as a player and manager. I needed a break, a complete change of scene and when a neighbour offered me a sales job at his printing company I took it. He hoped my name would open doors for us. It did, but all people wanted to talk about was football; they didn't want to buy anything.

Eventually, through that job, I met Bryan Bedson, who was then chairman of Brighton and Hove Albion. Bryan owned a successful printing business and I went to meet him for lunch one day. We got on very well and ended up talking more about football than printing. He soon realised how much I still loved the club.

A couple of months later, in May 1986, I got a phone call from Bryan asking if I'd like to come back as Brighton manager. I agreed to meet him at his home near the Bluebell Railway in Sussex. Once inside, he locked the front door and said he wouldn't let me out until I agreed to take the job. I liked Bryan. He was always joking around. But he was serious about my return to the Goldstone.

They say never go back but the truth was, I was missing football more than I'd ever thought possible. I was like an addict without his drug. I knew Brighton had severe financial worries and had gone downhill considerably since I'd left, but despite all that I agreed to return on half the salary I'd been earning five years before.

I took over as manager from Chris Cattlin, one of my former players. Considering the restrictions he'd been working under, Chris had left me a reasonable team who had finished eleventh in the Second Division. If we could have kept that side together and built on it, maybe we could have moved forward, but I was told right away to get rid of the high earners. I did it, but I didn't enjoy it.

Justin Fashanu, Graham Moseley and Alan Biley all went in a short period of time. Once again, I was involved in arguments and bitterness. I saved the club a fortune in salaries but, as a former professional myself, I had sympathy with the players. It was all very negative. I'd come back to coach the team, but I soon felt weighed down with the same headaches and hassles I'd faced elsewhere.

By the turn of the year, we were down at the foot of the table.

The playing squad was cut back to the minimum and I had no room to manoeuvre. Then I was told to sell Gary O'Reilly to Crystal Palace. The club needed the money to pay the next month's wages. I believe that left us with fourteen first-team players. It was hard, but I was still in there fighting. I was determined Brighton would not be relegated in my first year back as manager. I could not allow that. Everything was stacked against us, but somehow we'd survive.

I decided to push all the business and money worries to the back of my mind. It was time to get back to what I did best: working with the players. The big names had all gone, but there were still some very genuine lads at the club. If they started to believe in themselves again, we could climb to safety. I knew I could give them that belief. In a way, I was relishing the challenge.

We had a very good away win at Grimsby Town in January 1987, which gave us all some hope for the future. The following Monday, Bryan Bedson called me into the boardroom. I'm sure you'll think I was naïve, but I had no idea what was coming. Two other directors were waiting for us.

'We've decided to change the manager,' Bryan told me.

'I think the commercial manager's doing OK,' I said.

'No,' said Bryan. 'I mean you.'

The news came as a complete shock. I felt the colour drain from my face. This was nothing like my final argument with Mike Bamber. Then, I felt angry. Now, I felt weak. I don't remember much more of what was said. My teenaged son, Neal, had come to the ground with me. A friend on the staff saw the state I was in and offered to drive him home.

I went to my office and put all my belongings into a plastic bag. I said goodbye to the people I'd worked with and thanked them for their help, then walked to my car. I don't know where I went for the next four hours. I just drove aimlessly around. I remember sitting in a lay-by beside a busy road for ages, lost in my own thoughts.

Why was I back in this situation? I'd done everything the club had asked of me. Of course, the cuts had left the team struggling, but I could have pulled things round if the board had trusted and believed in me. Instead, I'd been stitched up. Again.

I didn't rant and rave. I felt numb.

Brighton were relegated that season. Maybe, having removed the high earners at the club, I'd served my purpose. Who knows? The only reason the board gave for sacking me was that I had not moved to Brighton as promised. It took me forty-five minutes to drive from home to the ground at that time. I'll leave you to draw your own conclusions.

In the past I would have bounced back from the Brighton fiasco. Maybe even laughed at their so-called logic. But it was different this time. I'd been through five horrible years. Now, at the scene of my greatest triumphs as a manager, I'd been fired. Another failure.

An endless stream of cars roared past the lay-by in the fading winter light.

I felt broken. I could see no future.

13

BACK FROM THE BRINK

For three months, after losing my job at Brighton, I was as close to a nervous breakdown as I have ever been. The days were cold and grey and they matched my mood perfectly. I withdrew into myself and felt surrounded by darkness.

I had a beautiful house in Banstead, Surrey, which I'd bought during the success of my early years at Brighton. It had five bedrooms, a private drive, almost an acre of land and a swimming pool in the garden. It was a dream home, but it became my prison.

I never went out. I sat in my study for days on end, staring at the walls. At nights I roamed the house unable to sleep. I hardly spoke to June or the children. I was in my own world. I'd drink through the night, staring blankly at the television or video. I didn't even want the alcohol, it just filled a void.

The phone never rang. When you are a manager you are inundated with calls day and night. Now everything went very quiet. I felt football had abandoned me. No job offers, no goodwill calls from friends in the game. Just silence. The players and managers I'd known for years all seemed to disappear. I don't know why. A few words of encouragement would have meant the world to me. Maybe they were too embarrassed to call after my run of failures. I thought someone might offer me a bit of scouting work, just to keep me involved, but nothing.

I'd enjoyed so much success in my life, now I felt like a failure.

It must have been a terrible time for my family, but I was too lost in myself to see it. June started to go out on her own more, but I hardly noticed. One night she came home and something in her face had changed. She told me she'd been going to meetings at a local church and had taken Jesus into her life. It was a major event for her and she looked so happy, but even at a time like that I was cold and distant.

'Good for you,' I said. 'It doesn't mean much to me, but if it makes you happy . . . fine.'

June asked me to attend some meetings, too. By this time I was bitter and nasty inside. I agreed to go, but I planned to wreck things, tear the people there apart for their beliefs, which I did not share. I was so screwed up, I actually felt excited when the night of the meeting came. I couldn't wait to cause some chaos, but another man got there first. He was obnoxious and argumentative all night and I ended up being impressed by the patient way the people from the church dealt with him.

I could have been the fool shouting my mouth off. Instead, I stayed to listen and I soon found myself looking forward to those meetings. I have no intention of preaching to you here. All I will say is that I eventually became a Christian, too. There was no miraculous change in my fortunes but when life was at its lowest ebb, my faith helped to pull me through.

I could have played up to my public image in this book: Mullers the colourful character with his strong opinions and endless stories about the game he loves. That is me, but only some of the time.

Life is not about one-dimensional cartoon characters. It's about real people facing what fate throws at them.

For my story to mean anything, it must include the pain.

It was spring 1987 and for three months I'd sat and moped at home.

'You must do something,' said June.

I could see the worry in her eyes.

'What can I do?' I asked. 'All I know is football and nobody in the game wants to know me.'

I was through the worst of my depression, but my confidence was still shot to pieces. I had no education to fall back on. I'd never passed a GCE in my life and had only very limited experience of the business world. My area of expertise was football and now that seemed to count for nothing.

I went to Tottenham just before the end of the season. It was the first game I'd seen since leaving Brighton. I enjoyed the match, but being at White Hart Lane emphasised how much I missed the game.

I met a Spurs director called Douglas Alexiou. 'Lovely to see you, Alan. Where have you been?' he asked. 'I haven't seen you at any of the games.'

He soon realised I was at a low ebb. He offered me some advice. 'You've got to get yourself to football matches where you think the manager may possibly be losing his job. Let people see you, keep yourself involved in the game.'

'I wouldn't want to prey on a situation like that.'

'Then you're going to struggle to find a job,' Douglas told me and he was absolutely right.

To be a successful manager, you need a strong inner belief, first-class health and stamina. I had none of these things. A wasted season at Charlton; stress and personal abuse at Palace; late night phone calls at QPR and the final insult at Brighton. All these had taken their toll on me. I couldn't go back into management. All my competitive edge had gone. Jovial, confident Mullers? I couldn't see him anywhere in my life.

But June was right. I had to do something. I did try coaching a south coast non-League team called Southwick, but even that was unsuccessful. In the end we bought a sports shop in Banstead. I'd had a similar part-time interest in my playing days and I thought it made sense to go back into something I knew a bit about. We ploughed what was left of our savings into setting up the business and buying our stock. The building in Banstead was on a twenty-year lease and the overheads were high, but we went into the venture with great enthusiasm.

The shop was our new start, but it was never a success.

Every morning as a player, I woke up looking forward to the day ahead. Even when I hit trouble as a manager, I always felt fully involved with the battle to put things right. I never visualised a future away from the game. Now I was a full-time shopkeeper, serving the general public six days a week. How could that possibly replace the life I'd known?

It was a strange time. Five years drifted past like a play on a stage. I saw everything that happened, but I didn't feel part of it. Little by little, we slipped into debt. By the early nineties, the shop had become a burden. It came as a relief when the owners of another sports shop offered to buy our lease. They took over the business and all our stock and said they would pay us over a two-year period.

I was pleased to get out. I was pining for the game and I needed a major new challenge, preferably something that would ease the constant strain of worrying about money. In early 1993, a dream opportunity arose. An agent offered me £50,000 a year tax-free to coach the Malaysian Armed Forces team in Kuala Lumpur. The job came with an apartment in a luxury complex, a car, six flights home for June and me every year, plus complete freedom to coach and select the team without any interference.

The contract was for two years. If I'd filled out a wish list at that time in my life, the Malaysian package would have ticked each and every box. I felt charged with energy and optimism. I couldn't remember when I'd felt so alive. The agent invited me to Kuala Lumpur in February to have a look around. On the flight out, I kept telling myself not to build my hopes too high. There was sure to be some kind of catch, but I was wrong. The people I met were very positive about me coming out and I couldn't wait to get started.

It was on that trip I heard the sad news that Bobby Moore had passed away. I spent a lot of time thinking about him on the way home. Mooro had always made the most of life and now I was determined to do the same.

As soon as I got back to England, June and I started to get ready for the big move. Samantha and Neal were both old enough to look after themselves and they were happy I had the chance to coach again and earn some much-needed money. I should have known things were going too well. Just before June and I were due to fly out, Neal came home from the sports shop, where he was still working, and said business was so bad he'd been made redundant.

I went to the shop with him the following Monday morning to try and get him some redundancy pay. We were shocked to find the business closed down. The shop was bare. We got all my stock back, but I didn't have the time or will to get the shop up and running again.

I put the whole affair in the hands of a solicitor and took off for Malaysia. I was glad to get out of England. Financial pressures were closing in on me. I had a big bank loan plus a mortgage. Our house in Banstead was expensive to run and now my income from the shop had fallen through. I had to start paying the lease again, plus all the other expenses involved with the property. It added up to a frightening amount of money going out every month. We were up to our eyes in debt.

I was so glad I had the job in Malaysia to look forward to. I arranged with Neal to send money home every month to pay our debts. I stood to earn £100,000 in the next two years and my expenses would be minimal. June and I agreed to save hard, so that when we returned to the UK in 1995, we would be in a position to pay off all our debts and start again. We were in dire straits, but at least we could see light at the end of the tunnel.

I can still remember the wave of relief that swept through me as we stepped out of the plane into the sticky air of Kuala Lumpur airport. OK, I thought, the future starts here. We were driven to our apartment, which was very comfortable, and went for a swim in the private pool in the grounds. England and all its worries seemed far away.

The first monthly cheque went into my account and I started work with the Malaysian Armed Forces side. Our training camp was just outside Kuala Lumpur and I drove myself there every day in the car I'd been given. The facilities were OK and the soldiers I was coaching were very fit. Their individual skills and team play needed some improvement, but that was fine. I was there to help them and they seemed keen to learn. Everything looked very promising.

I was so engrossed with my coaching it took me a few days to realise my second cheque hadn't been paid. I mentioned this to the officers running the team, but they said they could not help. Everything had gone through a third party. I had to speak to him about my money.

I'm not going to mention this character's name because I feel sick every time I hear it.

I searched all his haunts in Kuala Lumpur, but he was nowhere to be seen. He had disappeared off the face of the earth. June and I were broke; we had nothing to fall back on. I remember going to see the Armed Forces play a game out in the country and telling June she could have a Coke or a sandwich but not both, because we couldn't afford it.

'Buy them both and we'll share,' she said.

That answer was typical of the way June faced our troubles. But even her strength and resilience began to crumble during our final days in Malaysia. The Armed Forces were sorry to lose me, but once again I'd been cheated by someone I trusted. It's lucky I never found that individual, because I might have killed him for what he'd done to me and my family.

The Armed Forces kindly offered to fly June and me home.

We packed our belongings in silence, moving around the apartment like zombies. We thought this would be our home for the two years that would turn our lives around. Now we leaving with our plans in tatters. I went for one last walk in the tropical gardens and tears filled my eyes. I didn't want to go back to England. All that waited there was a web of debt and worry.

How many beatings can a man take before he cracks?

How many times can a woman share the misery of the man she loves?

Back in England – and this needs to be told – June and I came close to committing suicide.

How close?

I'd say the toss of a coin.

The financial pressures we came back to were worse than ever before. Every day brought a new pile of bills and we had no money to pay them. People were suing us. We were about to lose our house. Every time there was a knock on the door we thought it was the bailiffs. Reality became mixed with paranoia.

One night, I lay wide awake. It was dark in the bedroom. I had a shotgun in the wardrobe. Why not turn it on myself and end all this suffering, all this pain? Madness? Not to me. I longed to escape my misery and suicide was a definite option.

When June woke up, I told her what I'd been thinking. She said she didn't want to live without me. We cried and held each other like lost children. It seems incredible now, but during that bleak time we actually talked about the best way to do it. Should we use my gun? Maybe pills would be better? We were not frightened of dying; it seemed the easy way out. What pulled us back from the brink was our faith and our love for our children.

We couldn't put them through the shock and horror of our deaths. We couldn't leave them to clear up the mess we'd created. We had to somehow find a way forward. I can totally understand why people take their own lives. If it hadn't been for June and the kids, I would have joined that list of sad statistics. But we moved on and life was never so cruel again.

Leaving our house in Banstead was heartbreaking. Today that property must be worth a fortune, but it was washed away by a sea of debt. We moved to a small semi in Cheam, which never felt like home, but was far cheaper to run. Then I met a financial adviser called Richard Ashken, who worked with the Lennox Lewis management team. Richard proved to be a wonderful friend. He negotiated with our creditors and we were eventually able to settle with them all. I'll never be able to thank him enough for his help.

One by one our problems were being solved.

Now I needed to start earning again and I found an exciting new career in the world of radio and television. It wasn't planned, it just seemed to fall into place. My first big break was being offered the role Bobby Moore had previously filled at Capital Radio. Over the years I added my comments to the excellent match commentaries of Jonathan Pearce, Steve Wilson and Rob Wotton. (Jonathan and Steve are now with the BBC and Rob works for Sky Sports News.)

White Hart Lane, Highbury, Old Trafford and Anfield, I was commentating at all the famous stadiums I'd once played in. It was so good to feel part of the game again. I was back where I belonged and I loved it. People were glad to see me. I remember arriving at Maine Road to cover a City game. Francis Lee got out of his

Rolls-Royce and came over to shake me warmly by the hand.

'Great to see you, Mullers! Come and have a chat in the board-room.'

Boardrooms are still very formal. Smart suits are the order of the day. I was in an open-necked shirt and sports jacket.

'I'm not dressed for it,' I said.

Franny smiled. 'I'm the chairman and I decide who's welcome in our boardroom.'

The money I was earning from my media work was vital, but feeling wanted again meant just as much to me. Managers, players and fans all seemed to respect my opinion. My self-belief came flooding back. I have never set out to be controversial. I don't try to whip up interest in that way. Ask me a football question and I'll give you a straight answer. You may not agree with my views, but I'll always give you my honest opinion. TV and radio bosses seem to like that approach and, to this day, the work keeps rolling in.

I did go back into the game briefly in the mid-nineties as director of football at Barnet for a few months, but I ended up managing the team and I didn't want that, so I resigned. My future was in the media.

I'm at ease in front of microphones and cameras. It feels very natural to me. I like the thrill of being on the air, especially on live shows when the adrenalin really flows. Jonathan Pearce and I shared a few adventures when we were working on radio together.

Jonathan is the ultimate professional. Before every match he would check the equipment, then lay out all his notes for the game. He'd surround himself with sheets of paper filled with key facts. One night in Sheffield, we were sitting on the gantry high above United's ground. A minute before we were due on air, a gust of wind sent Pearcey's notes flying. The look of shock on Jonathan's face was classic, but he's such a good pro he went into his commentary without skipping a beat.

Another time Pearcey had all his notes ready, both our microphones were working, everything was perfect, except we couldn't see the match. We were up at Port Vale for their game with Crystal Palace. Jonathan was unhappy with the room we'd been given to commentate from because our view of the pitch was poor. It was a wet, misty night but Pearcey decided we'd have to work from a flat roof outside.

'Sorry, Mullers,' he said. 'Looks like we'll be getting soaked.'

'No problem, Pearcey,' I told him.

He was determined to do the best job he could and I respected him for that. He got busy moving all the radio equipment and covering it from the rain, so we didn't blow up halfway through the match. Soon we were all set to go. The rain stopped, the game started and everything was fine, then the fog came down. The referee didn't call the game off, so we kept going, even when the action was on the far side of the pitch and we couldn't see a thing.

'And Palace are really coming into this game now, Alan.'

'Definitely, Jonathan, this one could go either way.'

Somehow we got through it. We even got the final score right.

After what I'd been through in my private life, a few problems on live broadcasts were not likely to faze me. I've worked for LBC and Talk Sport, too and the golden rule is always the same: if you're broadcasting live, keep going whatever happens.

I ran into a similar test of nerve on one of my first appearances for Sky. I was booked for a half-hour slot previewing the weekend's matches with journalist Mark Saggers. Normally these shows are meticulously planned with questions on autocue and exact timings for every film clip. Minutes before we were due to go out live, the master computer crashed and we were left with no electronic material to work with.

'Looks like we'll have to just keep talking,' I said.

'Can't do much else, can we?'

We went ahead with the broadcast and talked for thirty minutes without a script. Mark and I worked well together and I enjoyed it. There was no stress. In fact, time seemed to fly by. I think Sky were impressed, because I've been working for them ever since.

The programme people always ask me about is *Soccer Saturday*. When Sky Sports first announced the new format it was slammed. Who would want to watch four former players staring at TV monitors and reporting on games the viewers could not see?

'Ridiculous,' said the cynics.

'Brilliant!' said the fans.

Soccer Saturday was a success from day one. I was delighted to be one of the pool of players invited to take part and I never cease to be amazed by the skill and charm of Jeff Stelling, the show's outstanding presenter. If ever a man was cool under pressure . . .

I've worked with some great players on the show, but my all-time *Soccer Saturday* dream team would be former Arsenal Captain Frank McLintock, George Best, Rodney Marsh and me. The atmosphere when we four got together was electric. Jeff Stelling was like a skilled conductor working with a volatile orchestra. We all had different personalities.

Marshy was over-the-top in everything he did, but he also had an excellent knowledge of football. Rodney is a very clever man and he had a good thing going on television because he was the character who upset people. He loved being controversial and it made the programme in many ways. Frank would disagree with Marshy's extreme views and I would come in with a few no-nonsense comments of my own. It got very lively at times.

George was always the quietest of the four. He'd listen to us argue then come in with an astute comment in that gentle Irish brogue of his. Georgie was always quite happy as long as the game he was watching on the programme was Manchester United. He loved the club until the day he died. I know George got a lot of bad Press for his drinking, but he was always sober when he arrived

14

PAST, PRESENT, FUTURE

'You should write a book!' So many people have said that to me over the years.

Now I've done it and it has been a far more profound experience than I ever expected.

'Be as honest as you can,' said Tony Norman, when we started work together.

Talking about my glory days as a player was a pleasure. Reliving dark times I'd long since buried at the back of my mind was far more difficult. Laughter and tears, they have both been part of my story.

I've never sat down and analysed my life with this level of intensity before. It's been quite a journey . . .

Past

If the German bomber had hesitated for a split second before dropping his deadly cargo on West London in 1941, there would have been no story to tell. But the bomb fell two streets away from my home and baby Mullery slept through the raid unharmed.

I was lucky.

That sums up my life for the next forty years. Every dream I had as a little boy came true. I wanted to be a footballer. I wanted to play for England and in FA Cup finals at Wembley and I did it all and more. Johnny Haynes, Dave Mackay, Bill Nicholson, Alf Ramsey, Bobby Moore and Pelé: they all have a place in my scrapbook of memories.

Then, at Brighton, I found success as a manager. I was on a magic-carpet ride. I'd go for a meal in a restaurant and find a grateful supporter had paid the bill for me. I was living in a different world and I thought it would go on for ever. But, in my fortieth year, it all came crashing down. From that point on, I started to fall, slowly at first but faster and deeper as the years wore on.

By 1993, I was ready to end it all.

Only my family knew the truth about that horrible time. I've never spoken publicly about it before, but I hope by talking frankly in this book I may offer hope to other people in that dark place. My advice is simple. There *is* always a future, never give up.

I moved on and, with the support of my family and friends, I've never looked back . . .

Present

I love my cell phone. It's my mobile office. Television directors, radio producers and newspaper journalists all have my number. I get calls every day asking me to make live appearances or to give a quote about a current issue in the game. It's good to reminisce about past glories, but the present is where I live and work. I love being part of football again.

I wonder if I was twenty-five now, would I survive as a player in the modern game? I honestly think I would. I recently read a newspaper article likened Steven Gerrard to me in my heyday. The writer said we both gave everything for the team and covered every blade of grass in a match. We could tackle and pass the ball well and score outstanding goals. I wouldn't put myself in Gerrard's class as a goal scorer but, if the other comparisons are fair, then I'm delighted to be linked with such a great young footballer.

I was lucky to work with some excellent managers during my career, but now I rate Arsène Wenger very highly. He is an intelligent man who knows how to build great teams and accommodate highly skilled individuals. José Mourinho is another superb tactician. He can be fiery at times, but don't let those displays of emotion fool you. Inside he is ice cool and totally focused.

I sometimes work for the government on the panel that decides if foreign stars are qualified to play in this country. Mourinho gave the presentation when Ghanaian Michael Essien joined Chelsea and he was immaculate. We were all given dossiers on the player, who was voted player of the year in France in 2004–05, and shown match action on José's laptop. Mourinho wanted Essien's registration approved and he left absolutely nothing to chance. Wherever José works, his players will get the best treatment available.

But are today's stars worth all the money they earn? Former players often hedge this issue and say they don't envy today's wages. Don't believe a word of it. Of course they envy a pay packet of, in the most extreme cases, £150,000 a week. Players now earn more in a month than we made in our entire careers. Money isn't everything but, as the saying goes, it's up there with oxygen. It matters, especially when your career is over.

Today's stars have the luxury of knowing they will never need to work again when they stop playing. My generation never had that level of security and I'm not the only one to have suffered in later life. I think some of the wages paid today are obscene. I think greedy agents are a blight on the game. Having said that, I do think that players should earn enough to protect them when they retire. It's all a question of balance.

I've had a lot of pain in later life, a legacy from my playing days. First I had to have an operation on my back. Then I went through agony with an arthritic hip. I went to the PFA but they were unable to help me. I had to wait on the NHS list and the hip deteriorated to the point where I could only walk with the aid of a stick.

I went to work for Sky Sports one evening in the autumn of 2004. I met Frank McLintock at the studio. We hadn't seen each other for a while and he was shocked by the state I was in. I looked pale and drawn due to the pain I was in, day and night.

'Why don't you have an operation?'

'I'm on the NHS list,' I said.

'Go private.'

'I can't afford it, mate,' I said, lowering my voice.

'How much would it cost?'

'About fifteen grand.'

'Have it done, Mullers,' said Frank. 'I'll pay.'

'I can't let you do that,' I told him. 'But thanks . . . thanks very much for the offer.'

I was deeply touched.

Frank and I are similar in many ways. Some people like us, others are happy to slag us off behind our backs. We both learned to live with that a long time ago. All I'll say is that I'm proud to have a friend like Frank McLintock. I'll never forget his kindness.

A couple of weeks later, I went to the Bill Nicholson Memorial Service at White Hart Lane. Once again, people were shocked to see me limping along with a stick. They told me I should have come to the club for help. Why hadn't I done that? One word: pride. But the concern of everyone at Spurs was very genuine; they were keen to look after one of their own. Today's Premier League clubs are often labelled as heartless money-making machines. I can tell you that is not true of Tottenham Hotspur.

Before Spurs could step in to help, my hip-replacement operation came through on the NHS. Even then, the club insisted on paying for me to have a private room, which I really appreciated. I'm pleased to say the operation was totally successful and I am now completely pain free and feel better than I have for ten years, which is just as well because life is busy. As well as my involvement with TV and radio, I also travel the country talking about my career. I don't see myself as an after-dinner speaker. I don't do jokes and gags. I'm a storyteller. I talk about the amazing cast of characters who have filled my life. I sometimes make appearances on cruise liners too, which is nice work if you can get it!

I love meeting people and talking football. I do just that at White Hart Lane and Craven Cottage throughout the season. I work for the match-day hospitality people at Spurs and Fulham. I answer questions about the past, present and future of the game. There's always plenty of laughter. Then I sit back and enjoy the match. I get paid for watching over forty games a season in the best League in the world. What could be better than that?

Future

I went back to Notting Hill last week. St Mary's Place, the road where I grew up. It has changed, of course, but all the familiar ghosts were there. The little boy in dungarees was still kicking his football down the street. I was back in my childhood, where it all began.

I saw my dad walking up to the pub. I wish we'd been closer. He told me he loved me for the first time on the day he died. It's never too late to hear those words, but we missed so much in the living years. I've tried to learn from that. My children, Samantha and Neal, know how much I love them and their families.

I saw my mum standing at the old front door in her floral pinafore dress, smiling and as full of support for me as ever. In my early life, she was my rock. June took up the mantle when we married forty-four years ago. I was a leader on the pitch and as a manager but, when my private life went into freefall, I was weak and June was strong. There were times when I did not deserve her love, but she was always true to me.

June is at the heart of my story.

I'm sorry to sound so sentimental, but looking back on my life has left me feeling that way. I am such a lucky man. Most people are happy to succeed in one career. I've had three. I travelled the world as a player, I saw wonderful times as a manager, then found a new life in the media. And more than all this, I have a family who love me.

June and I live in West Sussex now. We love our house and we've built a new life there. The way things stand, the mortgage won't be paid off until I'm seventy-two, but that's not a problem. I don't want to sit around and do nothing. I feel fit and full of energy.

And anyway, I believe the best is yet to come. I can't wait to see what that will be . . .

Players in photograph of the Football League dinner on p. 7 of the second picture section.

Back row (*l to r*): Kenny Dalglish, Ray Clemence, Pat Jennings, Johnny Haynes, partly obscured John Charles, John Barnes, Norman Hunter, Alan Mullery.

Next row (*l to r*): Colin Bell, Dave Mackay, Tom Finney, Arthur Rowley, Frank McLintock, Glenn Hoddle, Osvaldo Ardiles, George Hardwick, Liam Brady, Martin Peters, Terry Paine, George Cohen.

Next half row of six players (*l to r*): Trevor Francis, Nat Lofthouse, Cliff Jones, Paul McGrath, Ian Rush, Len Shackleton.

Front row (*l to r*): Alex Young, Neville Southall, Tommy Smith, Johnny Giles, Peter Shilton, Wilf Mannion, Stanley Matthews, Paul Gascoigne, Geoff Hurst, Alan Shearer, Malcolm Macdonald, Bryan Robson.

ACKNOWLEDGEMENTS

I would like to say how much I love and appreciate the three most important people in my life. My wife June has been a tower of strength. We have been married for forty-four years and I just don't believe any other person could have been so loving and loyal through all the trials and tribulations of my life. June has always been there as my friend, my lover and my wife. I love you dearly, darling. May God bless you at all times.

My daughter Samantha was the most beautiful baby from the day she was born, just like an angel. Thinking of the joy she has brought to my life brings tears to my eyes. When my son Neal was born, he weighed just four and a half pounds and was in an incubator for eight weeks. When he came out of hospital he was not much bigger than my hand. He has grown into a son to be proud of. I'm glad he never became a footballer like me. He is a man in his own right.

I'm so glad that God placed these three people in my life. I love you all.

I would also like to thank Tony Norman, who collaborated with me on the writing of this book. I could never have talked so frankly about my life to any other writer. Thank you for being a good friend.

Grateful thanks are also due to Alex Fynn for his original concept for this book and his subsequent advice, guidance and creative contribution. Many thanks also to David Wilson at Headline Book Publishing for all his support and encouragement and to Celia Kent, our excellent editor. I am also indebted to David Barber of the Football Association and Andy Porter, official historian of Tottenham Hotspur and Jack Rollin, editor of the *Sky Sports Football Yearbook*, for their invaluable help with facts and statistics relating to my career. Thanks also to the press office at Fulham Football Club for the professional way they have dealt with all enquiries. Medical information was provided by Dr Richard Sheaves BSc DPhil FRCP of the London Clinic. Many thanks also to Martin Chivers for the words he wrote for this book.

Finally, I would like to thank all the players and managers I played with and against during my career. Without them, this story could never have been told . . .

CAREER STATISTICS

Alan Patrick Mullery MBE, born Notting Hill, 23 November 1941. St John's Secondary School Notting Hill. Career: West London Schools, London Schools, Middlesex Schools, Fulham ground staff June 1957. Turned professional December 1958. League debut 14 February 1959 v Leyton Orient. Transferred to Tottenham Hotspur March 1964 (£72,500). Fulham loan March 1972. Transferred to Fulham June 1972 (£65,000). Awarded MBE, Football Writers' Association Footballer of the Year 1975. Retired May 1976. Brighton and Hove Albion manager July 1976 to June 1981. Charlton Athletic manager July 1981. Crystal Palace manager June 1982 to May 1984. Queens Park Rangers manager June 1984 to December 1984. Brighton and Hove Albion manager May 1986 to January 1987.

Club Honours:
Fulham Division Two runners-up 1958–59.

Tottenham Hotspur FA Cup winners 1967, League Cup winners 1971, UEFA Cup winners 1972.
Manager:
Brighton and Hove Albion promotion to Division Two 1976–77, promotion to Division One 1978–79.

Honours:
35 full England caps, 1 goal.
1964 v Holland
1967 v Spain, Austria, Wales, Northern Ireland, USSR
1968 v Scotland, Spain, Spain, Sweden, Yugoslavia, Romania, Bulgaria
1969 v France, Northern Ireland, Scotland, Mexico, Uruguay, Brazil, Holland, Portugal
1970 v Holland (sub), Wales, Northern Ireland, Scotland (sub), Colombia, Ecuador, Romania, Brazil, Czechoslovakia, West Germany (1 goal), East Germany
1971 v Malta, Greece, Switzerland

England Under-23s:
1960 v Italy
1961 v Holland
1962 v Belgium

Football League:
1964 v Italian League, Irish League

Representative:
1969 Rest of UK v Wales

SEASON	LEAGUE		LEAGUE CUP		FA CUP		EUROPE		OTHERS		ENGLAND	
	Apps	Goals	Apps	Goals	Apps	Goals	Apps	Goals	Apps	Goals	Apps	Goals
FULHAM												
1958–59	14	–	–	–	–	–	–	–	–	–	–	–
1959–60	36	2	–	–	2	–	–	–	–	–	–	–
1960–61	37	1	–	–	1	–	–	–	–	–	–	–
1961–62	40	6	2	–	7	–	–	–	–	–	–	–
1962–63	38	1	2	–	2	–	–	–	–	–	–	–
1963–64	34	3	1	–	2	1	–	–	–	–	–	–
TOTTENHAM HOTSPUR												
1963–64	9	1	–	–	–	–	–	–	–	–	–	–
1964–65	42	2	–	–	4	–	–	–	1	–	1	–
1965–66	40	1	–	–	3	–	–	–	–	–	–	–
1966–67	39	5	1	–	8	–	–	–	–	–	2	–
1967–68	41	2	–	–	5	–	3	–	1	–	8	–
1968–69	41	1	6	–	4	–	–	–	–	–	8	–
1969–70	41	4	1	–	4	–	–	–	–	–	12	1
1970–71	41	6	7	–	5	1	–	–	4	–	3	–
1971–72	18	3	3	–	–	–	7	4	2	–	1	–
FULHAM (loan)												
1971–72	6	1	–	–	–	–	–	–	–	–	–	–
FULHAM												
1972–73	40	8	2	–	1	–	–	–	–	–	–	–
1973–74	40	2	4	1	3	1	–	–	–	–	–	–
1974–75	42	9	3	1	12	–	–	–	–	–	–	–
1975–76	37	4	3	1	1	–	–	–	–	–	–	–
Totals	676	62	35	3	64	3	10	4	8	–	35	1

INDEX

memorial service 294
no sentiment when selling
players 170, 180, 222–3
no time for sentiment 11
philosophy as manager 11–12
players' injuries 165–6, 170
resignation 225–6
ruthless approach to older
players 32
signing AM transfer 156,
157–8, 160
tactician 237
Noades, Ron 268–70
Norman, Maurice 161, 164, 176
Norman, Tony 291, 299
Notting Hill, St Mary's Place
89–93, 95

O'Reilly, Gary 276
O'Sullivan, Peter 240
Osborne, Frank 104, 107–9, 110,
124–6, 154–5, 157
Osgood, Peter 196

Padilla, Clara 53
Parkes, Phil 29
pay for modern players 293
Pearce, Jimmy 205, 206
Pearce, Jonathan 286, 287–8
Pelé 42–3, 59, 60, 88
Penn, Frank 132
Perryman, Steve 24, 26, 179, 202,
205
Peters, Jim 7
Peters, Martin 6, 24, 29, 180–1,
205, 215
petty crime 135
Phillips, Leighton 267
pigeon shooting 266–7

Pointer, Ray 147
Powell, Jeff 47
Poynton, Cecil 5, 8, 9, 10, 169
Pratt, John 21, 177, 223
Pratt, Maurice 116
printing company 275
Purdy, Albert 111–13, 115
Purdy, Maude 111
'push and run' 11, 173
Puskás, Ferenc 102, 151, 214

Queens Park Rangers 101, 270–5

Ramsey, Sir Alf
'ahead of his time' comment
181
Bobby Moore 88
complacency, guarding against
37–8
England squad's quality 44
graciousness 219
key players 55
mind games 47–8
mistakes not tolerated 39
public relations skills 57
Rest of UK v Wales 203
specific role for every player
213–14
support for players 34–7
words of wisdom 237
World Cup 1966: 210
rats 114–15
Rattin, Antonio 37
Read, Charlie 128
Rest of UK v Wales 202–3
Richards, John 27
Rioch, Bruce 207
Ritchie, Andy 259, 260
Rivera, Gianni 25, 26